SUBURB
Neighborhood and Community in Forest Park, Ohio, 1935–1976

ℑ *Twentieth-Century America Series*

SUBURB

NEIGHBORHOOD AND COMMUNITY
IN FOREST PARK, OHIO, 1935–1976

by Zane L. Miller

KNOXVILLE
THE UNIVERSITY OF TENNESSEE PRESS

ఌ *Twentieth-Century America Series*
Dewey W. Grantham, General Editor

Clothbound editions of University of Tennessee Press books are printed on paper designed for an effective life of at least 300 years, and binding materials are chosen for strength and durability.

Library of Congress Cataloging in Publication Data
Miller, Zane L.
   Suburb : neighborhood and community in Forest Park, Ohio, 1935–1976
   (Twentieth-century America series)
   Bibliography: p.
   Includes index.
   1. Forest Park, Ohio—Politics and government.
   2. Forest Park, Ohio—History. I. Title.
   F499.F73M54 977.1'77 80-21828
   ISBN 0-87049-289-6

FOR RICHARD C. WADE
who first interested me in thinking about spatial relationships and territorial community in urban history.

PREFACE

This book stems from the growing contemporary interest in neighborhood and community history, in both academic and non-academic circles. The study began as a project in the Laboratory in American Civilization, an undergraduate research seminar in the Department of History, University of Cincinnati. This seminar was started in 1974, with approval of the head of the department, William D. Aeschbacher, and with a grant from the university's Education Council. Directed jointly by Henry D. Shapiro and me, lab participants define and explore problems in the history of American civilization, using the Cincinnati metropolitan area and its parts as subjects of investigation. Forest Park attracted our attention in an unorthodox way, however, as a problem defined for us by an outsider. In winter 1975, a member of the Forest Park City Council asked me if I would do a history of that city. I knew little about Forest Park, but it occurred to me that aspects of its history might make appropriate work for the lab; such work might produce a short city history—either a collection of essays by lab participants or a synthesis of their work, supplemented by a summer of additional research. On that basis, I secured a modest grant from the Forest Park City Council to defray our photoduplication and typing expenses and to hire Lyle Koehler as a research assistant for the summer.

During those first few months of research, however, I decided that sufficient materials existed for a larger study. What had begun as a short-term project leading to the preparation of a short history became a long-term project yielding a book. In the process, I received invaluable help from a number of sources.

During summer 1976, Helen Slotkin, now Archivist at Massachusetts Institute of Technology but then head of the Department of Special Collections in the University of Cincinnati Libraries, provided air-conditioned space in which I could work and helped me stock it with research materials. During fall 1976, the university granted me special leave, during which time I finished my research and started writing. A fellowship from the Newberry Library in Chicago during winter 1977 enabled me to complete the first draft of the manuscript, which Kristin Ruggiero typed. During summer 1977, Professor Dewey W. Grantham read the work and made several valuable suggestions for improving and shortening it. I completed the revision, which was typed by Susan Guzeman, during 1978, and submitted that version to Professor Grantham, who commented on its utility for those interested in twentieth-century United States history generally. Blaine A. Brownell also read and criticized the second draft, making observations which helped me to clarify the argument and rethink parts of the story.

At this point, Henry D. Shapiro read the manuscript. He made useful stylistic corrections, insisted that I make myself clearer on several points, and persuaded me to revise some of the text and to compose a new introduction and conclusion. Shapiro then read and criticized several drafts of the introduction and conclusion. So did Robert Fairbanks, Alan I. Marcus, and Judith Spraul-Schmidt, all of whom had worked as graduate assistants in the lab and all of whom were then writing papers or dissertations on Cincinnati topics, using the approach to the history of American civilization which we had worked out in the lab. My debt to these four, and especially to Shapiro, is enormous. For the central argument of this book is largely the product of our collaboration, which started in the lab with an idea of Shapiro's about how to "do" local history. I have tried to apply that idea in this attempt to understand Forest Park.

During summer 1979, while Evelyn Schott typed the last draft of the manuscript, Steve Aynes and Will McGriff, employees of the City of Forest Park; Judy Noorish of Forest Park, Inc.; and George Cummings of the U.S. Soil Conservation Service helped me gather maps and illustrations. Peggy Palange of the University of Cincinnati Public

Information Office made photographs or photographic reproductions of much of that material.

Others helped, too. Alice Vestal, Slotkin's successor as head of the Department of Special Collections in the University of Cincinnati Libraries, collected and made conveniently accessible in the university archives local materials which otherwise would have been dispersed in various locations. Laura Chace and Ed Ryder of the Cincinnati Historical Society guided me to an invaluable collection at the society, and Charles Leach secured for me important documents from Cornell University. I would be remiss, too, in failing to mention Saul Benison, Ron Applegate, Ellen Cangi, Bob Carroll, Paula Dubeck, Gene and Dottie Lewis, Patricia Mooney Melvin, Janet Smith Miller, Elaine Tillman, and Al Tuchfarber, who as friends, colleagues, or students have contributed to my thinking about the problem of neighborhood and community. The University of Tennessee Press provided welcome encouragement and advice while working out arrangements for acquisition and preparation of the book. Mavis Bryant, who edited the manuscript which became this book, did an extraordinarily helpful and diligent job. I am also grateful to the Greenwood Press for allowing me to use in this book parts of an essay I wrote on the concept and role of neighborhood in American cities, to be published in Peter Romanofsky and Robert Fisher, eds., *Community Organization for Social Change: A Historical Perspective*.

All of these people assisted me with patience, good humor, skill, and imagination. Without their assistance and the support of the institutions cited above, this book would not have had its present form—if, indeed, it existed at all. They share responsibility for its merits; I am responsible for its defects.

Cincinnati, Ohio   ZANE L. MILLER
March 1980

CONTENTS

ILLUSTRATIONS

INTRODUCTION

The white-collar people slipped quietly into modern society. Whatever history they have had is history without events; whatever common interests they have do not lead to unity; whatever future they have will not be of their own making. . . . Yet it is to this white-collar world that one must look for much that is characteristic of twentieth-century existence . . . they have transformed the tang and feel of the American experience. They carry, in a most revealing way, many of those psychological themes that characterize our epoch, and . . . every general theory of the main drift has had to take account of them.

C. WRIGHT MILLS, *White Collar: The American Middle Classes* (1951), p. ix.

. . . these communities are a product of the great expansion of the middle class, for the new suburbs have become a mecca for thousands of young people moving up and out of city wards. It is not these people, however, who are dominant. In his wanderings, the organization man has found in the suburbs an ideal way station.

WILLIAM H. WHYTE, JR., *The Organization Man* (1956), pp. 310–11.

After the 1960s people lost faith in public solutions. Now they are turning to what they can control [including vegetable gardens]. . . . in the garden friends are as obvious as the sun. Enemies are as real as the root borer. The goal is as tangible as a head of cabbage. You don't need a consultant to assess failure or success.

ELLEN GOODMAN, quoted in *Newsweek*, July 17, 1978, p. 90.

This book is a history of Forest Park, Ohio, a comprehensively planned new town in northern suburban Cincinnati. But this volume is about more than one city's history, and not simply because Forest

Park began as a New Deal greenbelt town, or because its developers and planners after World War II included men of national importance, or because Forest Park is a "representative" post-World War II new community or suburb. This book is about more than "merely" Forest Park because it treats a series of events in Forest Park and in the larger Cincinnati metropolitan area, as "symptomatic" of the ways Americans generally have defined their society and structured their territorial communities during the middle decades of the twentieth century, and because it analyzes the consequences of those definitions and that structuring.

The assertion that events in one locality point to more general patterns of thought and action, however, has not satisfied many of my friends, acquaintances, and colleagues, who remain puzzled about why an urban historian would be interested in such a small, new, little-known, and seemingly unimportant place as Forest Park. At first their mystification puzzled me, and at last it forced me to acknowledge that the meaning of "symptomatic" history was not self-evident, and that this kind of history is often misunderstood because of traditional assumptions about historical continuity and representative "case" studies. Both the symptomatic concept and the claim of this history of Forest Park to being more than merely "interesting" require explanation.

My experience with symptomatic history began in the late 1960s, when Henry D. Shapiro and I, in connection with the celebration of the sesquicentennial of the University of Cincinnati's College of Medicine, were asked by the committee in charge of the celebration to do a study of the college's founder, Dr. Daniel Drake. Although we knew little about Drake when we began, we soon discovered that he was not merely a physician who founded the College of Medicine, but also a scientist and builder of a variety of institutions during the first half of the nineteenth century. Therefore we decided to examine all facets of his career. Our study yielded a book in which we aimed at an "assessment of Drake's career in the context of the problems which beset American science and American society during his lifetime." However, we did not present him as a great man with extraordinary influence either in his own time or later. Nor did we treat him as a "representative" product of historical, social, economic, and political forces which determined the development of early nineteenth-century America. Rather, we presented him as an individual through whose life and work we tried to understand better the period in which his life occurred. We concluded, in short, that what Drake did was unique, but that how he did it was not. By centering our analysis on the "how," we could use his life and work as symptomatic of more general patterns of thought and action during the time he lived.[1]

The Drake project was our first attempt at symptomatic history, and it took as its subjects one person and the early nineteenth century. Since then, Shapiro and I have done another such study, this one of a locality, the Cincinnati neighborhood of Clifton, in the nineteenth and twentieth centuries.[2] That study, our other more recent work, the work of some of our students,[3] and our knowledge of the histories of other persons, events, and localities have persuaded us of the utility of a symptomatic history of one locality in explaining events in other places during the same time period.

Our experience with symptomatic history has also clarified our method. As I now understand it, we do three things which differentiate our symptomatic history from more familiar kinds of history. First, we take what might be called a "radically historical" posture toward the past. Second, we concentrate on "how" by centering our attention on structure. And third, we deal with process, or more specifically, the process of people defining and solving problems.

We take a radically historical posture toward the past, in that we do not look for the remote origins and evolutionary development of the ideas and social, economic, or other forces which many presume to have shaped the present and projected the future, through a great chain of continuity. Indeed, we doubt that past ideas and forces have shaped the present or influenced the future in that linear, causal, and evolutionary sense. For us, the past really is past, and it breaks into a series of discrete and discontinuous chronological periods separated by shifts in the ways people characterize reality. And I, at least,

1. Henry D. Shapiro and Zane L. Miller, *Physician to the West: Selected Writings of Daniel Drake on Science and Society* (Lexington: Univ. of Kentucky Press, 1970), viii-ix.
2. Shapiro and Miller, *Clifton: Neighborhood and Community in an Urban Setting. A Brief History* (Cincinnati: Laboratory in American Civilization, Dept. of History, Univ. of Cincinnati, 1976).
3. See, e.g., Shapiro, *Appalachia on Our Mind: The Southern Mountains and Mountaineers in the American Consciousness, 1870–1920* (Chapel Hill: Univ. of North Carolina Press, 1978); Miller, "Music Hall: Its Neighborhood, the City, and the Metropolis," in Zane L. Miller and George Roth, *Cincinnati's Music Hall* (Virginia Beach, Va.: Jordan and Company, 1978); Alan I. Marcus, "In Sickness and in Health: The Marriage of the Municipal Corporation to the Public Interest and the Problem of Public Health, 1820–1870. The Case of Cincinnati" (Ph.D. diss., Univ. of Cincinnati, 1979).

confess that I am unable to explain why people organized reality differently at different times. I seek merely to identify those moments of redefinition and to understand and explain the consequences of the new modes of thought.

In preparing symptomatic histories of localities, we have found that a shift in the way people organized reality usually manifests itself in a general disposition to change old institutions or create new ones. Having identified such a moment, we concentrate on structure, by which we mean (a) the units which people in the past, though generally without saying so, took as the basic components of society in their own times; and (b) how, through that inarticulate act of definition, they established a taxonomy of social reality within which to define problems, and then to think about, argue about, and act upon those problems. For us, therefore, as Shapiro recently put it, people cause things to happen; how they see reality determines how they think and act in it; and how they see reality includes what they see and do not see in it. In this kind of structural analysis, then, we look at what people said and did not say, and at what they did and did not do. But we have been especially interested in institutions and institutional relationships and in the territorial arrangements and relationships which people have created within a particular period.

If we stopped with chronology and structure, we would, of course, have a series of static cross-sections of the past, not a history. But we are also interested in the experience of people within a chronological and a structural framework. For that, we look both at how people created their institutional and territorial milieus and at how events unfolded within those milieus. In symptomatic history we call this *process,* meaning both the process of people defining certain things or phenomena as "problems" and their attempts to resolve those problems by choosing among a variety of possible solutions. Proceeding through time, we lay out that story to the moment at which we identify a shift in the taxonomy of reality; at that point, we start to work on the history of the next period, or we stop and leave that history to another article, essay, or book.

For us, then, symptomatic history has a distinctive form and focus. Shifts in the way people divide and order reality provide the chronology. A new taxonomy establishes a framework for thought, discourse, and action, from which stem the institutional and territorial milieus within which experience and ideas flow. The process of people defining and solving problems provides the plot. This process is the dynamic which produces, within a given period, a series of events and phenomena which we analyze and organize in a narrative called symptomatic history.

I have found while working on this project that Forest Park is an especially useful and interesting subject for this kind of history. Forest Park began as a separate urban settlement in the 1950s and grew rapidly. By the late 1970s, it contained roughly 19,000 inhabitants, most of them middle-class and 19 percent of them black. Except for the relatively high proportion of blacks in its population, Forest Park in the 1970s was not demographically distinguishable from thousands of other suburbs built between the end of World War II and the late 1970s. It did possess a particular claim to distinction, however, as a "comprehensively" planned post-World War II "community." To local journalists, as to social scientists and city planners, Forest Park seemed a special place, as it did, indeed, to its developer, its city officials, and many of its residents.

The fact that Forest Park's planners, builders, and residents self-consciously tried to create a sense of community and the institutions of community, and not merely a place in which to live, caught my interest first. Precisely what they meant by "community" proved elusive, however. Clearly, the term referred to the people, buildings, services, institutions, and organizations assembled in a particular territory. But it also meant something more intangible. As I began the study, this word seemed most often to connote something like the public interest—a civic interest above and beyond individual or group interests—for the advancement of which individuals and groups ought to be willing to sacrifice, by volunteering time to work on a "community" project, for example, or by approving tax increases. Initially, too, I thought the attempt to create community was a single problem. I soon learned, however, that the definition of the nature of community changed with changing taxonomies of reality, and that the history of Forest Park encompassed three such taxonomies. Thus the single problem of community turned out to be three problems of community, and this book attempts to explain the definition and nature of community in each of three taxonomic periods.

I also learned that the process of building Forest Park had involved the governments of Cincinnati, Hamilton County, the State of Ohio, and the United States. Those connections alone made Forest Park inextricably a part not only of the metropolitan area, but also of American political life in the middle decades of the twentieth century.

The study of Forest Park's history therefore involved consideration of a broad variety of events and topics.

This history treats many, though not all, of those events and topics, including issues of the sort often regarded by residents and students of urban America as public policy problems. For example, it deals with fragmented political authority in American metropolitan areas; urban renewal in the 1950s and 1960s and its metropolitan consequences; the difficulty of building low- and low-middle-income housing through the private market; high costs of utilities and urban services and these costs' political and social implications in new communities and suburbs; school costs rising as school-age populations mushroom; the problems created at the local and regional levels by basing planning decisions on concern for residential property values; the nature of suburban politics and its connections to big city and metropolitan politics; attempts to control the socio-economic composition of communities; the increased "urban" problems faced by suburbs as they grew older and suburbanites perceived that "urban problems" were not confined to the inner city; the divisions between the big city and its suburbs, and among suburbs themselves; the inter- and intra-metropolitan competition for "top-notch" residents; the effect of neighborhood organization on community life and city politics and government; and the question of race in the big city and suburbs. In considering these problems, however, this book treats the history of Forest Park as part of the larger history of community in suburban (and urban) America.

To place Forest Park's history in this larger perspective, it has been necessary to examine a number of conventional views of the nature of community in suburban America. Some of these views date from the 1950s and early 1960s, while others are of more recent vintage.

In the 1950s and 1960s, it was commonly believed that suburbs "rose" only after World War II. From this belief stemmed explanations of the meaning and consequences of suburbanization, including explanations which contrasted suburban community with "the city." These explanations usually treated planned and unplanned suburbs as products of different processes. But in both cases, the end result was presented as "suburbia," seen as a part of a larger metropolitan area and dependent upon, yet different from, "the city." For example, while some political scientists lamented the inefficient multiplication of local governments which was spawned by suburban growth, they nonetheless accepted the proliferation as a fact of life and divided the study of metropolitan politics into "city" and suburban categories. Many sociologists, filmmakers, novelists, and journalists took a similar tack. They characterized suburbia as a place of homogeneous settlements populated by rootless individuals with loose morals and hyperactive if shallow social lives who lived in a poorly planned and often squalidly designed and disorderly milieu. Whether posh enclaves or pastiches, however, these outlying settlements struck their students as uniform in character, comprising a culturally conformist and politically conservative community of broad lawns and narrow minds which undermined the diversity, liberality, sophistication, and cosmopolitanism which the suburban critique associated with "the city." In the 1950s and early 1960s, suburbia seemed a new unit of urban society, different from "the city"—a community with values which were or were becoming characteristic of an aspect of American civilization.

In the late 1960s and early 1970s, however, that view of the nature of community in the suburbs altered. By then, students of the metropolis had "discovered" the existence of working class and black suburbs, and had observed that older, upper-income, WASPish "establishment" suburbs like Evanston, Illinois, formed an inner ring of peripheral communities between big city boundaries and the newer lower- and middle-class "developmental" suburbs farther out. The emergence in the late 1960s, moreover, of substantial numbers of anti-Vietnamese War, civil rights, and women's liberation advocates from suburban places also discredited the conventional 1950s wisdom about suburban conformity and the conservative suburban influence. Finally, the 1970 census revealed that 75 percent of all Americans lived in metropolitan areas, and over 50 percent of metropolitanites listed suburban addresses. The magnitude of the numbers alone suggested that "suburbia" housed a diversity of people, that suburbs occurred in bewildering variety, and that the suburban explosion had freed peripheral places of their dependence upon metropolitan core cities, including the central business districts. By the mid-1970s, some scholars even projected a "doughnut" metropolitan configuration, in which a circle of suburbs surrounded a downtownless core.

The "doughnut" hypothesis particularly offended historic preservationists, whose interests centered on the central business districts and metropolitan core cities. These groups wanted to make money in real estate. They wanted to attract the upper and middle classes back to the big city and thereby "save" the central business district by making it as lively by night as by day. They wanted to buttress big-city revenue bases through the conservation and rehabilitation of old city neighborhoods in or around the central business district. And they wanted to remind people of the diversity of their "roots" by preserving diverse physical artifacts in older portions of the city. But both sides in the argument over the future of the center of the big city rested their cases on a new view of the relationship between city suburbs within the metropolis.

The new view deviated from its predecessor, because the older conception of "suburbia" as homogeneous and opposite "the city" in its way of life no longer seemed persuasive. Even the idea of "suburbia" as a particular way of life now seemed untenable, because the range of "acceptable" behavior among the upper and middle classes had expanded to the point that "doing your own thing," rather than conformity, now seemed "normal." After the mid-1960s, people tended to link "the suburbs" not with a particular place or way of life, but with a social grouping of upper- and middle-income people who displayed a diversity of lifestyles and who might live close to or well removed from the big city downtown. At the same time, people tended to associate "the city" not with urbanity or a particular way of life, but with "urban problems," particularly the problems of the poor and "different" residents of the metropolis, including blacks and other colored minorities, the elderly, the violent, the criminal. People tended to locate these problems spatially in the "inner city" or "core city" of a metropolis, and to classify them as "urban," even when they occasionally were seen to appear in the suburbs. After the mid-1960s, the suburbs seemed "places" distinguished in large part by their separation from these problems. It was from this view of the metropolis that "gentrification"—in which rehabilitation of old big-city neighborhoods drove real estate prices up and poor residents out—could be identified as an urban problem. For the poor wanted to share in the improved big-city environment yet could not afford it, and the middle classes were reluctant to make room for them in "the suburbs."

For a variety of reasons, then, the new view differed drastically from that of the 1950s. But there were similarities, too. The new view resembled the older "rise of the suburbs" thesis in suggesting that suburbs did in fact grow so rapidly and persistently after World War II that by the late 1960s and 1970s they represented the dominant sites (wherever located) and normal mode of life (despite the variety of lifestyles within them). In short, both views, while defining suburbs differently, presented them as something new (that is, as a post-World War II phenomenon) and as a unit of urban society which differed in one way or another from "the city." In the former view, suburbia seemed a homogeneous unit of urban society characterized by conformity in one sense or another. In the latter, the suburbs comprised a diverse unit of urban society, the inhabitants of which pursued a variety of lifestyles. In both, however, "suburbia" or "the suburbs" was contrasted with "the city," which in the 1950s and early 1960s represented diversity and urbanity, and in the late 1960s and 1970s represented "problems" and danger.

Although I have accepted 1950 and the early 1960s as benchmarks in urban and community history, my own view of the substance of that history differs from both of these conventional views, and those differences have influenced my own explanation of Forest Park's past. Both views present a truncated and therefore misleading history of suburbanization and of the consciousness of the suburb as a community different from the city. Both views rest on a misleading assumption that unplanned and planned suburbs (and cities) derive from different processes, one "natural" and the other artificial. And both views are misleading because they interpret the *discourse* about "suburbia" (or "the suburbs") and "the city" between 1950 and the mid-1970s to mean that people in fact *acted* as if those categories comprised fundamental units of American society.

In the first place, suburbanization is not a recent phenomenon. Indeed, it has characterized American urban growth from almost the beginning, and during the nineteenth century the proliferation of such peripheral places accelerated. To be sure, until the early twentieth century, annexation by cities of their hinterlands roughly kept pace with the outward sprawl of people, businesses, and industries, a process which retained politically-vital civic and fiscal resources within the larger municipal arena. Nonetheless, early twentieth-century big cities still possessed their circles of diverse outlying suburbs. In the late 1920s, moreover, Harlan Paul Douglass, in *The Surburban Trend,* sought to explain to his generation the meaning of the persistence of the outward drift. And while the Great Depression of the 1930s slowed the pace of suburbanization, it still struck New Deal policymakers as a "problem," albeit as part of the larger and more fundamental problem of metropolitan community. In short, suburbs "rose" long before the 1950s, and any urban or suburban history should acknowledge that fact. After all, our view of our own history, including the assumption that suburbs are new, influences what we make of that history.

In the second place, the consciousness of suburbs as distinctive communities integrally related to, yet different from, the city is also not a recent phenomenon. Its origin in the mid-nineteenth century coincided with the appearance of a new taxonomy of reality and a redefinition of the city as a social system consisting of mechanically interacting groups characterized by different behavioral patterns. According to this mode of thought, individuals might acquire and maintain the appropriate behavioral pattern through the practice of moral discipline in surroundings conducive to the cultivation of good character. Frederick Law Olmsted and others in the mid-nineteenth century manifested the new urban-suburban consciousness when they designed spacious and artfully landscaped suburban residential alternatives, including asylums of various kinds as well as park-like housing developments, for clienteles either eager to live in a morally uplifting environment or deemed appropriate, for character-building purposes, to be of but not in the city.

In the later nineteenth and early twentieth centuries, under a different set of assumptions about the nature of the city and its constituent groups and parts, industrialists like George Pullman, interested in making their work force and industrial operations more efficient, set up working-class factory towns or "satellite cities" on the urban periphery. Still others, catering to the same taste for class, racial, and "ethnic" segregation by residence, established quite exclusive commuter suburbs.

Later still, in the second quarter of the twentieth century, a mode of thought about cities and suburbs prevailed which took the metropolis as a basic unit of society. Regional planning enthusiasts, including Lewis Mumford, the Regional Planning Association of America, and the American Institute of Planners, encouraged the establishment of suburban greenbelt towns as sub-units of the larger and fundamental unit of urban society, the metropolis; during the 1930s, the Roosevelt administration created three such towns.

In short, not only suburbanization, but also the consciousness of suburbs as distinctive places of one kind or another, related to the city or metropolis in one way or another, appeared long before the 1950s.

In the third place, it would be inappropriate to treat "planned" and "unplanned" suburbs or cities as products of different processes. To be sure, Forest Park was and is a "planned" development, and I necessarily discuss and analyze its various plans and planners. As a result, this book can be seen as a contribution to the history of urban planning construed as the product of the activities of "professional" planners. But symptomatic history treats "professional" planning, as it would a building, neighborhood, city, or metropolitan area, as an artifact of the taxonomies of reality and modes of thought and action with which this book is really concerned. One could say both that this book's generalizations would have been the same if Forest Park had not been "planned" at all, and that the book's viewpoint sees everything, in a sense, as planned—that is, as the consequence of a particular, chronologically-bounded taxonomy of social reality and mode of thought, discourse, and action.

In the fourth place, the substance of the conventional approaches is no longer appropriate because those approaches themselves are artifacts and events in the history of urban and suburban community. As artifacts and events from the past, they, like any others, require interpretation as part of the past. Viewed in this way, and in the context of other artifacts and events, they tell us more than they say and something other than what they seem to say. Specifically, and most importantly for this history of Forest Park, they tell us that the presentation, both in the 1950s and early 1960s and in the late 1960s and 1970s, of "suburbia" (or "the suburbs") and "the city" as fundamental units of urban society cannot be taken at face value. Indeed, this division rested on an unarticulated assumption that individuals constituted the fundamental units of the social order. As we shall see, moreover, assumptions about the nature of those individuals differed in the two time periods, and those assumptions provided the unspoken basis for both shaping and interpreting reality in each time period. The differences in the two periods provide the rationale for my accepting as legitimate the chronology, if not the substance, of the conventional approaches I have described in this introduction.

This book, then, sees the history of Forest Park as several histories, each of them the product of shifts in the taxonomy of social reality and of the consequences of those shifts. It adheres, that is, to the principles of discontinuity, contending that the histories of Forest Park and of other cities and suburbs in the middle decades of the twentieth century are not part of, and do not grow out of, the histories of suburbs and cities in the mid- or late-nineteenth and early-twentieth centuries. Those earlier histories are separate histories, divided by fundamental chronological gaps, and therefore are antecedent to, but not precedents for, this account of Forest Park; consequently they are appropriately the business of some other book. A knowledge of those histories is not a prerequisite for understanding the Forest Park story; I have acknowledged them here in order to establish their historical distance and distinctiveness from this story, which begins in the 1920s and 1930s, in the age of the regional planning movement and New Deal greenbelt developments.

Our story starts, then, in the era of the *metropolitan* mode of thought, which lasted from the 1920s to about 1950, and during which the problem of community was seen as a fundamentally metropolitan issue. The story begins with the creation of Greenhills, Ohio, a place designed for lower-middle class people but occupied by members of the middle classes. Since the land now called Forest Park served as part of a greenbelt for Greenhills, this section of our story centers on the partition and sale of Greenhills, and on plans to make its undeveloped portion, then called North Greenhills and not Forest Park, a planned entity on the Greenhills model. The analysis of these events suggests that during this period people took the metropolis as a basic unit of society, as a community which shaped the desires, hopes, aspirations, and character of its residents and which should command their loyalty.

The analysis in this section also suggests that Greenhills and the first planning for North Greenhills were not part of a suburban development plan, but rather were part of a metropolitan strategy to deal with the basic problem of metropolitan community. That problem was how to design the social and spatial structure of the metropolis so that the latter, as a community, would foster in its residents good citizenship—a commitment to the welfare of the metropolis as a whole—rather than civic alienation. The analysis also helps explain why C. Wright Mills, in the last years of this period, wrote a book about the American middle classes in which he talked about the metropolis (he sometimes called it "the big city") and about suburbs as subunits of that basic entity, but not at all about "suburbia" or "the suburbs" as opposed to "the city."

The study next moves into the period of the *community of limited liability,* which runs from the early 1950s into the early 1960s, and in which the problem of community seemed less clearly to be an essentially metropolitan issue. This section deals with the purchase of North Greenhills, with the changing of its name to Forest Park, and with attempts to make a single community of the several subdivisions which made up Forest Park. The analysis suggests that people at that time posited autonomous individuals as the basic units of society. As autonomous individuals, people possessed the ability to make partial commitments to the welfare of a variety of communities, including territorial ones such as a neighborhood, big city, or suburb, as well as purely associational ones such as a labor union, professional organization or ethnic group. People also understood that autonomous individuals deserved a say in shaping their communities, for the assumption of autonomy implied the additional assumption that residents shaped communities, rather than the converse. In addition, people understood that autonomous individuals might legitimately devote greater or lesser time to one or another community as their personal circumstances dictated; hence the term community of limited liability.

The analysis in this section also suggests that while people still regarded suburbs (and neighborhoods) as dependent upon the big city, they now drew a new and sharper distinction between the big city and its suburbs (and neighborhoods). In this mode of thought, suburbs and neighborhoods themselves, as communities of limited liability, seemed to possess a measure of autonomy. This phenomenon I have called "the rediscovery of local community," which manifested itself in a new concern with civic participation in, and for the sake of, the welfare of suburban (and neighborhood) community; I attempt to show how that rediscovery influenced events in Forest Park. In addition, the analysis presented here helps explain why William H. Whyte, Jr., in the middle 1950s, wrote a book about one segment of the American middle class, and in it talked more about "the new suburbia" and the appropriateness of a new individualism than about "the metropolis" or the problem of metropolitan community.

The story concludes in the era of the *community of advocacy,* the mid-1960s through 1976, an era in which the concern with the problem of community lost its civic focus. Now we deal with the question of race, the transformation of neighborhood organizations, and the appearance of the word "metroplex" (a neologism designating an area in which agencies deliver services to individuals) in Forest Park. The analysis suggests that people still drew a distinction between the city and the suburbs. But they defined that distinction in a fashion eliminating the assumption of suburban (and neighborhood) dependence on the city, rendering ambiguous the spatial connotations of the big city-suburban distinction, and transforming the nature of the neighborhood organization movement just as it reached Forest Park. People still took individuals as basic units of society and still assumed that those individuals shaped their communities. But a new definition of the nature of those individuals as "liberated" rather than autonomous relieved them of the obligation for even a partial commitment to civic participation for the sake of community welfare (as opposed to individual well-being). This new assumption I have called the *turning-inward tendency,* and I attempt an interpretation of its consequences for Forest Park as symptomatic of the condition of American society generally. This view also helps explain how Ellen Goodman could write about American society in the 1970s in terms of gardens, heads of cabbage, root borers, friends, and enemies, instead of the civic welfare or public interest.

This book, then, is not local history, but symptomatic history. Its central concerns are changing taxonomies of social reality and the consequences of those changes for community in urban society. And while this work is written with special reference to Forest Park and the Cincinnati metropolitan area, it is in the final analysis an attempt to understand central aspects of American civilization since the 1920s. It also presents Forest Park as a useful setting for examining a part of the neglected history of those whom Mills, in the epigraph which begins this introduction, called "the white-collar people" who "slipped quietly into modern society." Unlike Mills, I found that their history had events, and that they strove with determination to make their own future. This book does not pretend to be the kind of history which teaches us usable lessons from the past, however. For a past which is really past can teach no usable lessons for the present or the future. But one may hope that this kind of study of the past can help free us from assumptions of historical determinism and thereby help us to think in new ways about the present and the future.

CHRONOLOGY

I have compiled this chronology for several reasons. First, it should be useful as a guide through the maze of plans, zone changes, organizations, political campaigns, and governmental units which play a part in this history of Forest Park. Second, it should prove useful as a convenient reference for Forest Parkers, who have not had a list of events necessary for the preliminary examination of Forest Park's past, and who may wish to consult this chronology as a step in developing their own history of their community. Third, it should prove useful to those who share with Shapiro and me the conviction that any understanding of a particular history begins with a laying out of events which may be important in that history. Fourth, by arranging events in three time periods, it points to the fundamental organizing principle of this book, the principle of chronological discontinuity. That discontinuity is not the result of preparing this list, however, nor is it "intentional" in an *a priori* sense. Rather it emerged in the process of laying out, sifting, and making connections among events, a process which occurred while I was writing this book and *before* I compiled this chronology.

This chronology, then, is an artifact of the process of research and thinking involved in the writing of this book. Like all chronologies (and histories), it is selective. I have included some things, and omitted others. What I have included is arranged both by year and by the era in which it occurred. Some events are listed simply to help readers keep the details of the story straight. Others are listed as guides to the "plot"—because they proved particularly useful in making sense out of other events in their eras and in discovering the fundamental chronology on which this history rests. Though readers will not be able to distinguish between "detail" events and "plot" events until they have completed the book, the inclusion of both kinds in this chronology should make it a useful reference during the reading of this book. Having finished the book, readers should find the chronology a convenient reminder of both the plot and the details.

I. METROPOLITAN COMMUNITY

1925   City of Cincinnati adopts comprehensive plan
1929   Hamilton County Regional Planning Commission established
1935   Roosevelt administration establishes greenbelt town program; Cincinnati area selected as one of three greenbelt town sites
1938   Greenhills completed
1946   Federal government prepares to dispose of undeveloped portions of greenbelt towns
1947   Justin Hartzog prepares plan for North Greenhills
1948   Cincinnati Metropolitan Master Plan published
        Cincinnati Citizens Development Committee (CDC) urges sale of North Greenhills in one tract
1949   Congress passes legislation to sell greenbelt towns
1950   Greenhills Home Owners Corporation buys part of Greenhills
1951   Cincinnati city manager's office seeks developer for North Greenhills
        Cincinnati voters approve $1,350,000 Urban Redevelopment Bond Issue
1952   CDC negotiates for purchase of North Greenhills
        Cincinnati Community Development Corporation (CCDC) secures option to buy North Greenhills
        Ladislas Segoe prepares North Greenhills plan for CCDC's first developer
        First developer drops out
        Warner-Kanter Company joins CCDC to consider developing North Greenhills

II. COMMUNITY OF LIMITED LIABILITY

1953   Warner brings in Philip Klutznick as consultant on North Greenhills development
        Warner hires Hartzog to do another plan for North Greenhills

Warner presents preliminary development proposition to CDC and
requests its support

CDC refuses to "front" for the CCDC/Warner-Kanter combine

CCDC and Warner start negotiating for local subsidies

1954 CCDC buys North Greenhills and transfers the property to Warner-
Kanter for development

Warner negotiates with Hamilton County Commissioners for roads and
sewers

Cincinnati/Hamilton County water contract assures water for North
Greenhills

Warner negotiates with Hamilton County Regional Planning Commission on zoning in North Greenhills

Greenhills residents and officials object to proposed zoning

Warner-Kanter agrees to pay school subsidy to Greenhills School
District

Wanter-Kanter changes name of North Greenhills to Forest Park

1956 Forest Park's first subdivision (Cameron Heights) opens

Forest Park dedication ceremonies

1957 Forest Park's first anniversary celebrated

Forest Park Women's Club, Forest Park Civic Association, and Forest
Park Baseball Association organized

1958 Western portion of Forest Park rezoned from residential to commercial

1959 Union Central Life Insurance Company buys land in western portion of
Forest Park for office building

Warner-Kanter contract with CCDC expires

Warner-Kanter partnership dissolves, Kanter gets Forest Park

Kanter forms The Kanter Corporation to continue development of
Forest Park

Kanter meets with Civic Association to discuss development of Forest
Park

Movement starts to create Forest Park Volunteer Fire Department

1960 Forest Park population, 8,405

Kanter moves to Forest Park

Forest Park Fire District established

Forest Park Medical Center opens

Kanter sponsors "Country Fair"

1961 Greenhills attempts to annex western portion of Forest Park

Forest Park incorporates as a village

First village election (July)

Kanter confers with village representatives on planning and zoning for
Forest Park

Hartzog revises Forest Park master plan for The Kanter Corporation

Second village election (November)

1962 Village council hires Paul Christiansen as consultant to review
Hartzog's 1961 master plan

Kanter proposal to expand shopping center rejected by village

"C" section residents protest housing development in adjacent area

Christiansen presents review of Hartzog's 1961 master plan

1963   Village hires Christiansen to prepare a master plan for Forest Park
       Civic Association disbands
       Organization of Forest Park Police Association
       Christiansen presents master plan
       Kanter objects to Christiansen's master plan
       Village council adopts amended version of consultant's 1963 plan
       Third village election
       Kanter starts *Forest Park News*
1964   Kanter organizes Forest Park, Inc., to continue development of Forest
          Park
       Mayor Donald English disagrees with several council members over
          development of Forest Park
       Philip White runs as candidate for precinct executive in Democratic
          primary
       Kanter announces plans for an office-research park
1965   Forest Park Beautification Committee established
       Organization of Forest Park Businessman's Association
       Fourth village election, Philip White elected mayor
1966   Kanter announces plans for an "apartment colony"
       Forest Park chosen as site for a branch of the Public Library of
          Cincinnati and Hamilton County
       Recreation tax levy fails
1967   *Village Voice* folds
       First blacks move to Forest Park
       The Cellar (Forest Park Youth Center) established
       Council designates Labor Day as Community Recognition Day
       Smaller recreation tax levy passes
       Fifth village election
       Charter Commission established to draw up charter for city govern-
          ment
       Forest Park annexes land around freeway interchange
       "Industrial park" district designated in western Forest Park
1968   City charter adopted

III. COMMUNITY OF ADVOCACY

1969   The Cellar closed
       First neighborhood association organized in "K" section
       First city council election
1970   Forest Park population, 15,174
       Black population reaches 2.8 percent
       First earnings tax proposal defeated by voters
1971   City approves planned unit development (PUD) across from Municipal
          Building

Citizens Forum established and initiates "Ecology Drive"
Second earnings tax proposed by council
Second earnings tax defeated by voters
Second city council election
1972 Kanter announces a "grand design" (including PUD) for Forest Park
Second PUD requested
Council criticizes city manager
City manager resigns (October)
1973 Third PUD proposed
White resigns as mayor
Fred Lamb elected as mayor
Michael D. Kadlecik chosen as city manager
Council creates Advisory Committee on Housing
Council passes fair housing ordinance
Third city council election
City manager issues fiscal report
1974 Black population reaches 10.7 percent
Kanter requests approval of Kemper-Mill PUD
Council issues fiscal report
Council establishes Community Development Department
Third earnings tax proposal approved by voters
1975 Black population reaches 12 percent
Forest Park secures federal "701" planning grant
Advisory Committee on Housing issues first report
Council commissions history of Forest Park
Council bans display of real estate "for sale" signs
Council approves Kemper-Mill PUD
Council approves Wright Farm PUD and cancels Kemper-Mill PUD
Fourth city council election
1976 Council rezones Wright Farm from PUD to R-1 single family
Metropolitan Area Religious Coalition (MARC) sponsors metropoli-
tan school desegregation forum in Greenhills Presbyterian Church

SUBURB

Neighborhood and Community in Forest Park, Ohio, 1935–1976

*. . . when a city expands beyond a certain size
it reaches the point of diminishing returns in
terms of the advantages which a city, as a
social community, should provide for its
inhabitants. . . . . The chief purpose of the Plan
for an integrated system of communities is to
reintroduce in Cincinnati as a metropolitan
center the advantages of the self-contained city
of medium size.*
CINCINNATI CITY PLANNING COMMISSION,
Metropolitan Master Plan, 1948

METROPOLITAN COMMUNITY, GREENHILLS, AND PLANNING FOR NORTH GREENHILLS

Forest Park is the product of a series of plans, and its "planners" include the Suburban Division of the U.S. Resettlement Administration, the federal Public Housing Authority, the Cincinnati City Planning Commission, the Cincinnati Citizens Development Committee, the Cincinnati Community Development Company, the Warner-Kanter Company, the Kanter Corporation, the Forest Park municipal corporation, and the residents of Forest Park. The Resettlement Administration came first, however. Its decision to make what is now Forest Park part of a new town's greenbelt derived from a conception of the city which appeared in the 1920s and flourished into the 1950s. That view abandoned neighborhood and city as basic units in American society, replaced them with metropolis and region, and suggested that planning in urban areas ought to start with the metropolis, conceived as a heterogeneous system of specialized, differentiated, interdependent, and organically related parts.

Expressions of the tendency to think and act in metropolitan terms appeared in a variety of places and took varied forms. In Cincinnati, for example, reformers assaulting urban housing problems in the 1920s began to look on a metropolitan strategy of slum clearance, inner-city public housing, and the creation of suburban new towns as preferable to big-city tenement-house regulation and construction of model homes.[1] In Cincinnati, too, political reformers, who before 1920 had concentrated on municipal reform, in the 1920s began to chart countywide reform campaigns. Meanwhile, the city itself in 1925 adopted a comprehensive plan suggesting the wisdom of regional planning "in the interest of proper development of the metropolitan area embracing Cincinnati and the communities adjacent to it."[2] And in 1929, after a series of discussions between the secretary of the Cincinnati City Planning Commission and the Hamilton County Commissioners, eleven units of local government in Hamilton County joined together to form a Hamilton County Regional Planning Commission.[3]

Manifestations of the new metropolitan focus occurred outside Cincinnati as well. Between 1921 and 1929, public or private regional planning commissions appeared in virtually every major metropolitan area in the nation, the most famous, perhaps, being the New York Regional Planning Commission, financed by the Russell Sage Foundation and after 1923 directed by Fredric A. Delano, an uncle of Franklin D. Roosevelt.[4] In addition, important theoretical work was done in the 1920s. Professor Norman S.B. Gras at the University of Chicago began to work out a metropolitan interpretation of economic history. President Herbert Hoover established the Committee on Social Trends which published R.D. McKenzie's *The Metropolitan Community*. Harlan Paul Douglass published a study called *The Suburban Trend*, which sought to differentiate the emerging conditions of the new metropolitan life from the emerging conditions of the new rural life. And Harvey Warren Zorbaugh wrote *The Gold Coast and the Slum*, which deemphasized the significance of "neighborhood" and nominated residents of Chicago's Gold Coast as the group most likely to shape the future city conceived as a metropolis dominating

1. On this point I am indebted to Robert B. Fairbanks, who is a doctoral candidate in history at the University of Cincinnati and is completing a dissertation on public housing in the Cincinnati area between 1920 and 1960.

2. Judith Spraul-Schmidt, "Local Government and the Urban Community: Cincinnati and Hamilton County" (seminar paper, Dept. of History, Univ. of Cincinnati, typescript, June 1977); Cincinnati City Planning Commission, *Official Plan of the City of Cincinnati* (Cincinnati: Cincinnati City Planning Commission, 1925), 6.

3. Paul M. Cholak, "Hamilton County's 'Urban Gap': Problems and Prospects for Intergovernmental Cooperation" (M.A. thesis, Univ. of Cincinnati, 1963), 112–13.

4. Joseph L. Arnold, *The New Deal in the Suburbs: A History of the Greenbelt Town Program, 1935–1954* (Columbus: Ohio State Univ. Press, 1971), 12–15.

the life of a region. Zorbaugh, moreover, specifically endorsed the concept of comprehensive city plans, including those which, like New York's, encompassed the region around the city. The significance of such a plan, Zorbaugh wrote, was twofold:

> It tends toward an increasingly realistic conception of city life. But beyond this, as city plan commissions resort to publicity to arouse public interest, the plan begins to give the city a conception of itself—a self-awareness, a sense of its history and role, a vision of its future—in short, a personality. And only when the city has achieved self-consciousness, only when the mosaic of cultural worlds which compose it come to think of themselves, not as over against one another, but as related to a vision of the city as a whole, can the city adequately act.[5]

In the 1930s people continued to talk and act as if territorial community existed or ought to exist in America, and to think of that community as a unit which, though larger than the traditional neighborhood, nonetheless molded the desires, values, aspirations and personalities of its inhabitants. And just as this mode of discourse made it possible to talk about and act upon "the South" and "the West" as cultural regions, the same mode of discourse made it possible to talk about and act upon cities in new ways. Indeed, by the 1930s the metropolis itself seemed to constitute a pluralistic community with a distinctive culture, whose principal characteristics and tendencies were laid out tersely by Louis Wirth, the prominent "Chicago school" sociologist, in his essay on "Urbanism as a Way of Life." The new culture, in Wirth's view, might move in either of two directions. One grimly raised the specter of a "mass society" rendered pathologically unstable by anomie and alienation, while the other raised the brighter prospect of a new era of cosmopolitanism, urbanity, and tolerance.[6] In the 1930s, the existence of these two possibilities spurred various attempts to coordinate or consolidate metropolitan area political units and social agencies, with the goal of establishing a "healthy" and "balanced" community life and a sense of community within the metropolitan framework. And while the same mode of thought allowed for the existence of territorial subcommunities within the larger and basic territorial (metropolitan) community, it did not posit those subcommunities as autonomous,

5. Harvey Warren Zorbaugh, *The Gold Coast and the Slum: A Sociological Study of Chicago's Near North Side* (Chicago: Univ. of Chicago Press, 1929; Phoenix Edition, 1976), 272–73.

6. Louis Wirth, "Urbanism as a Way of Life," *American Journal of Sociology*, Vol. 44 (July 1938), 1–24.

self-contained, or primordial social forces, but rather as interdependent and changing components of a larger and pluralistic metropolitan community of competition and cooperation.

In this context of concern for the condition of community in both rural and urban environments within a metropolitan regional framework, it is not surprising that the Roosevelt administration, in 1935, consolidated several rural land use and community construction agencies into the Resettlement Administration. Nor is it surprising that in the same season Rexford G. Tugwell, a member of Roosevelt's "brain trust," convinced the president to undertake as one resettlement program the construction of several "greenbelt" communities on the outer edges of metropolitan areas, as a means of demonstrating what enlightened planning could do to help solve pressing rural and urban problems. Through the various resettlement programs, Tugwell hoped to save marginal but economically viable farms, persuade rural families to move from unproductive to more fertile land, and create new communities on the outer rim of metropolitan areas, as alternative places of residence for thousands of Americans either driven off their land or trapped in the crowded slums of the nation's cities.[7]

Within the Resettlement Administration, the Suburban Division formulated the greenbelt program. Those who worked on it varied in their assessments of the precise role of the new towns in the metropolitan scheme of things. Some saw them as balanced communities offering not merely residential facilities but also industrial and agricultural jobs. Others coupled residence with industrial development only, while still others saw the new towns as essentially commuter suburbs for low- and moderate-income families. All, however, conceived of them as places of sufficient population (projections varied from 7,000 to 30,000 residents) to support public and commercial facilities and a "healthy" community life. It was agreed, too, that these towns should be protected from the encroachment of urban sprawl by greenbelts of forest, farms, or gardens, some parts of which could serve, if necessary, as sites for future development to bring the total population up to an appropriate level.[8] Underlying all the planner's schemes was the basic metropolitan and regional perspective. "My idea," Tugwell once said, "is to go just outside centers of

7. Arnold, *The New Deal in the Suburbs*, 24–25; Paul K. Conkin, *Tomorrow a New World: The New Deal Community Program* (Ithaca, N.Y.: Cornell Univ. Press, 1959).
8. Arnold, *The New Deal in the Suburbs*, 83–103.

population, pick up cheap land, build a whole community, and entice people into it. Then go back into the cities and tear down whole slums and make parks of them."[9]

The greenbelt planners, however, had to work within the $31-million budget allotted to the Suburban Division, and that fact restricted both the size and the number of the towns. Tugwell once estimated that the country needed 3,000 greenbelt towns, but the New Deal constructed only three, none of which was built to the size deemed appropriate by planners at the time. One, Greenbelt, was situated in Maryland, outside Washington, D.C., and another, Greendale, in Wisconsin, outside Milwaukee. The third, Greenhills, was located on a 5,930-acre tract of farmland eleven miles north of downtown Cincinnati, in Springfield Township, Hamilton County, Ohio. The site lay northeast of Mt. Healthy and west of Glendale, a nineteenth-century commuter suburb and the home of some of the Cincinnati area's wealthiest and most influential people, but not far either from the factories of the Mill Creek industrial belt.

The Suburban Division acquired the land at a cost of $1,615,222 and divided it into two parts. At the time of purchase, the land contained one hundred farms ranging from 1 to over 120 acres in size. Rolling topography provided natural surface drainage, but the soil stood "in a seriously depleted condition . . . because of continuous cultivation by successive generations of owners who were uninformed as to proper methods of soil fertilization and crop management. . . ." Since the smallest and least efficient farms lay in the south and south-central portions of the tract, the planners placed the village of Greenhills there, preserving forty-eight larger properties in the northern part for rural development as places of part- or full-time employment for some residents of the new town. Most of the rest of the land was to be reforested for conversion into a woods, and a smaller piece went to the Hamilton County Park Commission for use as a park and golf course.[10]

These general specifications, which made what is now Forest Park the farm portion of the Greenhills greenbelt, provided the guidelines for the construction of the new town. Upon completion in June 1938

9. Quoted in Mark I. Gelfand, *A Nation of Cities: The Federal Government and Urban America, 1933–1965* (New York: Oxford Univ. Press, 1975), 133.

10. "Analysis of Cincinnati Land Acquisition," typescript, Feb. 8, 1937, and "Substantiation of Recommendation for Agricultural Development, Greenhills Project," typescript, n.d., in Justin R. Hartzog Papers, Dept. of Manuscripts and University Archives, Cornell Univ. Hereinafter cited as Hartzog Papers.

Greenhills consisted of 676 dwelling units. In fall 1939, its residents secured from the State of Ohio a charter incorporating the village as a municipality. In the 1940s the town developed into a white, middle-income suburb, despite the fact that Cincinnati's slums, whose inhabitants were supposed to be among Greenhills' major beneficiaries, contained large numbers of blacks.

In retrospect, the most astonishing feature of the process of making Greenhills was its speed. Building a new town in a metropolitan area is, and in the 1930s was, a complicated business. Creating Greenhills involved not only acquiring a large plot of suitably priced land and designing a comprehensive plan, but also eliciting active cooperation within the Resettlement Administration, and among that agency, the Hamilton County Regional Planning Commission (an advisory body), the government of Hamilton County, the City of Cincinnati, local utility companies, and building, real estate, civic, and political interests. Without the support of all those groups, the project could have been aborted or the greenbelt idea compromised beyond recognition. And while Tugwell and others tended in the 1950s and 1960s to remember most vividly the difficulties they encountered while working on the project, more recent analyses emphasize the smoothness of the entire operation.[11]

At mid-century, however, the greenbelt idea, as embodied in Greenhills, faced and surmounted a serious threat to its integrity. In the 1940s federal officials considered breaking the towns into smaller parcels for sale to private parties. In 1942, the Federal Public Housing Authority (FPHA) assumed control of all three of the greenbelt towns and, after World War II and in accordance with the program's original intent, prepared to dispose of the three new communities. In connection with that procedure, FPHA engaged Justin R. Hartzog, who had been the chief planner of Greenhills, to make a plan for the town's enlargement which might guide its future development, and to advise the FPHA on whether to dispose of the town piecemeal or as a single unit.[12]

Hartzog's plan proposed adding a 1,099-family extension to Greenhills and constructing to the north of Greenhills two entirely

11. Charles Bradley Leach, "Greenhills, Ohio: The Evolution of an American New Town" (Ph.D. diss., Case Western Reserve Univ., 1978), 178–217; Robert B. Fairbanks, "Cincinnati and Greenhills: The Response to a Federal Community, 1935–1939," *The Cincinnati Historical Society Bulletin*, Vol. 36 (Winter 1978), No. 4, 223–41; Arnold, *The New Deal in the Suburbs*, 142–44.

12. Arnold, *The New Deal in the Suburbs*, 229–35.

new settlements of 1,379 and 1,593 families respectively. All three settlements would be brought together under one municipal jurisdiction known as "Greater Greenhills." For each of the two new settlements, Hartzog suggested a town center, two neighborhood centers, two local business centers, grade and high schools, an athletic field, a park and playing fields, and meeting places for social organizations and religious groups. He also wanted to set aside 160 acres on the eastern edge of Greater Greenhills for light industry, 250 acres for an airport, and space for a hospital, cemeteries, and a state or county police station to serve adjacent portions of Hamilton County as well as Greater Greenhills itself. Hartzog proposed, in addition, to retain park and forest land as a greenbelt for the new entity. And he recommended the disposition of the entire Greenhills tract as a single unit.[13]

When Hartzog completed his plan in 1947, both it and Greenhills attracted the interest of the Cincinnati Citizens Development Committee (CDC), a group of some of the most influential businessmen in the Cincinnati area. Among these leaders were Joseph B. Hall of the Kroger Company; Fred Lazarus, Jr., of Shillito's Department Stores; John J. Emery of Emery Industries, Inc.; Frederick V. Geier of the Cincinnati Milling Machine Company; and Stanley M. Rowe of the Fifth-Third National Bank. Established to assist in post-World War II economic reconversion and reconstruction, in the late 1940s the group participated in the making of a new master plan for Cincinnati and subsequently took as its chief objective "the promotion of public interest in and the execution of the objectives of 'The Cincinnati Master Plan' " of 1948. The committee's executive secretary, Sherwood L. Reeder, was a former city manager of the Wisconsin greenbelt town and had also served as director of the Metropolitan Master Planning Division of the Cincinnati City Planning Commission, the agency most directly responsible for the preparation of the 1948 master plan. In addition, he had chaired the American Institute of Planners (AIP) Committee on Greenbelt Towns.[14]

The Citizens Development Committee's commitment to the

13. Hartzog, "Greenhills Development Plan: A Report and Program of the Extension and Development of the Village and General Tract," typescript, 1947, Hartzog Papers.

14. Earle J. Wheeler, president, Cincinnati Community Development Company, to John Taylor Egan, commissioner, Public Housing Administration, April 10, 1952, Hartzog Papers; George P. Stimson, "They Cared—The Citizens Planning Association, 1944–1948," and Stimson, "The Citizens Development Committee, 1948–1968," typescripts, Citizens Development Committee Collection, Cincinnati Historical Society. Hereinafter cited as CDC Collection, CHS.

Metropolitan Master Plan of 1948 meant that the CDC would also be interested in the fate of Greenhills. A document symptomatic of the metropolitan mode of thought, the plan emphasized redevelopment of the existing urban structure rather than the creation of a new form. One of the plan's major goals was to assure Cincinnati's dominance of a region encompassing Huntington, West Virginia; Lexington and Louisville, Kentucky; Indianapolis, Indiana; and Dayton and Columbus, Ohio. The plan defined the Cincinnati metropolitan area as consisting of Hamilton County in Ohio and Kenton and Campbell Counties in Kentucky (see Figure 1). That territory was described as a "mature" metropolitan community with modest prospects for economic and population growth, but one within which the automobile's popularity would encourage a continuing outward drift of the population (Figure 2). The plan also divided the metropolitan landscape into two parts, one for "living" and one for "making a living." An "industrial policy" addressed the latter area, calling for "growth on a selective, quality basis." Activities should be encouraged whose introduction or expansion would shore up the existing economic base (Figure 3), as a foil against competition from rapidly growing cities in the southern half of Cincinnati's metropolitan region. Expansion, then, stood as a "means to an end rather than the end objective itself," and " 'service activities'—utilities, finance, insurance, real estate, communication, government, etc." were ranked as the most desirable industries from the standpoint of their potential contribution to the metropolitan economy. The plan also posited a rigid separation of industrial land use areas from both the central business district and residential areas.[15]

The residential strategy of the 1948 plan spoke directly to the future of Greenhills. This strategy rested on the premise that "when a city expands beyond a certain size it reaches the point of diminishing returns in terms of the advantages which a city, as a social community, should provide for its inhabitants. . . ." To gain maximum advantages, and to establish a sense of community at both submetropolitan and metropolitan levels, the plan proposed (Figure 4) to organize Cincinnati's metropolitan residential areas into "communities" of about 20,000 to 40,000 population, not self-governed but

15. Cincinnati City Planning Commission, *The Economy of the Cincinnati Metropolitan Area* (Cincinnati: Cincinnati City Planning Commission, 1946); Cincinnati City Planning Commission, *Cincinnati Metropolitan Master Plan 1948* (Cincinnati: Cincinnati City Planning Commission, 1948).

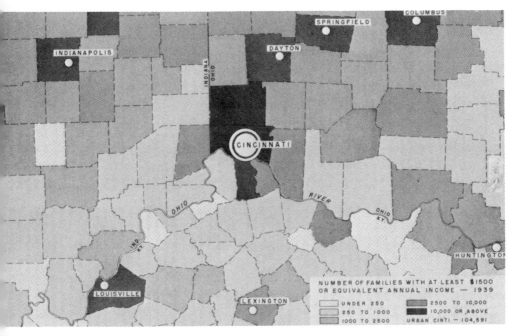

FIGURE 1. The Cincinnati metropolitan region, 1948, as depicted in *Cincinnati Metropolitan Master Plan, 1948*, p. 18.

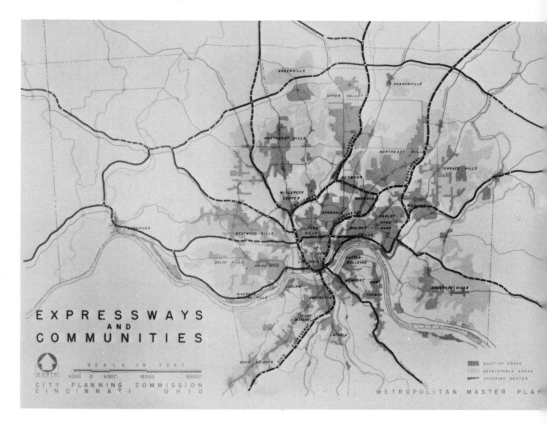

FIGURE 2. The Cincinnati metropolitan area, 1948, showing the relationship of proposed new subcommunities to proposed expressways. The expressways were seen as necessary to accommodate longstanding and ongoing "outward movement" and were designed "to provide for and guide this peripheral development." Source: *Cincinnati Metropolitan Master Plan, 1948,* p. 30.

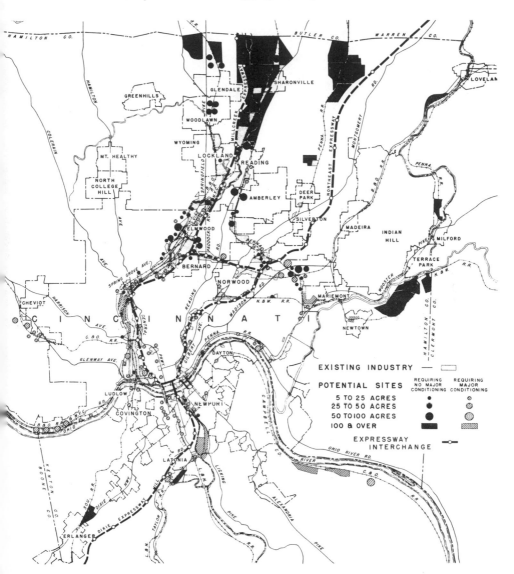

FIGURE 3. This map of actual and potential industrial areas reveals a desire on the part of planners in 1948 to link industry with railroads and with selected expressways only. The map projects considerable industrial activity in the upper Mill Creek Valley east of Greenhills. It also underscores the plan's commitment to segregating industrial areas from residential ones. Source: *Cincinnati Metropolitan Master Plan, 1948*, p. 74.

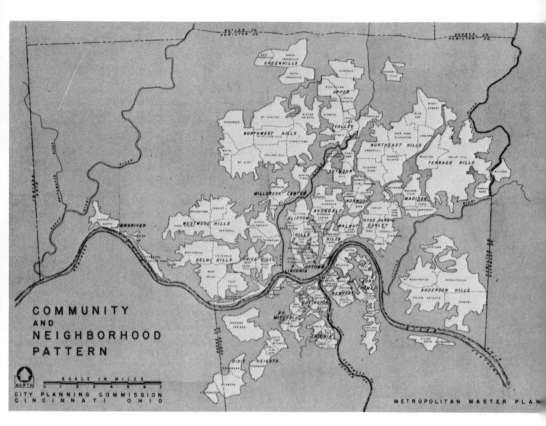

FIGURE 4. This map shows the merging of "neighborhoods" required to achieve the ideal "community" population of 20,000 to 40,000. The names of the "traditional neighborhoods," as the planners referred to them, appear in the small type. Source: *Cincinnati Metropolitan Master Plan, 1948*, p. 26.

"self-contained in respect to the everyday life of their inhabitants except for such facilities and services as will continue to be located in or supplied by Cincinnati as the central city, and by institutions serving the Metropolitan Area." This reorganization would involve clearing inner-city slums and creating a network of expressways and thoroughfares to knit together the elements of the metropolitan fabric. Existing neighborhoods were also to be merged into communities large enough to support secondary business districts, a set of elementary schools and a junior high, and other services such as branch libraries, health centers, post offices, police and fire stations, and "sometimes" community center buildings. The plan identified one of those communities as Northwest Hills; within its boundaries lay the three settlements envisaged in Hartzog's plan for Greenhills, two of them undeveloped and bearing the label "Federal Public Housing"[16] (see Figure 5).

In light of the Citizens Development Committee's commitment to the 1948 master plan, Reeder's experience and position as CDC executive secretary, and the plan's proposal for the treatment of Greenhills, it is not surprising that Reeder watched carefully as the federal government prepared to dispose of Greenhills. By mid-summer 1948 he sensed trouble, for in July he informed the CDC and the AIP Committee on Greenbelt Towns that the Public Housing Administration (PHA), which now controlled the greenbelt towns, was contemplating selling the properties in ten parcels "to the highest bidder without any restrictions regarding the original concept of these communities as demonstrations of a desirable scheme of living for moderate income families." Such action not only violated his own and his employers' plans for Greenhills, but also ran contrary to previous AIP recommendations on the disposition of the greenbelt towns. Reeder therefore tried to stall the disposition until the AIP could contact key congressional leaders to secure new disposition regulations.[17]

Meanwhile, the AIP committee prepared a special report urging the sale of each of the towns as a unit to one large investor, so that the original intent of the experiment could be preserved (see Appendix

16. Cincinnati City Planning Commission, *Cincinnati Metropolitan Master Plan 1948*, 11, 27–34, Fig. 17.
17. Sherwood L. Reeder to members of the AIP Committee on the Greenbelt Towns, July 7, 1948, Hartzog Papers.

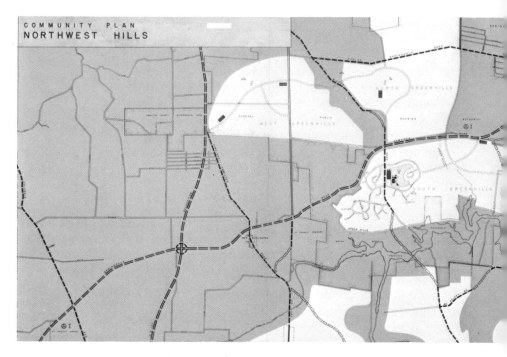

FIGURE 5. Portion of map of the proposed community of Northwest Hills. Shows the Greenhills tract, as in Hartzog's 1947 plan, divided into three neighborhoods. West and North Greenhills, which later became Forest Park, are slated for federal public housing. Just below South Greenhills, where the village of Greenhills lies, is a proposed reservoir which became Winton Woods Lake. Source: *Cincinnati Metropolitan Master Plan, 1948*, p. 51.

A).[18] The committee followed this report with a set of more specific recommendations for the disposition of the greenbelt towns. Drawn up by Clarence Stein, perhaps the foremost early-twentieth-century American planner of new towns, the recommendations urged that each property should be sold as a whole after competitive bidding, and that future additions to the towns should follow the general provisions of plans already drawn up by PHA consultants, including Hartzog in the case of Greenhills.[19]

Despite the views of the CDC, the AIP, Stein, and Hartzog, Congress enacted disposition legislation which jeopardized the greenbelt ideal. Passed in May 1949, the bill contained two key provisions. The first gave the PHA's disposition commissioner power, "by means of negotiated sale . . . and without competitive bidding or public advertising, to sell and convey, at fair market value . . . to such purchaser or purchasers as he deems to be responsible, all right, title and interest of the United States in or to *all or any part* [my emphasis] of the suburban resettlement projects known as Greenbelt, Maryland; Greendale, Wisconsin; and Greenhills, Ohio." That provision made it possible to break up each of the projects. The second key section required the commissioner to "give a first preference in such negotiated sale . . . to veterans groups organized on a nonprofit basis."[20] This latter stipulation identified prime purchasers in such a way as to exclude the CDC but, if veterans groups failed to acquire an entire project, left open the disposition of what remained.

Yet for a time, and without the intervention of the CDC, it appeared that the Greenhills tract might be kept intact. In 1950, the Greenhills Home Owners Corporation (GHOC), an organization which combined veterans with ordinary citizens, attempted to purchase both the village of Greenhills and its greenbelt. Unable to muster the financial resources necessary to close the deal, however, the group settled instead for title to all the houses in the village, the commercial center, the town hall, and 601 acres of undeveloped land, at a price of $3,511,300. A year later, the PHA transferred another 400 acres of undeveloped land to the Hamilton County Park District, leaving 3,400

18. American Institute of Planners, "Report of Committee on the Greenbelt Towns," typescript, n.d., Hartzog Papers.
19. Reeder to members of the AIP Committee on the Greenbelt Towns, July 28, 1948, Hartzog Papers; Clarence Stein, "To preserve the character of the Greenbelt towns . . . ," typescript, n.d., Hartzog Papers.
20. 81st Congress, 1st Session, Public Law 65, Chapter 127, p. 31.

acres of farmland north and east of Greenhills in the PHA's posses-sion.[21]

The separation of the village of Greenhills from the 3,400-acre greenbelt territory (by then called North Greenhills) brought the CDC back into the picture. In 1951, C. Russell Cravens, PHA assistant commissioner supervising real estate disposition, asked Charles H. Stamm, the Cincinnati city manager's assistant in charge of urban redevelopment, for his views on the best disposition policy for North Greenhills.[22] Then Cravens came to Cincinnati to take a closer look at the situation. During that visit, Cravens met with Stamm, who had worked on Greenhills in the 1930s and participated in the GHOC purchase of the village;[23] George W. Hayward, who now served as CDC executive director and who in the 1930s had worked on the Wisconsin greenbelt project; Walter S. Schmidt, president of the Frederick A. Schmidt Company (realtors); and Albert J. Mayer, Jr., a partner in Theodore Mayer Sons Company (realtors). All these men told Cravens that North Greenhills should not be broken up, and that a "group or company" should acquire it from the government. Stamm offered to sound out other organizations and individuals about their willingness to participate in the purchase, adding, however, that planning studies would have to be made before the project's feasibility could be determined. In a subsequent letter to Cravens, Stamm said that Hayward was confident that the CDC might be willing to form a company to make the purchase, and asked Cravens how he felt about such a plan, whether the sale of the property to such an organization could be negotiated, and what terms might be arranged.[24]

Cravens apparently doubted the wisdom of Stamm's proposal, for a month later Stamm wrote John Taylor Egan, PHA commissioner, seeking more information and a more sympathetic hearing.[25] Specifi-

21. Arnold, *The New Deal in the Suburbs,* 236; Charles H. Stamm to author, interview, June 1, 1976.

22. Stamm, "A Plan to Acquire a 3,400 Acre Tract of Land Owned by the Federal Government," Mar. 5, 1952, typescript, CDC Collection, CHS.

23. Stamm to author, interview, June 1, 1976; "Analysis of Cincinnati Land Acquisition," Hartzog Papers; Gregory V. Keller, "Charles Stamm and Urban Redevelopment in Cincinnati," (senior thesis, Dept. of Urban Planning and Design, Univ. of Cincinnati, 1976), 45–47.

24. Stamm to Col. C. Russell Cravens, Oct. 18, 1951, CDC Collection, CHS; George W. Hayward to author, interview, May 20, 1976.

25. In November 1951, the City of Cincinnati submitted a $1,350,000 Urban Redevelopment Bond Issue to a popular vote. Its passage started the urban renewal projects which would reduce the city's housing stock. See *Citizens Development Committee Bulletin,* Vol. VIII, No. 4 (Oct. 1951), 3.

cally, Stamm asked if disposition of North Greenhills could be delayed until April 1, 1952, by which time he thought a feasibility study could be completed, and if the PHA would negotiate a sale along the lines indicated in his correspondence with Cravens. Egan agreed to the April 1 deadline and said a negotiated sale would be possible, but he refused to make a firm commitment on the price or conditions of a sale.[26]

Stamm next turned to the CDC, persuading its Housing and Urban Redevelopment Subcommittee to tour the site with him on March 1, 1952.[27] The subcommittee listened politely and decided to consider the matter at a more formal meeting on March 19. Before that session, however, George Hayward distributed to the CDC a memorandum summarizing the results of inquiries to Stamm and the director of the Cincinnati Metropolitan Housing Authority about the relationship between the Cincinnati area's housing shortage and proposed expressway construction. In a "fair meeting of the minds on needs and prospects," Hayward reported that 4,248 families would be displaced by completion of the Mill Creek Expressway through the West End black ghetto and the construction of the downtown Third Street distributor and its connections. The memo also projected a metropolitan dwelling shortage of 2,500 units over the next two years.

Hayward also argued that blacks, who occupied "the bottom of the private . . . market where profit is lowest," constituted the most neglected group of people caught in the housing crunch. To meet their needs, the memorandum suggested immediate establishment of a contemplated relocation center; a search for a developer to construct new low-income housing; assignment to the Cincinnati Metropolitan Housing Authority and the Cincinnati City Planning Commission of the task of finding sites to accommodate black families; and cooperation with the Better Housing League in securing home financing for blacks. Then, in a separate recommendation, Hayward urged that "all possibilities for sound, large-scale housing developments for *general relief* of the housing shortage must be encouraged," including the "proposal to develop the federally-owned 3,400-acre Greenhills tract according to a coordinated plan under single ownership."[28] The emphasis is mine, and the implication seems clear. North Greenhills

26. Stamm to Egan, Dec. 24, 1951, CDC Collection, CHS; Egan to Stamm, Jan. 22, 1952, CDC Collection, CHS.
27. CDC, "Minutes," Vol. 3 (1952–53), Housing and Urban Redevelopment Subcommittee, Mar. 1, 1952, CDC Collection, CHS.
28. Hayward, "Housing Program for Hamilton County," n.d., CDC Collection, CHS.

would not provide housing for blacks uprooted from their inner-city neighborhoods.

Stamm, meanwhile, prepared a fifteen-page brochure for the CDC's Housing and Urban Redevelopment Subcommittee. In the introduction, he stated that his own "thorough review of the city's housing problem in the past, present and future," and the "trouble the City is having today in carrying out Master Plan recommendations due to lack of relocation housing" had convinced him that "the large assembly of land constitutes one of the greatest potential assets this community possesses." In the body of the brochure, Stamm drew on his considerable development experience, including his 1930s work on Greenhills, to defend the idea of building North Greenhills along the lines of the original greenbelt towns.[29]

Stamm considered North Greenhills ideally located for such a program (see Figure 3). The property stretched from Hamilton Avenue (U.S. Route 127) on the west, to Springfield Pike (State Route 4) on the east. Its center lay 4 miles west of the proposed Mill Creek Expressway; 13.5 miles north of Fountain Square in the heart of Cincinnati's central business district; 11.5 miles south of the center of Hamilton, Ohio; 2 miles west and 1 mile north of Glendale; 3 miles north and 1 mile east of Mt. Healthy; and 6 miles north of Cincinnati's north corporation line at North Bend and Winton Roads. Over good county roads, North Greenhills' center was only ten to fifteen minutes by automobile from the remotest point in the Mill Creek industrial belt, and thirty minutes by car and fifty minutes by bus from Cincinnati's central business district.

To Stamm, providing the area with public utilities and services looked difficult, though not impossible. Water and electric lines approached it from Cincinnati and Hamilton, in Butler County to the north of North Greenhills, and although no gas mains penetrated the location, a trunk gas line between Hamilton County and the City of Hamilton could be tapped if sizable development took place in North Greenhills. As for sewers, Stamm estimated that it would cost $100,000 to build a mile-and-a-half extension along the east boundary of the village of Greenhills, but the western half of the tract, which rested in the Great Miami River watershed, would have to be taken care of separately, delaying development there for several years.

Schools, Stamm admitted, could be a problem, too, for the area lay within the Greenhills School District, which possessed but one build-

29. Stamm, "A Plan to Acquire 3,400 Acres," introduction, CDC Collection, CHS.

ing housing all grades from kindergarten through senior high school. But Stamm rated Greenhills' police, fire, waste disposal, and shopping services adequate to serve North Greenhills, and he raved about the area's recreational facilities, which included Hamilton County's 1,856-acre Winton Woods park and an eighteen-hole golf course opened during summer 1951. In addition, Stamm noted, the village itself contained fifty acres of parks, sixteen acres of athletic fields, and "one of the finest swimming pools in this part of the country."

Stamm then addressed the housing shortage. Was the metropolitan area housing market strong enough to make the development of North Greenhills viable economically? He answered with an "unqualified yes." In 1951, Stamm observed, Hamilton County accommodated 235,000 families, up 26,000 from 1940. Over that decade, 30,140 new units had gone up, enough to take care of the family increase. But at that rate of building, the worn-out units in the total inventory had not been replaced. Assuming one hundred years as the normal life of a dwelling unit, Stamm argued, at least one percent of the total inventory should be built each year for replacement alone. Given the current inventory of 235,000 units, Stamm calculated that from 1940 to 1950 the area needed 23,500 new units as replacements and another 26,000 to accommodate new families. The total came to 49,500 new units, well above the 30,140 units which were in fact constructed.

But that assessment of the magnitude of the housing shortage, Stamm noted, covered just one aspect of the housing problem. The Metropolitan Master Plan of 1948, in which the CDC was so intensely interested, recommended extensive expressway construction and slum clearance. Those projects would cut sharply into the already short housing supply, and particularly into the stock available for low- and moderate-income families. *"Not until replacement housing is built,"* Stamm emphasized, *"Will the city be able to go ahead with master plan projects, such as the Expressway which eliminates housing by the thousands [sic] and slum clearance which is so long overdue."*[30]

The last section of Stamm's CDC brochure took up the delicate question of money. Stamm estimated the average cost of appraising, acquiring, and administering the original 6,000-acre Greenhills site at $300 per acre, and from that calculation suggested that $1 million ought to cover the 3,400-acre North Greenhills location. He believed,

30. Stamm, "A Plan to Acquire 3,400 Acres," CDC Collection, CHS.

too, that the PHA would accept such an offer, provided that it was accompanied by a complete program for development of the tract. To help hold down initial costs, Stamm suggested a staged development of the project, early payment by industries of 50 percent of the site improvements for the light industry district, and county participation in laying the needed sewer. A tentative agreement with the PHA, Stamm concluded, provided for a negotiated sale on terms of "perhaps" one-third down, with the balance payable in 300 equal monthly installments, at 4 percent interest.[31]

On March 19, 1952, with Hayward's memorandum and Stamm's brochure in hand, the CDC's Housing and Urban Redevelopment Subcommittee convened to consider the acquisition of North Greenhills. At the meeting, Walter S. Schmidt reported that he had found a possible developer who possessed the experience, knowledge, and capital necessary to carry out the project. Impressed by Schmidt's report and Stamm's and Hayward's presentations, the subcommittee decided to endorse the acquisition scheme. It also recommended, however, that some local "civic group" should prepare a general plan and prospectus for presentation to the PHA, acquire the property, and secure a developer to execute the scheme "according to a strict agreement of compliance with the plan prepared by the civic group."[32]

With the PHA's April 1 deadline for receiving a proposal for purchasing North Greenhills just two weeks away, Stamm pressed forward. Two days after the March 19 meeting, he sent Hayward the name of another potential developer, the Warner-Kanter Company, which had carried out major housing projects in Birmingham, Alabama; St. Louis; and Cincinnati. Although Stamm urged a meeting between Warner-Kanter and the Housing and Urban Redevelopment Subcommittee "at the earliest possible time," Hayward forwarded the nomination to Joseph Hall and Stanley Rowe of the CDC, advising them to keep the matter confidential and to defer the meeting with Warner-Kanter "until after the more complicated introductory phases of the proposal have been solved." He was referring, of course, to the problem of finding an appropriate civic group to purchase North Greenhills from the PHA. Meanwhile, Stamm wrote PHA Commissioner Egan requesting an extension of the April 1 deadline and

31. *Ibid.*
32. CDC, "Minutes," Vol. 3 (1952–53), Housing and Urban Redevelopment Subcommittee, Mar. 19, 1952, CDC Collection, CHS.

enclosing a letter from Hayward suggesting that the CDC itself might agree to function as the civic group which would purchase and supervise the development of North Greenhills.[33]

The Hayward letter, however, somewhat misrepresented the case. The CDC actually wanted another organization, the Cincinnati Community Development Company (CCDC), to take on the task of buying and overseeing the development of North Greenhills. CCDC had been created in 1948, on the initiative of Cincinnati Mayor Albert Cash, as a limited-profit company to "aid in community growth and development by helping to alleviate shortages of housing that may, from time to time, exist, and by providing housing within the City of Cincinnati and its environs."[34] CCDC carried the CDC endorsement, several members of the CDC served as its officers, and Rowe, Stamm, and Schmidt had been among its early sponsors.

On March 13, 1952, just six days before the March 19 meeting between Stamm and the CDC Housing and Urban Redevelopment Subcommittee, Hayward discussed the 1947 Hartzog plan for North Greenhills and the proposal to purchase the entire tract with Lawrence H. Tucker, a former Greenhills city manager and, since December 1948, manager of the CCDC. For a variety of reasons, CCDC seemed a reasonable choice as the "civic group" to buy North Greenhills and oversee its development. But in 1952 CCDC lacked the capital necessary to undertake the North Greenhills venture on its own.

To surmount this obstacle, CCDC offered to form a subsidiary corporation to acquire and participate in the development of the North Greenhills property. Under this proposal, CCDC would hold preferred shares of stock bearing a nominal return of about 5 percent, in return for which CCDC reserved the right to examine and approve all plans for land use and physical development within the tract. Additional capital would be generated by selling common shares to a developer, who would select a majority of the board and conduct the subsidiary's business, subject only to the control over plans and physical development exercised by the preferred shareholder. The creation of the subsidiary corporation, therefore, would make it possible to raise money to purchase North Greenhills and also vest

33. Stamm to Hayward, Mar. 21, 1952, CDC Collection, CHS; Hayward to Joseph B. Hall, Mar. 28, 1952, CDC Collection, CHS; Stamm to Egan, Mar. 27, 1952, CDC Collection, CHS.

34. "Articles of Incorporation of The Cincinnati Community Development Company" [copy], n.d., CDC Collection, CHS.

control over its planning and development in the hands of people from the Cincinnati metropolitan area.[35]

This proposition was worked out in summer 1952. That fall, CCDC secured from PHA an option in the form of a land purchase contract to buy North Greenhills for $1,200,000; the option prevented other interests from acquiring all or part of the land until CCDC was ready to make the purchase. At the same time, CCDC invited the developer Schmidt had mentioned in the March 19 meeting to draw up a plan for North Greenhills, in preparation for being brought into the subsidiary corporation. The developer turned out to consist of Robert Gerholz, a nationally-known builder from Flint, Michigan, who had constructed more than 6,000 homes; Richard T. Selzer, a builder and investment banker from Philadelphia and a former president of the Urban Land Institute (ULI), a non-profit research organization representing the entire range of occupations interested in urban land development; and Schmidt himself, who had been a founder (in 1936) and former president of the ULI.[36] As their first step, and before formally joining the subsidiary corporation for the development of North Greenhills, the group hired Ladislas Segoe, a planner with a superb local and national reputation, to draw up a master plan for North Greenhills.

Segoe had served as chief planning consultant for Cincinnati's 1925 and 1948 master plans, had headed the staff of the Research Committee on Urbanism of President Roosevelt's National Resources Committee, had consulted with the Resettlement Administration on the site and guidelines for Greenhills, and in 1941 had edited and written substantial parts of the International City Managers Association's manual on city planning, a volume widely regarded as the most influential planning book published in the United States during the first half of the twentieth century.[37] Segoe fervently believed in the

35. Lawrence H. Tucker to Hayward, Mar. 13, 1952, CDC Collection, CHS; "Report to the Stockholders of the Cincinnati Community Development Company," Dec. 1948, CDC Collection, CHS; Tucker, "Historical Notes: The Cincinnati Community Development Company," Aug. 26, 1953, CDC Collection, CHS; Cincinnati Community Development Company, "Statement Regarding Formation of the Cincinnati Community Development Company," Apr. 22, 1948, CDC Collection, CHS; Hayward to Hall, Mar. 28, 1952, CDC Collection, CHS.

36. Earle J. Wheeler to Egan, Apr. 10, 1952, CDC Collection, CHS; "Preliminary Proposal for Purchase and Development of Greenhills Tract, Submitted to the Public Housing Administration by the Cincinnati Community Development Company," Apr. 10, 1952, CDC Collection, CHS.

37. Richard High, "Five Decades of City Planning," *Clifton: The Magazine of the University of Cincinnati* (Winter 1976), 4–5; Ladislas Segoe to author, interview, July 18, 1975.

concept of the metropolis "as an organism in which all things are related in one form or another." He also insisted that any plan "confined to arbitrary city limits cannot be sound . . . ," for the "organic unit is the whole of the urban complex."[38] His firm's plan for North Greenhills, which he later called "the best to come out of my office in fifty years,"[39] reflected his commitment to these principles.

Segoe's 1952 plan projected a "new predominantly residential community, reasonably self-contained, but still a component of Metropolitan Cincinnati and in many respects dependent upon the central city . . . , composed of homes for families of various income levels, but mainly single-family in the medium price range."[40] It would accommodate 36,085 people in six neighborhoods built to a pedestrian scale and equipped with an elementary school, a shopping area, and at least one church. In addition, the plan called for construction of four elementary schools and one junior and one senior high school. On the extreme eastern portion of the site, 240 acres were reserved for light industry, and just west of that, 85 acres were set aside for a regional shopping center. Finally, the Segoe proposal included fire stations, recreation facilities, meeting places for social organizations, a hospital, and a cemetery. Here a person could be born, be raised, work, and die. But in stressing the need for good highways through the Mill Creek industrial belt and into Cincinnati, the plan also recognized North Greenhills' dependence for work, cultural, and recreational attractions on the larger metropolitan area of which it was a part.[41]

The Segoe plan offered potential residents the combined benefits of neighborhood, community, and metropolis in a detailed package he calculated to be economically realistic.[42] The plan's execution, however, depended on retaining a private developer willing to push through such a program, and by the end of 1952, the enthusiasm of

38. Quoted in High, 5.
39. Segoe to author, interview, July 18, 1975.
40. Ladislas Segoe & Associates, "Report Pertaining to Development Plan and Related Studies for North Greenhills Community [,] Cincinnati, Ohio," typescript, January 10, 1953, files of the Laboratory of American Civilization, Dept. of History, Univ. of Cincinnati, p. 1. Hereinafter cited as LAC Files.
41. *Ibid.*, 1–35.
42. Having been chief consultant on Cincinnati's 1948 master plan, Segoe knew full well that its implementation would uproot large numbers of black families who lived in the West End. He later claimed that he had hoped that at least some of them might find a place in North Greenhills. Thus, North Greenhills could have served as a "reception area" on federal property, outside the jurisdiction of local government units, and no one could effectively have objected. Segoe held the city, county, and CDC responsible for not

Schmidt, Selzer, and Gerholz had subsided. Selzer's health had declined, leading him to withdraw from all but absolutely essential activities.[43] But the most serious problem was a report by the Urban Land Institute, which the developer had brought in to evaluate the feasibility of Segoe's plan. That report was skeptical of the possibility of attracting industry to the site and emphasized the need to secure costly local subsidies for utilities and services to make the venture profitable.[44] The ULI report closed the case. Although they had spent almost $100,000 on Segoe's fee and ULI expenses, Gerholz and Selzer pulled out.

The CCDC and Stamm were left with the task of finding another developer, if they were to meet the terms of the land purchase contract with PHA. They turned to the Warner-Kanter Company, which, on January 20, 1953, just ten days after the Segoe plan was officially submitted, agreed to consider the project and put up $25,000 in earnest money. With this assurance of Warner-Kanter's commitment, CCDC negotiated an extension of the PHA's land contract deadline to January 20, 1954.[45]

Signing the Warner-Kanter Company as a potential developer for North Greenhills marked the end of one era in Forest Park's history as an urban community and the beginning of another. Throughout most of the first period, Forest Park was farmland, serving as a greenbelt for a New Deal new town conceived as a subcommunity of a larger, organic metropolis. The 1950 division of the Greenhills property and sale of the village of Greenhills led to the idea of North Greenhills and left the future of the Forest Park area in doubt. Both Hartzog and Segoe designed plans for the area—plans compatible with the greenbelt notion and the larger assumptions about metropolitan community underlying both the greenbelt concept and the Cincinnati Metropolitan Master Plan of 1948. By bringing in Warner-Kanter, CCDC sought to assure development of North Greenhills as one step in

---

assuring this outcome. Segoe to author, interview, July 18, 1975. Yet none of this was made explicit in the plan his firm submitted, and none of the other parties to the project seems to have been committed to the goal of making North Greenhills a racially integrated community.

43. Segoe to author, interview, July 18, 1975.

44. Stamm to author, interview, June 1, 1976; Tucker, "Historical Notes"; Tucker to author, interview, Aug. 12, 1976; Marvin L. Warner to Cincinnati Community Development Company, Feb. 25, 1953, CDC Collection, CHS.

45. Warner to Cincinnati Community Development Company, Feb. 25, 1953, CDC Collection, CHS; Tucker to author, interview, Aug. 12, 1976.

implementing the Metropolitan Master Plan of 1948. Yet the CCDC agreement with Warner-Kanter not only brought new actors onto the stage but also coincided with a general redefinition in America of the nature of metropolis. These events opened the second period in the history of Forest Park.

Even to the superficial observer the modern metropolis is a collection of little worlds and local communities.
MORRIS JANOWITZ,
The Community Press in an Urban Setting
(1952)

THE REDISCOVERY OF LOCAL COMMUNITY AND THE PURCHASE OF NORTH GREENHILLS

It took three years to plan and build Greenhills, but four years were required merely to acquire the land and develop a plan for North Greenhills. It is tempting to attribute the difference to bureaucratic red tape and bungling, or to ineptness or lack of ability or perseverance among the participants. In fact, Charles Stamm, George Hayward, the CDC, and the CCDC applied themselves assiduously and imaginatively to the North Greenhills project. And both Congress and the PHA reacted with reasonable speed and flexibility to the proposals put to them for the disposal and development of North Greenhills. Yet from its outset the project floundered, and the floundering continued after the Warner-Kanter Company became the CCDC developer. Indeed, it took a full year for Warner-Kanter and CCDC to complete the purchase of North Greenhills and to create a new plan for its development. The delay stemmed from difficulties in securing cooperation among the various local actors in the process. Those difficulties arose from a national phenomenon, the rediscovery of local community in America and the appearance in the 1950s of a new mode of thought about the metropolis.

The rediscovery of local community in America took place within the framework of a new conception of American society and the city's place in it. By mid-century, the old organic metaphor had fallen out of favor, and with it the view of the metropolis as a basic component of the social order. Replacing the organic image was a more mechanistic

28

conception of society which drew on physics rather than biology.[1] This outlook held that individuals constituted the fundamental units of society and thus comprised the only "real" entities appropriate for study and concern. The clash of individual interests, values, and aspirations, to be sure, produced classes, institutions, associations, organizations, and even territorial communities of a sort. But nothing similar to the turn-of-the-century formulation of neighborhood and city, or to the subsequent casting of metropolis and region as "natural" elements in the social order, was deemed to exist.

In this perspective, individuals possessed or ought to possess the sort of autonomy that David Riesman and his colleagues wrote about in *The Lonely Crowd* (1950), the ability to become what they wanted as a consequence of personal decisions insignificantly influenced by their associations, residences, and histories. In territorial terms, this meant that where you came from no longer determined who you were. Instead, who you were—or decided to be—determined where you went, and wherever you went, you sought a degree of autonomy sufficient to maintain your security and self-defined sense of identity. You deserved, in other words, to be consulted about what happened to you and your chosen environment.

This new view, emphasizing individuals and their varied personal needs, had significant implications for post-1950 efforts to reconstruct metropolitan areas. The revision implied a new respect for diversity and a new tolerance for both mixed and segregated socioeconomic, racial, ethnic, and land-use patterns. The new view in the 1950s drew a particularly sharp distinction between the city and its suburbs, with the city characterized in terms of heterogeneity, concentration, specialization, tension, and drive, and the suburbs characterized in opposite terms. In this context, as William H. Whyte, a prominent student of urban life in the 1950s, put it, there could be "people who like cities," just as there indubitably existed people who liked silk-stocking, middle-class, or industrial suburbs, or exurbia.[2] In this view, too, a slum need not be a mere hotbed of pathology entrapping and demoralizing its inhabitants; the slum could also be a staging ground for mobility or a location chosen by people because it fit their self-defined needs. Similarly, the central business district of the me-

1. The "mechanistic" notion is adapted from Werner Stark, *The Fundamental Forms of Social Thought* (New York: Fordham Univ. Press, 1963).
2. The Editors of *Fortune, The Exploding Metropolis: A Study of the Assault on Urbanism and How Our Cities Can Resist It* (Garden City, N.Y.: Doubleday, 1958), vii.

tropolis need not be exclusively a place of business and entertainment; it could also be, like New York's 57th Street, a place of residence for those to whom "midtown" epitomized the prototypically desirable characteristics of "the city." And while people could and did continue to use the word "community," the term no longer designated a powerful social and cultural force. It now meant merely a place where people chose to live for the purpose of satisfying their personal economic, psychological, professional, or civic needs, or some combination of the four.

The emergence of this new vision of society had profound consequences, not the least of which was a rediscovery of local community. While this rediscovery was a general phenomenon, Morris Janowitz, a University of Chicago sociologist, characterized it as bluntly as anyone. In *The Community Press in an Urban Setting* (1952), Janowitz argued for the existence of a local community orientation—a sense of civic connection—among some people in what he conceded to be a mass society. He posited the metropolis not as a basic territorial unit of community, but as a congeries of localities, each functioning as a "community of limited liability." Within this kind of local community, individuals and families with social and psychological commitments to a variety of other "communities"—churches, fraternal and social organizations, ethnic and labor groups, businesses, and professions—could identify and interact, participating or withdrawing (whether by moving or by adopting a passive attitude toward local affairs) as their interests, perceptions of community conditions, and stage in the family cycle dictated. In a forthright attack on the old metropolitan mode of thought, Janowitz wrote:

> Our community is clearly not one of completely bureaucratized and impersonalized attachments. In varying degrees, use of local facilities is accompanied by community orientations. The extent and character of these attachments are in good measure linked to the individual resident's predispositions and acts. Raising a family and, to a lesser extent, length of residence and local social contacts predispose him to an acceptance of local community institutions and social controls. In the process, purely 'rational' and 'instrumental' relations are modified. In this regard, individuals vary in the extreme; some are more capable (or have more need) than others of developing these orientations.[3]

The new mode of thought about urban areas emphasized the validity of local community and the distinction between big city and

3. Morris Janowitz, *The Community Press in an Urban Setting: The Social Elements of Urbanism,* 2nd ed. (Chicago: Univ. of Chicago Press, 1967), 211.

suburbs. This mode involved a way of dividing up and ordering society which implicitly legitimized the fragmented metropolis and opened an era of intense conflict and competition among local units of government in metropolitan America generally, including the Cincinnati area. It was in that context that the Warner-Kanter Company approached the task of purchasing and planning North Greenhills. Under its arrangement with PHA, the firm had one year to complete the process.

Marvin L. Warner and Joseph H. Kanter were to become two of the Cincinnati area's most sensational mid-twentieth-century citizens. They ranked with three other men as the city's premier entrepreneurs in the posh times following World War II. One, J. Ralph Corbett, was a millionaire who made his fortune in the home accessories business during the suburban explosion of the 1950s and 1960s. His philanthropic activity, most notably his passion for refurbishing Cincinnati's Music Hall, had endeared him to metropolitan civic leaders. Robert and Carl Lindner had parlayed a string of United Dairy Farmers stores into a sizeable financial empire, but they preferred to keep their good works private. While Corbett and the Lindners enjoyed respectable reputations, Warner and Kanter struck the press and other local observers as somewhat less than genteel.

Both Alabama natives, Warner came from Birmingham and Kanter from Tarrant, not far from Birmingham. Both attended the University of Alabama and George Washington University. In the U.S. Army during World War II, Warner served as a lawyer with the War Department's Legal Division, while Kanter was staff sergeant with the 102nd Infantry Division. After the war, Warner sold insurance in Birmingham, then used his savings and money borrowed from his family to build a 101-unit apartment house. Finally, he and Kanter formed a partnership to construct low-cost, Federal Housing Authority-insured apartments in the Birmingham area. After saturating that market, Warner and Kanter scoured the country for other places with a housing shortage and few contractors willing or able to take on FHA projects. They found the East Coast, Florida, and California "covered," as Warner put it later, but "for some strange reason, the Midwest seemed untouched." By the 1950s they had projects in St. Louis, with Kanter in charge, and in Cincinnati, where Warner ran things.[4]

4. *Cincinnati Post,* Aug. 30, 1976; *Cincinnati Enquirer,* Sept. 6, 1977; Forest Park, Inc., "Joseph H. Kanter Biography," May 29, 1975, LAC Files.

The way Warner ran things distressed many people in Cincinnati. As he once said, he "wasn't winning any popularity contests in those days." His lack of popularity stemmed in large part from his unconventional, high-pressure construction techniques. Before 1953 he had finished two large FHA apartment projects in Cincinnati, the 910-unit Stratford Manor and the 350-unit Canterbury Gardens. While building these projects, Warner fought with local labor officials to secure union membership for his imported plumbing, electrical, and heating workers; offended plasterers by introducing dry-wall construction to the area; and annoyed local custom builders by designing "repetitive buildings" from rough lumber prefabricated in Ft. Payne, Alabama, and shipped to Cincinnati. And he drove his crews relentlessly. "Hell," he once recalled, "I was out there riding a bulldozer, and somebody'd say to me, 'We can't pour that foundation, it's too wet,' and I'd say, 'The hell you can't, get up there and do it.' " When his two projects were finished, moreover, the rents undercut those of other developers (Stratford Manor provided two-bedroom apartments at just $75 a month). And he finished both jobs in suspiciously short order. For example, Canterbury Gardens, which FHA officials had estimated as a year-and-a-half project, took Warner just ten months to complete. Time was an important factor financially because, under the FHA program, a developer could take out a mortgage against the FHA-estimated value of a project after its completion. If the project was built in less time or for less money than estimated, the developer could keep the difference between estimated and actual costs, but he took the loss if a project failed to meet the cost estimates. Warner excelled at finishing under the estimates and garnering the so-called "overloans," and his success aroused suspicions that he took unwise short-cuts. But William Mitchell, president of the Central Trust Bank in Cincinnati, after finding Warner early one morning up to his knees in mud at the Stratford Manor site, declared Warner a good risk, and took him on as a client.[5]

Warner, with his usual energy and thoroughness, took major responsibility for the North Greenhills project, while Kanter attended to the company's business outside the Cincinnati area. Warner talked with Gerholz about the reasons he and Schmidt had withdrawn from the project. He consulted with an old friend, Philip M. Klutznick, who had developed the Chicago suburb of Park Forest, a place given

5. *Cincinnati Post,* Aug. 30, 1976.

national notoriety in William H. Whyte, Jr.'s sometimes acid but generally sympathetic study, *The Organization Man* (1956). Warner also visited Levittown, Long Island, outside New York City, and Levittown, Pennsylvania, outside Philadelphia, two additional "package" suburbs of the post-World War II era. Finally, he brought Klutznick to visit the North Greenhills area to review both the Segoe plan for North Greenhills and the Urban Land Institute report on it.

Klutznick was inclined to agree with the ULI that the Segoe plan was unrealistic. Reporting to Warner, Klutznick noted that it "is my understanding that the principal objective which you have . . . is to provide substantial quantities of housing for the lower-middle income group" and to "encompass within this objective the provision of modern amenities—water and sewage disposal, schools, churches, recreational areas and adequate shopping facilities." But, he said,

> You cannot afford to expend $33 to $45 per lineal foot of utility and road cost. The Segoe preliminary study predicated upon the provision by the developer of all sewer and water and roads under present county specifications would indicate just such a cost. It must not be forgotten that when you add to his cost a fair interest rate during the construction period, the inescapable cost of school subsidies and contribution to stimulate the development of churches, that you would have a gross cost that would make it impossible to develop the area for the lower-middle income group unless the housing structures themselves were totally inadequate.

To get down to a more reasonable $20-per-lineal-foot utility and road cost, Klutznick suggested several possibilities. First, the City of Cincinnati might provide all water and sewer facilities. Second, Greenhills might buy water from Cincinnati at wholesale prices and secure free access to sanitary sewer trunk lines in the Cincinnati disposal system, then expand its own water and sewage disposal facility into North Greenhills by issuing revenue bonds. Third, a private utility owned and financed by Warner-Kanter might work out an arrangement like that suggested for Greenhills. To get down to the $20-per-lineal-foot range, however, it would also be necessary for the county to lower its road specification requirements. Or failing that, North Greenhills could be annexed to Greenhills with an "understanding" about road construction regulations.[6]

Despite Klutznick's warnings about the need for subsidies from local government units, Warner emerged from his preliminary inves-

6. Warner to Cincinnati Community Development Company, Feb. 25, 1953, CDC Collection, CHS.

tigations with guarded optimism. He wrote CCDC a letter indicating that he and Kanter thought the project feasible and that they stood ready to "give our time, our effort, and to invest and risk our funds." They could not go it alone, however. It was essential, Warner added, to determine "the extent of the moral, the civic, the political, and the economic support which we can expect" in order to overcome the obstacles foreseen by Klutznick. To drive home the point, Warner reminded CCDC that it could be five or six years before the Warner-Kanter Company would realize any returns from its investment and emphasized that

> . . . it is essential that the project be burdened by as few overhead costs as possible, since, . . . besides the community facilities which are essential, it is the type of house that we will build and the price that we ask for it which will determine the success or failure of this undertaking . . . .
>
> Underwriting our business interests in the potential development of North Greenhills is a sincere and urgent desire on our part to make this community possible as our contribution toward easing the housing problems of Greater Cincinnati and the resultant social problems which spring therefrom. I am honest in stating that the civic considerations are, to me, equally important as the commercial considerations.[7]

The CCDC agreed that if the CDC would help secure the necessary local subsidies, the CCDC would sign an agreement under which Warner-Kanter would put up money for the term purchase of the land, with a mortgage to the PHA. Warner-Kanter would also have to agree to pay CCDC $50 per housing unit to cover five years of supervisory costs and salaries of the CCDC director and his secretary. After five years, CCDC would step out of its supervisory role and turn the project over to Warner-Kanter. All this remained contingent, however, upon the preparation of an "economically feasible master plan" acceptable to CCDC, and it left the questions of schools, churches, sewers, water, and roads to be worked out with local authorities.[8]

For the planning, Warner first approached Ladislas Segoe, but the two men, both strong-willed, could not agree on the nature of the plan. Warner then hired Justin Hartzog, who in 1947 had drawn up a general North Greenhills plan for the federal government, to prepare the new master plan and to map out what cooperation from public agencies would be required. Briefly, they hoped to secure water at wholesale from Cincinnati, trunk sewer construction from Hamilton

7. *Ibid.*
8. Tucker, "Historical Notes"; Tucker to author, interview, Aug. 26, 1976.

County, and assistance on road construction from county, state, and federal agencies.[9]

By early fall 1953, CCDC and Warner-Kanter were ready to approach the CDC to ask for its aid in securing local subsidies. On September 10, Warner and CCDC Director Lawrence Tucker met with the CDC Housing and Urban Redevelopment Subcommittee. Warner laid out the plan, which called for phased construction of a new town with five "self-sufficient neighborhoods, each having central shopping and other community facilities." When completed, the town would accommodate a population of 41,000 in 11,000 units, 13 percent of which would be in multiple-family dwellings. Lot size for the typical detached single-family home would be 60 x 110 feet, and the house itself would contain three bedrooms and one-and-one-half baths, with a stove, refrigerator, and optional washer and dryer. Prices would run from $12,000 to $18,000. Warner thought that the provision of one or more swimming pools and "other public features" in the new town would make these houses compare favorably with more expensive homes elsewhere owned by people who could afford country club memberships. Financing the purchase of such homes would be difficult, he added, and would require "arrangements for down payments . . . . of 5 percent in contrast to the 20 percent down payment currently required for homes in the vicinity of $15,000."

In the meeting with CDC, Warner stated that Cincinnati Gas & Electric would extend its utilities, contingent upon construction of a sufficient number of dwellings in the initial phase. He also announced that the developer could not afford improvement costs for roads, water, and sewers in excess of $25 per front foot. Tucker then explained that to meet the $25-per-front-foot figure they needed subsidies from the city and county for the development of the entire tract. Cincinnati, he suggested, could either invest $2,973,000 in water mains and tanks, or supply water wholesale to the developer who would, in turn, build a water system for its retail distribution. The county would need to grant a variance from its policy of requiring sewers to drain according to the natural watershed, so that the western portion of North Greenhills could use the Mill Creek system. Even with that variance, however, the county would have to invest $700,000 for the construction of new sewers outside the project area

9. Hartzog, "North Greenhills Development: Preliminary Check List of Procedures, Master Plan Approvals, and Public Agency Conferences," typescript, n.d. [circa Aug. 1953, marginal notation], Hartzog Papers.

to connect North Greenhills with the Mill Creek trunk sewer. In addition, Tucker wanted the county to assume "specific important" highway improvement costs, where such costs would exceed those usually assessed to abutting property owners. The county was also asked to make an advance payment to the City of Cincinnati for topographical mapping of the project area. Finally, Robert Goldman, CCDC's lawyer, reminded the subcommittee that time was running out for North Greenhills; PHA's deadline for selling North Greenhills to CCDC and Warner-Kanter was January 20, 1954.

Joseph Hall of the CDC subcommittee congratulated CCDC on its presentation, but also observed that its projected improvement costs paralleled those of the first prospective developer. The rest of the conversation centered on the CDC's role in working out the needed subsidies and other arrangements. CCDC maintained that the CDC should "take the lead in any negotiations on behalf of CCDC," to which Hall responded that "this was the problem of CCDC with its developer, for which it must necessarily take full responsibility and assume the lead." Fred Lazarus concurred, remarking that the CDC could "not act as a 'front.' " But both Lazarus and Hall agreed that the CDC could make arrangements for and attend meetings and offer support for the CCDC proposal. After Warner and Tucker left, the CDC, meeting in executive session, heard Hall repeat his objections to CDC's assuming "the initiative"; unanimously agreed not to do so; assigned Executive Secretary Hayward to work with CCDC on materials and meetings; and agreed that the CDC chairman or some other representative would attend such meetings.[10]

The CDC's commitment to the project, though limited, satisfied both CCDC and Warner. Spurred on by the approach of PHA's January 20 deadline, they now pushed hard to get local government subsidies and to rezone the area where they wanted to build the first subdivisions. Negotiations with the county for sewer and road subsidies proceeded quietly but not very successfully. The CCDC and Warner failed to receive either the drainage variance or the $700,000 sewer construction commitment. Primarily because their proposal meshed with previous county plans for county roads, they did secure help on the construction of Southland Road, a new artery critical to the first phase of construction.[11]

10. CDC, "Minutes," Vol. 3 (1952–53), Housing and Urban Redevelopment Subcommittee, Sept. 10, 1953, CDC Collection, CHS.
11. *Ibid.*, Nov. 13, 1953; Tucker to author, interview, Aug. 12, 1976.

Warner and the CCDC also failed to get all the water subsidy they wanted from Cincinnati. Worse still, these negotiations turned into a public controversy involving the question of race; the publicity complicated resolution of the water and the zoning problems.

In the November 1953 Cincinnati City Council elections, the Charter Party emerged with a five-person majority.[12] Almost thirty years before, the Charter Committee had ousted the Republican Party machine and replaced it as the dominant force in Cincinnati politics. More than any other political group, the Charterites had stood for centralization and efficiency in local government. Since the mid-1920s they had strongly supported the city-manager form of city government, with a nine-person city council elected at large through a system of proportional representation. The Charterites had made periodic efforts to reduce governmental fragmentation at the local level by securing consolidation and coordination of services on a countywide basis. And large numbers of Charterites had served on the board of the Cincinnati Bureau of Governmental Research, a non-profit organization created in the 1920s to improve the theory, practice, and efficiency of public administration in Hamilton County.

In short, from the 1920s to the 1950s, the Charterites had seen themselves as Cincinnati's special champions of the metropolitan mode of thought. They conceived of the metropolis as a basic and coherent social organism composed of interdependent parts, and they pursued in various ways the logical extension of that position—some form of federated metropolitan government. Although the Cincinnati Metropolitan Master Plan of 1948, which Charterites had supported enthusiastically, made no explicit mention of metropolitan government, it did spell out guidelines for the development of the entire metropolitan area and so seemed likely to contribute to a reduction in the political fragmentation of the metropolis and especially of Hamilton County. By one count, the county alone in the 1950s contained eighty-nine governmental jurisdictions.[13] On the basis of their party's

---

12. *Cincinnati Enquirer,* Dec. 2, 1953.

13. For partial accounts of the Charterites' commitment to efficiency and centralization and their efforts to extend those principles into the county, see Charles P. Taft, *City Management* (Port Washington, N.Y.: Kennikat Press, 1971); Ralph Straetz, *PR Politics in Cincinnati* (New York: New York Univ. Press, 1958); William A. Baughin, "Murray Seasongood: Twentieth Century Reformer" (Ph.D. diss., Univ. of Cincinnati, 1972); and *Cincinnati Enquirer,* Jan. 19, 1954. The last source describes city administration and city council discussion of annexation possibilities, including acquisition of up to fifty square miles of territory in five townships.

record, then, the Charterites ought to have been willing to cooperate enthusiastically with Warner-Kanter and CCDC, for the North Greenhills project seemed consonant with the city's Metropolitan Master Plan of 1948 and with the idea of the metropolis as an interdependent socioeconomic organism.

As it turned out, however, the Charterite majority on the Cincinnati City Council was in an unexpansive mood during fall, winter, and spring 1953–1954. As the new council took office in December 1953, the city faced a severe fiscal crunch. The crisis stemmed from the familiar confluence of urban sprawl, which ate away at the city's revenue base, and inflation generated by World War II and the Korean conflict. Consequently, in December 1953, the council's Finance Committee was contemplating various means of meeting the crisis. The committee was chaired by Charterite Theodore Berry, the council's only black member, who in the 1970s would become Cincinnati's first black mayor. Suggestions for alleviating the financial strains included cutbacks in the city's donation to cultural institutions, which everyone knew served the entire metropolis, and the imposition of an income tax[14] on the earnings of all who worked in Cincinnati, whether they lived in the city or not.

To complicate matters, Berry himself had just had an unpleasant brush with the CDC. In 1949, a group of twenty black veterans had formed the Cedar Grove Development Corporation, hired Berry as their lawyer, and, using a white buyer, acquired a small tract of land just east of North Greenhills for a housing development. White resistance to the plan surfaced immediately. Attempts were made to buy out the blacks or trade the Cedar Grove land for another tract close to Lincoln Heights, one of the largest all-black suburbs in the nation. And Berry and his clients also failed to secure financing from Cincinnati banks.[15] In summer 1952, Berry had approached the CDC for help in getting a loan to carry out the $3 million building program. A CDC delegation toured the site but ended up offering no assistance except to recommend that members should "act individually on behalf of the project to the extent of their resources." Berry and his colleagues eventually raised the money outside the Cincinnati metropolitan area, and in 1958, homes in the $14,000 to $25,000 range

14. *Cincinnati Enquirer,* Dec. 2 and 24, 1953; Jan. 20, 1954.
15. Theodore M. Berry to author, interview, May 16, 1976; Allen L. Bivens, Jr., "Housing Migration of Black Cincinnatians in the 1950's and 1960's" (M.A. thesis, Univ. of Cincinnati, 1971), 51–52.

began to go up in what became the middle-class black suburb of Hollydale.[16]

The Cedar Grove experience left Berry exasperated with the CDC, but it also had raised fears in the northern part of the county about the "dangers" of an influx of blacks. These fears were fed by publicity which connected the North Greenhills project with the razing of much of the West End black ghetto to make way for expressways, and which used the planning jargon term "integrated" to denote the comprehensiveness of the North Greenhills plan. This publicity, combined with Warner's reputation as a builder of low-cost housing, kept alive the race question and complicated CCDC-Warner negotiations with the city and other local authorities.[17]

At the same time, the North Greenhills project got caught up in another controversy, the great water fight between Cincinnati and its suburbs. For years the Cincinnati waterworks had possessed the capacity to process more than enough water to meet the needs of Cincinnati consumers. Under an agreement with Hamilton County and county municipalities, Cincinnati traditionally had sold water to "outside" consumers at the flat rate of 15 cents per hundred cubic feet, while charging Cincinnatians a maximum of 10 cents, on a sliding scale which put heavier consumers in lower rate brackets. The basic agreement had expired in 1946, however, and since then the city had been trying unsuccessfully to negotiate a new contract with higher rates for outside consumers. In 1950 the city proposed a rate schedule which retained city consumers' 10-cent maximum but raised their minimum rate, while placing outside consumers in three brackets at 25, 22, and 14 cents. At once the county and several suburban municipalities objected, not to rate differentials *per se,* but to what they regarded as excessively high differences in rates for residents of different places. Amid talk of new water systems to be built in the county, the Bureau of Governmental Research proposed that the city sell water "wholesale," i.e., sell water at negotiated rates, if some other public or private entity would retail the water, maintain the water lines, and, where necessary, create and expand the distribution system. The City of Norwood, a heavy user of water for industry,

16. Berry to author, interview, May 16, 1976; Bivens, "Housing Migration of Black Cincinnatians," 52–53; *Cincinnati Post,* May 12, 1976; CDC, "Minutes," Vol. 3 (1952–53), July 1, 1952, and July 17, 1952.

17. See, e.g., the *Cincinnati Enquirer,* Mar. 1, 1954; and a City Planning Commission report on the North Greenhills plan, quoted in Max Schamer, "Forest Park Water Rights, Part II," typescript, Mar. 1976, LAC Files.

already had its own lines and did in fact work out such a wholesaling agreement. But as of winter 1953–1954, an agreement had not been reached for consumers in the rest of the county.[18]

The absence of a general water agreement forced CCDC and Warner to seek a negotiated settlement with the city. In November 1953, CCDC approached the Cincinnati City Council with a request that the city spend $3 million for a water distribution system in North Greenhills, beginning with a $300,000 water tank for the first 2,700 housing units. The city was also asked to provide water to North Greenhills "wholesale."[19] The proposal faced immediate and strident opposition, led by an unlikely alliance of a liberal Charter-Democrat, John J. Gilligan, and a conservative Republican, Donald Clancy, both of whom called the proposal too expensive.[20]

With no support on the council for the proposal to have Cincinnati build a water system for North Greenhills, CCDC and Warner suggested an alternative plan. Warner-Kanter would create a North Greenhills water company to retail and distribute water purchased from Cincinnati at a wholesale rate. On December 19, the council's Public Utilities Committee reported favorably on this arrangement for the first 2,700 housing units. Berry, however, wanted a stipulation that the city would participate in determining planning standards at each stage in the development of North Greenhills. That proposal sent the entire question back to committee. Finally, on December 24, the council considered the matter again. This time two council members, Charterites Berry and Dorothy Dolbey, tied the agreement to a proviso that the master plan for the new community would have to be approved by the Cincinnati City Planning Commission. When Stanley Rowe, then CCDC president, suggested that the North Greenhills project would be "seriously jeopardized" if Warner-Kanter had to adhere to city building and zoning codes, Berry, apparently referring to Warner's previous low-income projects, replied that he merely wanted a safeguard against "short-cuts" which might eventually make North Greenhills an "eyesore."[21]

18. Cincinnati Bureau of Governmental Research, "The Water Question: Cincinnati and Hamilton County," typescript, July 31, 1951, Cincinnati Bureau of Governmental Research Papers, Urban Studies Collection, Archival Collections of the University of Cincinnati; *Cincinnati Enquirer,* Dec. 16, 1954.

19. CDC, "Minutes," Vol. 3 (1952–53), Nov. 13, 1953.

20. *Cincinnati Enquirer,* Dec. 10, 1953.

21. Berry to author, interview, May 16, 1976; Segoe to author, July 18, 1975; Schamer, "Forest Park Water Rights"; *Cincinnati Enquirer,* Dec. 24, 1953.

To meet Dolbey and Berry's reservations, the City Planning Commission hastily reviewed the North Greenhills master plan and on January 6, 1954, reported favorably. The planning commission suggested that the council cooperate on the water question, but only if Hamilton County provided assurances that sanitary sewage would be provided for the entire tract, that the necessary zoning would be secured, and that county authorities would exercise subdivision control to insure that the development proceeded according to the master plan's guidelines.[22]

A week later, the city manager sent the council a report recommending that the city charge uniform water rates throughout the county.[23] The signal seemed clear. The city would "cooperate" on the North Greenhills zoning and development problem; it would also renegotiate a water agreement, thereby forestalling the creation of additional waterworks plants in the county and making city water available to suburbs at rates lower than the 1950 schedule had proposed. Though the issue was scarcely resolved, the prospect of an imminent city-county water contract or a negotiated arrangement with the city encouraged CCDC and Warner-Kanter to purchase North Greenhills.

With less than a week left before the PHA deadline, Kanter and Robert Goldman, CCDC counsel, went to Washington to close the deal with the PHA, under terms which permitted them to do the project in phases. In a hectic all-day session the federal authorities agreed to a contract by which CCDC would pay for only part of the property and receive an option to acquire the rest in a specified series of purchases over time. Right on the deadline, January 20, 1954, CCDC closed with the government and the same day transferred to Warner-Kanter both the property and the responsibility for the PHA mortgage covering the unpaid portion of an eventual $1,200,000 for purchase of 3,400 acres.[24]

The purchase of North Greenhills, however, did not mean that construction could begin, for Warner-Kanter still had to get water from the city. In April 1954, the council considered an ordinance authorizing a water contract between the City of Cincinnati and

22. Schamer, "Forest Park Water Rights."
23. *Ibid.*
24. Joseph H. Kanter to author, interview, July 3, 1975; Tucker, "Supplemental Historical Notes," n.d., CDC Collection, CHS; Robert E. Wildermuth to author, June 17, 1976, LAC Files; Arnold, *The New Deal in the Suburbs*, 236.

Warner-Kanter for the North Greenhills project. The ordinance's preamble recognized the need for "medium-priced" housing in the Cincinnati area, and the rest of the ordinance provided for sale of 17-cent city water to a North Greenhills water company for redistribution and use in North Greenhills. The council deferred action until May, then authorized the contract.[25]

Two terms of the May ordinance indicated that some deal with the county on general water rates might be imminent. The first item declared that if the city and the county adopted a contract providing standard rates and services outside Cincinnati, those standards would apply to North Greenhills. The second clause stipulated that if the city-county contract also provided for "non-restriction and non-discrimination because of race, religion, ancestry, or national origin in the sale, lease, use, rental, or occupancy of housing in areas receiving city water," that clause, too, would apply to North Greenhills.[26]

On June 3, the council authorized negotiations between the city and the county on a standard water contract. The talks ran until December 15, when the two sides agreed on a thirty-six-year pact. The county water area was defined as all of the unincorporated territory in the county, plus ten specified villages and cities. The city rate for water rose from 10 to 15 cents per hundred cubic feet and the county rate from 25 to 30 cents. Future rate adjustments were left to the city, with the understanding that the county's rate for equivalent services should be double that of the city. And responsibility for water main construction and services was divided between city and county, but the problem of distribution mains outside the city was left to the county commissioners. The agreement said nothing, however, about non-discrimination in housing within the county water area.[27]

The new city-county contract looked good for North Greenhills. It meant 30-cent water and city maintenance of the system. It also meant that CCDC and Warner-Kanter would deal with the county commissioners and not the city council (some members of which distrusted Warner and wanted to impose non-discrimination controls on the development) on the questions of who would build the water distribution system within North Greenhills and under what terms. During the council's consideration of the water ordinance, Berry had

25. *Cincinnati Enquirer*, May 25, 1954.
26. Schamer, "Forest Park Water Rights."
27. *Ibid.*

tried unsuccessfully to retain some leverage for the city by inserting an escape clause permitting either party to terminate the agreement. And Berry and Dolbey both had tried to make city approval of the contract contingent upon the county's agreeing to handle any sewer problems which might develop as a consequence of pumping more water into the county. But the council had gone along with Councilman Gilligan, who had chaired the Public Utilities Committee which worked out the arrangement with the county. He had argued that water and sewer problems, like other city-county problems such as annexation, police work, and poor relief, should be treated separately and not tied together in such a way as to block progress in one field because of insuperable difficulties in another.[28]

Meanwhile, Warner and CCDC had been working with Hamilton County and Greenhills officials to change some of the zoning regulations covering North Greenhills. This process took seven months. In April 1954, Warner took a rezoning request to the Hamilton County Regional Planning Commission. He asked that 675 acres of the 3,400-acre tract be rezoned from R-A, which stipulated lots of 20,000 square feet for residential sites, to R-C, which permitted residential construction on lots as small as 6,000 square feet. He also requested the conversion of 100 acres in the eastern and western parts of North Greenhills from residential to industrial and commercial use.[29]

The rezoning proposal ran into immediate, heated, and persistent objections from Greenhills residents, not because of its provisions for industrial development, but because of the potential ramifications of the requested residential down-zoning. At the first planning commission public hearing, George Hayward of CCDC made a plea for the changes, on the grounds that the development would "take care of those made homeless by slum clearance projects." Opponents of North Greenhills, however, claimed that Greenhills, not the county, possessed jurisdiction over zoning in the area.[30] After the meeting the furor mounted. By early June, the *Cincinnati Post* reported that a majority of people in Greenhills opposed the construction of the new town because they feared that "low-cost housing" would force up school property taxes to accommodate a sudden influx of families into the district. The second planning commission public hearing attracted over one hundred Greenhills residents, featured "verbal

28. *Cincinnati Enquirer,* Dec. 16, 1954.
29. *Greenhills Journal,* Apr. 16, 1954.
30. *Ibid.,* May 14, 1954.

fireworks," and elicited pledges from Warner to protect property values, to preserve topsoil and trees, to build on lots no smaller than 7,200 square feet (despite the request for a 6,000-square-foot minimum), and to construct houses in the $13,000 to $14,500 price range.[31]

Ignoring these assurances, Greenhills officials remained adamant in their opposition to the project. Nevertheless, the rezoning request cleared the planning commission and went to the county commissioners.

While the commissioners deliberated, disturbing rumors circulated in Greenhills. The mayor, for example, wondered out loud if Warner-Kanter really would resist the temptation to build homes on 6,000-square-foot lots. The *Greenhills Journal* raised another specter. It reported a "fear" that Greenhills might be persuaded to annex successive developments on the North Greenhills site, one by one, in order to secure added revenue for municipal services. This scheme, the paper noted, would allow the completion of undeveloped tracts under county rather than Greenhills zoning authority and eventually permit the newcomers to take over the Greenhills City Council.[32] At a final hearing before the county commissioners, however, the Greenhills mayor and city solicitor based their objections to the zoning changes on the school problem. The alterations, they insisted, would drive Greenhills property taxes up and permit outsiders to use the schools without paying a fair share of the costs.[33]

Despite the Greenhills resistance, the county commissioners approved the zoning changes. The rezoning left Greenhills but one avenue of protest, a referendum to overturn the new zoning regulations. Support for a referendum evaporated, however, after the *Greenhills Journal* ran a story that the school board and Warner-Kanter were negotiating an agreement under which the corporation would subsidize the construction of school facilities for North Greenhills residents.[34] Shortly thereafter, on October 13, 1954, the school board accepted a Warner-Kanter proposal to pay the school district $100 for each house constructed in the initial subdivision.[35]

The school pledge concluded the preliminaries. After years of

31. *Cincinnati Post*, June 5, 1954; *Greenhills Journal*, June 25, 1954.
32. *Greenhills Journal*, July 9, 1954; Sept. 3, 1954.
33. *Cincinnati Enquirer*, Sept. 15, 1954; *Greenhills Journal*, Sept. 17, 1954.
34. *Greenhills Journal*, Oct. 1, 1954.
35. *Greenhills Journal*, Jan. 4, 1957.

planning and months of negotiations, CCDC had secured a developer, purchased the land, and worked out local arrangements for utilities and services. Warner now stood ready to start constructing a new community. To be sure, the CCDC and Warner had failed to secure water, sewer, and road commitments necessary to do the entire tract according to the 1954 Hartzog plan, and the school situation remained volatile. But the land was theirs, they had a plan, the general economic and urban trends seemed to be running in their favor. The housing shortage persisted, and the passion for suburban life burned as brightly as ever. By this time, too, everyone knew about I-275, a freeway projected to circle the metropolitan area and cut across the edge of North Greenhills. The freeway was expected to hasten the spread of people, business, and industry into the northern suburbs. The new community might yet become another Park Forest, a community of limited liability for uprooted organization men and their families.

As if to assure that outcome, Warner and Kanter took another step in forging the public image of their new town. They dropped the name North Greenhills, which evoked memories of the Great Depresssion and New Deal low-income housing projects, and dubbed their new town Forest Park.

Ideals of community living will be of primary consideration in the program.
MARVIN WARNER,
Cincinnati Post, May 5, 1953

COMMUNITY WITHOUT SELF-GOVERNMENT: AN EXPERIMENT IN SUBURBAN LIVING, 1956—1961

The Warner-Kanter Company had no difficulties attracting residents to Forest Park. The first residential area, Cameron Heights, was completed in 1956 and contained 400 families. By the end of the decade, two more subdivisions had gone up. Though Forest Park in 1960 still contained 3,000 acres of undeveloped land, it already housed 4,800 people, an impressive increase even in an era of burgeoning suburban growth generally.

But Warner and Kanter wanted to build more than mere suburban subdivisions. They wanted to built a *community,* a single cohesive unit in which the residents of the subdivisions would participate in common activities and cooperate with the developer in the essentially civic enterprise of fostering the general welfare and prosperity. In the age of the community of limited liability, this aspiration meant that Forest Park had to be a suburb distinguishable from all others, and not merely a series of unrelated subdivisions. Moreover, if leisure activities were to be the medium through which a sense of community was created, Forest Park had to offer leisure activities suitable for a community of autonomous individuals—channels for developing and expressing the cultural, charitable, and civic impulses which the residents as responsible "citizens" presumably possessed. And since Forest Park lacked self-government, the developer and first residents had to cooperate closely to generate the types of participation which would make community-consciousness through civic participation the town's most distinctive characteristic. The effort to make Forest Park a civic community without self-government persisted for half a decade, only to collapse in 1961 when unforeseen events resulted in Forest Park's incorporation as a village.

From the beginning, Warner-Kanter worked hard to insure that Forest Park would not be merely a well-planned development, but rather a place designed and equipped to engender in its residents a sense of connection to, and responsibility for, a civic community without self-government. In March 1957, for example, Warner-Kanter donated seven acres of land with swimming pool and club, touting this facility as the first of several neighborhood leisure centers. To point up the donation's significance, Warner noted that the "responsibility of providing for such facilities cannot be borne entirely by public agencies"; he capped the occasion by announcing plans for a medical center, including six doctors and an infirmary, to be the first of its kind in the northern section of Hamilton County.[1]

The leisure center donation and medical center announcement proved to be only two events in the campaign to attract the "right" kind of people and inspire in them a sense of Forest Park's special nature. To celebrate the opening of Cameron Heights in 1956, for example, Warner-Kanter brought in Steve Allen,[2] a musician, writer, wit, and versatile television celebrity whose late-night talk show had built for him a strong following among the nation's college-educated middle classes, and who, unlike Sid Caesar or Milton Berle, had established a reputation through his television show as a well-informed citizen responsibly concerned with urban and community problems.

In September 1956, to mark the opening of Forest Vue Estates,[3] Warner-Kanter held a grand three-day dedication of Forest Park, an event with a "country fair atmosphere" attended by an estimated 30,000 to 35,000 persons. The ceremonies featured appearances by Miss America, Marian Ann McKnight, and Judge James Garfield Stewart, justice of the Ohio Supreme Court and former mayor of Cincinnati. The pair represented, on the one hand, the wholesome charm and beauty of "responsible" femininity, and, on the other hand, the majesty of the law and the dignity of civic statesmanship. Since there was little to show except groups of houses arranged in

1. *Cincinnati Times-Star,* Mar. 22, 1957; Mar. 26, 1957.
2. *Cincinnati Enquirer,* May 25, 1956.
3. *Cincinnati Enquirer,* Aug. 12, 1956.

what appeared to be two ordinary subdivisions, the company's press releases focused on what would be, rather than what was. One described a "New City Spawning," spoke of ultimate expenditures of $300 million, a population of 50,000, homes priced from $14,000 to $75,000, an industrial center of 239 acres, and plans for swimming and wading pools, ice-skating facilities, tennis and badminton courts, and baseball diamonds. Another release emphasized the natural screening of ridges and trees between projected subdivisions; Warner-Kanter's intention to establish a large park and a shopping center for the whole area; and plans to equip all Forest Park houses with clothes dryers and garbage disposals to eliminate lawn and street clutter.[4]

The dedication ceremonies peaked with the unveiling of the Forest Park monument. The concrete and brick structure served as foundation for a flagpole and housed a "time capsule" containing three copies of Cincinnati newspapers, literature about Forest Park, and a letter from Warner.[5] The front of the monument displayed a plaque with a brief inscription which sought to establish Forest Park's distinctiveness by celebrating the commonplace:

> History affords ample recognition to statesmen, soldiers, and inventors, whose leadership and creativeness helped build America. But little acclaim has been given the wage earner and the home maker—the families of the American home. They are America—for them, Forest Park, Ohio, is planned and gratefully dedicated.[6]

After the dedication, the developer continued his effort to implant in residents a commitment to the creation of civic community in Forest Park. In late November 1956, Warner-Kanter announced that it would sell, "at a substantial discount," five acres of land for church sites.[7] The first full year's promotion of Forest Park as a civic community reached a climax with a first anniversary celebration in late September 1957. On this occasion, the company's news releases paid special attention to the swimming pool donation, to Cincinnati Gas & Electric's purchase of an industrial site, and to the bus service which

4. *Cincinnati Enquirer*, Sept. 20 and 30 and Oct. 1, 1956; *Cincinnati Post*, Sept. 28, 1956; *Cincinnati Times-Star*, Oct. 1, 1956. Also see *Business Week*, Sept. 22, 1956; *Engineering News Record*, Oct. 4, 1956.
5. *Cincinnati Enquirer*, Sept. 29, 1956.
6. Flagpole monument, Forest Park, Ohio.
7. *Cincinnati Enquirer*, Nov. 29, 1956; *Greenhills Journal*, Dec. 7, 1956; Jan. 4, 1957. Warner-Kanter reserved sites for Catholic, Protestant, and Jewish edifices, but let the Council of Churches determine when the demand warranted the creation of a congregation. Kanter to author, interview, July 5, 1975.

now connected Forest Park's first three subdivisions to each other. Reporters noted that an estimated 500 families already lived in Forest Park, while more were moving in every day, and pointed to the existence of several voluntary associations as indications that the development was becoming a cohesive community different from and superior to a mere residential subdivision.[8]

Indeed, Warner-Kanter's enthusiasm for creating a civic community gradually caught on with Forest Park residents. One early settler, Eileen Kieffer, a self-styled crusader for "our 'model city' idea," expressed optimism about creating community in Forest Park. In a guest editorial in the *Greenhills Journal* written on the occasion of Forest Park's first birthday, Kieffer thanked Greenhills for extending Forest Parkers a warm and generous welcome into that city's schools, churches, and organizations. She frankly recognized Forest Park's deficiencies as a community and its dependence on Greenhills. She closed her remarks, however, by challenging Greenhills to compete in "this wonderful drama of growth" which must eventually lead to practical if not legal independence for Forest Park. "No business organization or community stands still," she declared. "It either slips backward or charts a course for continuous, vigorous growth."[9]

Kieffer's commitment to severing Forest Park's dependence on Greenhills for community facilities must have gratified Warner-Kanter. To be sure, Greenhills' existence on the southwestern edge of Forest Park's first subdivisions constituted an invaluable convenience to both Warner-Kanter and the pioneer residents of Forest Park. Without Greenhills, the company itself would have had to provide the basic services necessary to a rapidly growing settlement. The existence of Greenhills saved Forest Parkers both money and trouble, for they could enjoy its schools, shopping center, churches, and organizations without paying the taxes or spending the time necessary to build up and sustain such facilities. Greenhills made Forest Park's mid-1950s rawness more palatable, which pleased Forest Park's first residents, and settlement in Forest Park more attractive to prospective home buyers, which pleased the developer.

Yet Warner-Kanter did not want the dependence of Forest Park on Greenhills to persist, for it ran against the grain of the developer's practical idealism. Like Philip Klutznick in Park Forest, Warner and

8. *Cincinnati Times-Star,* Sept. 18, 20, and 27, 1957; *Cincinnati Enquirer,* Sept. 29, 1957.
9. *Greenhills Journal,* Oct. 18, 1957; June 19, 1959.

Kanter wanted to make money, preferably lots of it. The partners saw the completion of Forest Park as a twenty- or thirty-year project; therefore they wanted to create early in the process a community structure and a sense of community among Forest Park's residents strong enough to support the long-term stability and prosperity without which money could not be made. Warner and Kanter believed that the mere possession by residents of a thirty-year mortgage made little difference if Forest Park remained a collection of strangers, a large proportion of whom led the fluid existence of corporate employees subject to sudden transfer or lay-off and accustomed to the rapid acquisition and disposition of real property. Warner and Kanter, moreover, doubted the efficacy of "neighborhood," the mere juxtaposition of similar people in subdivisions, to generate a sense of responsibility for Forest Park as a whole.

Unlike Klutznick's Park Forest, however, which was a real town with real problems, Warner-Kanter's Forest Park was not incorporated as a village or city, and so lacked a basic ingredient of self-government through which to develop a sense of identity, civic participation, and commitment.[10] To compensate, Warner-Kanter augmented its civic build-up campaign by attempting to develop voluntary civic associations in Forest Park as surrogates for the traditional functions of participating in a legally constituted self-government and to stimulate a sense of belonging, possession, and community. To begin with, Warner-Kanter turned its recreation center over to an association of residents, but that organization quickly turned into a private swim club indistinguishable in form, program, or operations from others scattered throughout metropolitan Cincinnati. In 1957, however, at Warner-Kanter's instigation, two more promising organizations appeared.

The Forest Park Women's Club, which in 1964 claimed to be "the oldest civic organization in the Village," took root in spring 1957. Marvin Warner invited every woman in Forest Park to meet with him at Dixie Dale Farms, his estate in Forest Park's southwest corner, for the purpose of forming a club. Roughly one hundred women responded to the call, and out of that meeting came a group which took as its motto "Happiness through Service,". elected two members from each subdivision to its governing board, and aimed to "unite the

10. For Klutznick's views and experience with civic participation, see William H. Whtye, Jr., *The Organization Man* (Garden City, New York: Doubleday, 1956), 320–27.

women of Forest Park into an organization for the promotion of the intellectual, cultural and social betterment of the community."[11]

The early vigor of this organization led a *Cincinnati Post* reporter to conclude, after interviewing the club's president, that "for sheer enthusiasm about their community, the people of Forest Park stand near the top of the list."[12] During its first few years, the club's 100 to 125 members helped two doctors find temporary quarters in Forest Park, assisted in a rezoning effort, sponsored "koffee klatches" to introduce newcomers to their "new (and wonderful) community," raised money for recreational activities, listened to talks, threw parties, gave dinners, held fashion shows, and in general tried to keep track of, welcome, entertain, and accommodate the seemingly endless tide of people moving into Forest Park's three subdivisions.[13]

The Women's Club concentrated its most relentless effort, however, on charitable activities and humanitarian causes. In 1959 its members gave 1,099 hours of voluntary service, a figure estimated as equal to one-fourth of all the time volunteered to "welfare" activities in the Cincinnati area in 1958–1959.[14] Service of that intensity, if the club's motto can be believed, must have made its members very happy; it also encouraged them and others to think of humanitarianism as an essential civic trait of Forest Parkers.

The other organization for the elevation of community consciousness through civic participation was the Forest Park Civic Association. The association began on April 12, 1957, when a Warner-Kanter vice-president met with five men, all middle-management or research personnel for General Electric, General Motors, or the Avco Corporation, to discuss organizing an association of Forest Park residents. The new association initially identified itself as interested in working with other communities for the mutual benefit of the entire north Hamilton County area.[15] And at one of the group's first meetings, its members heard Iola Hessler, executive director of the Hamilton

11. Mary Elizabeth White, "History of the Forest Park Women's Club," typescript, 1975, LAC Files, p. 1; *Greenhills Journal,* June 7, 1957; *Cincinnati Post,* July 3, 1957; *Forest Park Newsletter,* Nov. 1964; *Forest Park News,* Apr. 8, 1969.

12. *Cincinnati Post,* Oct. 4, 1958.

13. White, "History of the Forest Park Women's Club," 1; *Forest Park Newsletter,* Mar. 2 and May 14, 1958; June 1960; *Forest Park News,* May 29, 1964.

14. *Forest Park Newsletter,* Mar. 2 and Apr. 16, 1958; *Cincinnati Enquirer,* Apr. 14, 1958; *Greenhills Journal,* Dec. 4, 1959.

15. *Greenhills Journal,* Apr. 12 and 26, 1957; *Cincinnati Times-Star,* May 28, 1957.

County Good Government League, speak on the relationship of Forest Park to the Cincinnati metropolitan area.[16]

But the resident group's intitial metropolitan focus soon gave way to a more parochial spirit. By May 1958, the association was calling itself the Forest Park Civic Association and had taken as its official objective the task of making Forest Park a "Better Place in Which to Live." To achieve that end, it set up eleven standing committees for three broad activity areas—association operations (membership, program, finance, and publicity committees), leisure pursuits (recreation, fine arts, and garden committees), and community affairs (legal, development, education, and safety committees). Several of the leisure and community affairs committees regularly came into contact with "outside" groups, such as the authorities of the newly-renamed Greenhills-Forest Park School District, the Springfield Township Trustees, the county sheriff, or Warner-Kanter, but they did so to promote the welfare of Forest Park as a self-contained community, not as a part of northern Hamilton County or the metropolis generally.[17] The association, in short, functioned as a quasi-public body, the closest thing to self-government within Forest Park and the critical crucible within which to forge civic consciousness among a collection of otherwise unrelated individuals.

The Civic Association's officers and standing committees also assumed that creating civic consciousness obliged them to make the people of Forest Park "more closely knit" by organizing and contributing members to more specialized subgroups made up of residents from all three of Forest Park's subidivisons. To that end, the association generated a whirlwind of activity. In its first annual report, the association credited its Recreation Committee with having set up mixed bowling, duplicate bridge, boys' and men's softball, and knothole baseball leagues, as well a summer playground, beginner's bridge classes, and a Teen Club to encourage a "more responsible attitude in teenagers." The Fine Arts Committee proved only slightly less active, listing among its first year's achievements the founding of Theater Forest Park, the Sketch Club, a Great Books Discussion Group, and a Music Group.[18] In the next few years, the association

16. *Forest Park Newsletter,* Jan. 14, 1958.
17. *Forest Park Newsletter,* Aug. 1962; Forest Park Civic Association, "First Annual Report," May 15, 1958.
18. *Forest Park Newsletter,* July 1960; Forest Park Civic Association, "First Annual Report"; *Greenhills Journal,* Dec. 4, 1959.

applauded the appearance of a variety of other groups, including two garden clubs, a Baby Sitters Club to "combat the high cost of gala-vanting," a Toastmasters Club, a Co-op Nursery Center for pre-schoolers, and a Forest Park chapter of the Child Conservation League. Indeed, by summer 1961 so many groups existed that the Civic Association formed yet another one, the Forest Park Coordinating Council, to act as a clearinghouse in arranging meeting times for more than twenty-five organizations.[19]

Clearly, however, the Baseball Association ranked as the most popular of Forest Park's first batch of voluntary associations. A spin-off of the Civic Association, it enrolled 200 boys during 1959 alone. Because of the large number of families reached by its programs, the Baseball Association's officers became familiar figures throughout Forest Park, devoting much time to fund-raising events. In 1959, in addition to charging an activity fee of $4 per child, the organization sponsored three social events which garnered $1,500. Plans were also announced for other activities to raise money to cover the next year's needs, which included a total budget for uniforms of $1,100.[20]

Although the Baseball Association eventually came to compete with the Civic Association in producing community leaders, the Civic Association continued to play the leading role in arousing a sense of civic, as opposed to special-interest, consciousness in Forest Park residents. Indeed, the Civic Association's drives for community improvements such as baseball diamonds and uniforms, traffic signals, and more business and industry constituted the organization's principal reason for existing. Since Forest Park as a community lacked the legal power to do things for itself, the Civic Association had to persuade others to do things for it. To be effective, its leaders argued, required the attention and cooperation of a large proportion of Forest Parkers. And as the chief instrument in securing that cooperation, the association started the *Forest Park Newsletter*.

The *Newsletter* devoted generous amounts of space to the issues of membership and participation in Civic Association affairs. Though the organization's membership roster grew steadily, increasing from 217 in January 1958 to 351 in October 1959, the *Newsletter* persis-

19. *Greenhills Journal*, Feb. 28, 1958; Nov. 20, 1959; Dec. 4, 1959; *Millcreek Valley News*, Sept. 17, 1959; and *Forest Park Newsletter*, May 14, 1958; Jan. 16, 1960; Oct. 1960; July 1961; Aug. 1961.
20. *Forest Park Newsletter*, February 13, 1960.

tently lamented the size of these figures. It pointed out, for example, that 351 family memberships in 1959 represented just 37 percent of the total of 960 occupied homes, and that two subdivisions enrolled just 33 and 29 percent of their families, while the third returned 45 percent.[21]

Part of the *Newsletter's* urgency in promoting widespread interest in the Civic Association stemmed from the latter's anxiety about raising money to meet operational costs and to keep various groups and activities going. Yet the need for funds was neither immediate nor critical. In 1958, the association took in over a thousand dollars— $810.25 in dues, $166.54 raised at a Valentine's dance, and a $100 donation from Warner-Kanter—but spent only $750.49. By February 1960, moreover, the association directors announced that their policy of saving a little each year had led to the accumulation of a "Fund for the Future." Although a use for this fund had not yet been determined, the directors could see that a time might come when "a real community center will be needed"; such a center was an expensive item which "no one is going to give to us."[22]

A more important source of the association's concern for a large membership and consistently high level of participation than its need for money was its eagerness to display the representativeness, strength, and tenacity of its constituency. The association president made this point clear during his inaugural addresss in fall 1959. "It has been said," he noted, without indicating when or by whom, "that every American has a right to a place to live and place to play, where he can rid himself of the pressures and burdens of business life, a place to recuperate from nervous tension." Forest Park, he thought, "fulfills these requirements." Nevertheless, he argued that a "new community" needed a "banding together of individual citizens" so that the association's demands and activities "will represent the action of the majority, rather than the desires and efforts of a few."[23]

Newsletter editor Charles Dawson, who during his extraordinarily long residence in Forest Park functioned as the occasionally acerbic but always lucid public conscience of the community, repeated the idea more bluntly a year later. The Civic Association, he stated flatly, needed a large membership representative of all of Forest Park, as

21. *Forest Park Newsletter,* Jan. 14, 1958; May 15, 1958; Oct. 17, 1959.
22. Forest Park Civic Association, "First Annual Report"; *Forest Park Newsletter,* Feb. 13, 1960.
23. *Forest Park Newsletter,* Oct. 17, 1959.

evidence that the organization spoke for a majority and not just a few "hot-heads," in order to influence "the developer, or the Sheriff, or the Township Trustees." In spring 1960, moreover, Dawson responded heatedly and defensively to "gossip" that the Civic Association was "run by a clique—that outsiders do not have a chance." The truth, he asserted, was "that the officers and directors have come from a small group that is willing to do the work"; he invited the participation of current non-members, to relieve the pressure on those who bore an unfair burden of activism. A year later he was at it again, complaining about people who would not do their share of the work in the association's committees and sponsored organizations and urging these people to join and participate.[24]

Despite its chronic worrying about Forest Parkers' lack of a spirit of responsible citizenship and about its image as a representative organization, the Civic Association claimed that its civic protests got results. It said that it had forced builders to cease "stacking houses" by utilizing the smallest lots permitted under zoning regulations, and had stopped them from using vacant lots for dumps. It took credit for prying "Stop" and "No Parking" signs out of recalcitrant township trustees and for playing an "instrumental" role in the passage of three bond issues for the Greenhills-Forest Park School District. And the association congratulated its Development Committee for securing street lights along Kenn and Southland Roads and said that these lights, when viewed at night from high ground above Forest Park, "proclaim the birth of a city."[25]

Curiously, the Civic Association's policy of civic action seldom brought it into serious conflict with the developer. During its first two years, the nearest the group came to a confrontation with Warner-Kanter took place in spring 1958, when the association sponsored a public panel discussion with Lawrence Tucker, who was then both manager of CCDC and director of planning for Warner-Kanter. To stir up interest, the association's *Newsletter* ran a provocative piece emphasizing the unfulfilled promise of the 1954 Hartzog master plan.[26] The meeting, however, quietly came and went. Tucker predicted that the rate of new house construction in the coming year would be three times that of the past two years. He announced that

24. *Forest Park Newletter,* Mar. 19, 1960; Apr. 1961.
25. *Greenhills Journal,* Dec. 4, 1959; *Forest Park Newsletter,* Dec. 17, 1959; May 13, 1960; July 1960.
26. *Forest Park Newsletter,* Apr. 16, 1958.

West Sharon Road would be widened to four lanes from Winton to Northland and then extended northeast to the proposed Tri-County Shopping Center and, ultimately, to Circle Freeway. In response to a question about the slow pace of commercial and business develop-ment in Forest Park, he seemed less certain, talking generally about expectations for a shopping center, an industrial park, and an office-medical park to accommodate both physicians and a proposed Warner-Kanter office building.

Far from reacting with dismay to Tucker's vagueness about the prospects for non-residential development and to the obvious lack of real progress on the commercial and business front, the Civic Associ-ation passed a motion in favor of all three "expected" projects, declaring that the projects fit the best interests of both Warner-Kanter and the residents. The *Greenhills Journal,* which took bitter conflict between developers and inhabitants in other suburbs as the norm, termed the action "a unique resolution." The *Newsletter* was just plain pleased, congratulating the association's Development Commit-tee for so ably representing the residents' interests in their discus-sions with Warner-Kanter.[27]

The affirmation by Warner-Kanter and the Civic Association of joint interest in commercial and business development made simple good sense. Both Warner-Kanter and the association's constituents owned property and paid taxes, and the bulk of the taxes they paid went for schools. Business and industry produced tax revenue with-out increasing school enrollments and educational costs. And any measure which helped retard the rise of school taxes made Warner-Kanter's new homes more attractive to potential customers, while enhancing the resale value of homes already owned by Forest Park residents. This line of thought, as much as any other, formed a cash nexus between Warner-Kanter and the residents. In 1958 that alliance proved useful in easing the way for the first important deviation from the development's original master plan.

Hartzog's 1954 plan had scheduled the western portion of Forest Park principally for residential use. In 1958, however, Warner-Kanter approached the Women's Club, then better organized than the Civic Association, for help in persuading the county to rezone almost 200 acres in this area from residential to commercial. Later the coopera-

27. *Forest Park Newsletter,* Feb. 12 and May 14, 1958; *Greenhills Journal,* June 20, 1958.

tion of the Civic Association was secured as well.[28] The rezoning effort proved successful, paving the way for the suburbanization of the Union Central Life Insurance Company.

Union Central, with assets over $850 million, had been a Cincinnati firm since 1842. In the mid-1950s, the company began talking about leaving its traditional headquarters in a skyscraper in the heart of downtown Cincinnati. Officers wanted a "modern and more efficient" building on a larger site and, after canvassing both Cincinnati and suburban locations, decided to abandon the center city. The reasons for the suburban choice, the company's board chairman explained, included parking problems and the difficulty of working in a tall vertical building where employees led "a 'leap frog' existence, moving through several floors and passing through various other departments in order to get where they were going." Another important factor was that, "with world unrest spreading rapidly and tensions building steadily, the Union Central and its people would be better served moving away from a highly industrialized complex such as Cincinnati which would be a logical target for enemy air attacks."[29]

Given those assumptions, Forest Park looked ideal, and in 1959 Union Central purchased 190 acres on the northwest periphery of Forest Park, abutting the planned Circle Freeway route. A 360,000-square-foot "monumental type building," surrounded by a generous expanse of open space and parking lots, was designed for the site.[30] On learning of the purchase, the Women's Club and the Civic Association both expressed their delight.[31] As the *Newsletter* indicated several years later, Union Central's move to Forest Park added the equivalent of 500 homes to the tax duplicate without any concomitant increase in the school population.[32]

Despite the Union Central coup and the spirit of civic cooperation between residents and developer, in the late 1950s and early 1960s affairs in Forest Park and the Greenhills area took a turn which jeopardized the entire effort to build a model community. The crisis stemmed in large part from the era's baby boom. Given the legal

28. White, "History of the Forest Park Women's Club"; Forest Park Civic Association, "Second Annual Report," May 15, 1959. Warner-Kanter contributed $25 to the association during its second year.

29. John A. Lloyd to Brian C. Strachan, May 29, 1975, LAC Files.

30. *Ibid.*

31. White, "History of the Forest Park Women's Club."

32. *Forest Park Newsletter,* May 1964.

injunction that each child must attend a school, public schools in urban areas across the country were flooded with pupils. School construction began to eat up a disproportionately large share of local government tax resources and strained the abilities of townships, counties, villages, and suburban cities to provide adequate police and fire protection, recreation, and street and road construction and maintenance. In rapidly growing suburban areas such as northern Hamilton County, these stresses made local governments as interested in commercial and business development as Warner-Kanter and Forest Park's resident boosters. In Forest Park, the baby boom and its attendant strains created suspicion between developer and residents; set Forest Park at odds with Springdale, its neighbor to the northeast, and with Greenhills; and ultimately ended Forest Park's attempt to develop civic community without self-government.

Resident suspicion of Warner-Kanter first appeared because the developer failed to attract a shopping center to Forest Park. The Forest Park master plan had called for the construction of a regional shopping center, and Warner-Kanter had tried hard to land the Tri-County development,[33] one of the first such enterprises proposed for northern Hamilton County. Yet the facility went to Springdale. By the end of the 1950s, this loss, and Warner-Kanter's failure to provide a satisfactory substitute, had made a shopping center a point of contention in the community. As it did in Klutznick's Park Forest, a regional shopping center had been expected to function as the focal point of Forest Park, and the construction of Tri-County in a neighboring location made development of such a shopping center in Forest Park unlikely. The loss, then, forced a reconsideration of Forest Park's basic layout and economic viability, from the perspectives of the developer, tax-hungry units of local government, and school-hungry residents of Greenhills and Forest Park. It also created tension between the developer and the Civic Association, especially after the association released the results of a 1960 poll claiming that 97.8 percent of the residents wanted a shopping facility of some sort in Forest Park,[34] and that most of those who responded to the poll wanted a center of regional rather than merely local dimensions.

33. Tucker to author, interview, Aug. 12, 1976.
34. *Forest Park Newletter,* Oct. 1960; Kanter to author, interview, July 5, 1975; Raymond J. Burby III and Shirley F. Weiss, *New Communities U.S.A.* (Lexington, Mass.: Lexington Books, D. C. Heath, 1976), 77, 297–320.

Although Union Central's move to Forest Park seemed partially to compensate for the loss of Tri-County, the firm's construction schedule left a four-year gap between land purchase and the time when the company would begin to contribute to the tax duplicate. The school population explosion, in contrast, was immediate. The Greenhills-Forest Park School District was in a perpetual financial crisis, unable to meet mounting demands for more classrooms in both Greenhills and Forest Park. People in Greenhills, dissatisfied with this state of affairs, tended to identify Warner-Kanter as the culprit responsible for bringing a sudden infusion of students into their schools.

Warner-Kanter tried to mollify the Greenhills critics in several ways. The developer kept its agreement to pay a $100 subsidy to the school district for every completed house, turning over an initial check for $10,900 in 1956. In winter 1957, the firm pledged to continue this practice and urged other builders in the school district to follow suit. The next spring, moreover, Warner-Kanter agreed to provide, on a guaranteed repurchase contract, three houses in Forest Park as temporary school structures.[35]

None of these gestures mitigated the anger growing in Greenhills, and in May 1957, when Warner-Kanter approached the county for additional rezoning, resentment turned into indignation. The developer wanted to change 7 acres from residential to commercial, and, because of the potential increases in school tax revenues, no one objected. But Warner-Kanter also wanted to add 8.6 acres to an apartment tract, and, in another one-square-mile area, to change the minimum residential lot footage from 20,000 to 6,000 square feet. In a "spirited" public hearing before the Hamilton County Regional Planning Commisson, Greenhills city officials, school board members, and Greenhills Citizens' Association representatives charged that the "unrestricted rate of construction" contemplated by the zoning changes would place the school district in a "critical condition." They predicted an increase in the unpopular practice of "double-shifting" first and second graders on half-day schedules, higher school taxes, and reluctance among Greenhills voters to support future tax levies to improve district schools. Although Warner-Kanter paid another subsidy of $21,000 to the Greenhills-Forest Park School District in July 1957, the rezoning's approval by the county

35. *Cincinnati Post*, Oct. 5, 1956; *Cincinnati Times-Star*, Oct. 19 and Dec. 27, 1956; *Greenhills Journal*, Jan. 4 and Mar. 1, 1957.

59

commissioners in August elicited an unsuccessful effort by disgruntled Greenhills residents to place the new zoning code on referendum ballot in November.[36]

The problem of school financing would not go away. In winter 1958, the Greenhills-Forest Park Board of Education asked voters to pass a $560,000 bond issue to finance a school in Forest Park. Despite the 1957 protests over rezoning and school crowding, the 1958 bond issue carried 60 percent in the district as a whole; it was, of course, more popular in Forest Park, where it passed by an overwhelming 95 percent of the votes cast. This bond issue was the third new school levy approved by Greenhills-Forest Park voters in four years.[37]

In 1959, however, when the school district placed yet another levy on the ballot, this time for a new elementary school outside Forest Park, concern over school financing and management spread to Forest Park itself. The school superintendent justified the measure by pointing out that district enrollments were expected to rise by 585 pupils per year through 1961, with 400 of those each year being elementary students. That levy passed, but during summer 1959 the superintendent shocked Forest Park parents with an announcement that the double-shifting of their first and second graders would continue, because the new Kemper Heights School in Forest Park would not be completed until June 1960. After complaining, the parents finally accepted a compromise which eliminated double-shifting by using Forest Park Chapel Methodist Church as a temporary school site. Even the completion of the new elementary school gave taxpayers no financial relief, however, for in 1960 the school board decided that the high school, built in 1953 before the baby boom began producing teenagers, needed an addition. The board placed a $570,000 bond issue for that purpose on the May ballot, and it, too, passed.[38]

While Forest Parkers fretted over the high cost of education, grumbled about the need for commercial and industrial development to help offset that cost, and wondered if their needs were being met equitably by a school board they saw as dominated by Greenhills residents,[39] two other concerns emerged to test their faith in the idea

36. *Greenhills Journal*, May 29, June 7, July 5, and Aug. 2, 1957; *Cincinnati Times-Star*, July 8, 1957.

37. *Forest Park Newsletter*, Jan. 14, Feb. 12, Mar. 12, and May 14, 1958; *Greenhills Journal*, Jan. 17, Feb. 14, Apr. 11, and May 9, 1958.

38. *Greenhills Journal*, Mar. 27, Apr. 24, June 5, June 19, August 29, and May 6, 1960; *Forest Park Newlsetter*, Mar. 19, 1960.

39. *Greenhills Journal*, Nov. 20, 1959.

of civic community without self-government and intensify their distrust of the developer.

In 1959, the Warner-Kanter contract with CCDC expired, leaving the two partners free, if they wished, to redesign or even abandon the 1954 master plan. Yet it had been the promise embedded in that document, coupled with the knowledge that Warner-Kanter was legally bound by the CCDC agreement to adhere to the spirit if not the precise substance of the plan, which had played a key role in upholding the dream of realizing civic community among Forest Parkers. Now that old assurance was gone, and the uncertainty engendered by its disappearance was intensified by the simultaneous dissolution of the Warner-Kanter partnership. Warner remained in Cincinnati, pursuing a variety of business interests. In the 1970s, he served on the Ohio Board of Regents, which oversaw public higher education, as an appointee of Democratic Governor John J. Gilligan; and as United States Ambassador to Switzerland under President Jimmy Carter.

Joseph Kanter, head of the new Kanter Corporation, now took over Forest Park.[40] The Forest Park Civic Association invited Kanter to appear before a general meeting of the residents in October 1959 to tell them, as Eileen Kieffer put it, "what's in store for our town."[41] As it turned out, Kanter himself seemed not entirely sure what was in store for Forest Park. He answered in a non-committal manner what the *Newsletter* called "several pages of questions" on the present status of, and future plans for, Forest Park. Although he was fairly specific about residential development, when the questioning turned to the critical area of non-residential plans, Kanter announced that work on the Union Central building would begin the next spring and then lapsed into generalities, explaining that he had no immediate or firm plans for securing a shopping center, restaurant, medical center, or other businesses and industries. He also refused to make an area originally designated as residential available to the Civic Association Recreational Committee for construction of tennis courts. He would not say whether he would build another swimming pool.

Kanter closed the session by indicating that he hoped to work with the Civic Association, as the group representative of the residents' views. He would like to answer the questions of Forest Park residents

40. *Greenhills Journal,* Apr. 10, 1959; *Cincinnati Post & Times-Star,* May 16 and June 20, 1959; *Cincinnati Enquirer,* June 14, Aug. 9, Sept. 6, and Sept. 13, 1959; *Cincinnati Post,* Aug. 30, 1976.
41. *Greenhills Journal,* Nov. 6, 1959.

personally, he remarked, but because his time was limited, he urged those present to approach him in the future through the Civic Association.[42] Apparently Kanter would continue the experiment in civic community without self-government, utilizing the Civic Association as a surrogate for a legally constituted governmental entity.

Kanter soon took steps apparently designed to show that he, like Warner before him, wanted Forest Park to be more than just one development among many. In 1960, Kanter moved his family into Dixie Dale Farm. That summer and fall, he personally announced the opening of the Forest Park Medical Center (though the staff consisted exclusively of general practitioners, an obstetrician and pediatrician were expected to join it soon); and he presided over the opening of Northland Road, a major east-west artery on the north edge of the developed portion of Forest Park. He leased twelve acres of land to the Baseball Association for one dollar per year and gave $275 needed to lay out three baseball diamonds for Little League and community play. In September, in cooperation with the Civic Association, Kanter put on a "Country Fair" featuring a horse show and rodeo, pony raffle, exhibits by industries and the U.S. Army, amusement rides, pony track, pet show, pie contest, and displays of arts and crafts by Forest Park residents. Though several voluntary organizations raised money from the event, its real intent, as the *Newsletter* put it, was to "let people know that Forest Park is not just another 'bedroom suburb', but a tightly knit community with a high degree of civic pride. . . ."[43]

Well into 1960, then, the Civic Association seemed inclined to go along with Kanter's version of Forest Park as a civic community without self-government.[44] But the association had begun to express a new concern with non-educational public services, particularly fire protection, which some thought might be improved by Forest Park's incorporation as a village. For fire protection purposes, Forest Park had been divided into two parts served on a contract basis by the Greenhills Fire Department and the Springdale Fire District. By 1959, however, the growth of both Greenhills and Springdale, not to mention Forest Park, made it difficult to continue the arrangement. The Civic Association emphasized, however, that Forest Park could have

42. *Ibid.*; *Forest Park Newsletter,* Oct. 17, 1959.
43. *Forest Park Newsletter,* Sept., Oct., and Nov., 1960; *Millcreek Valley News,* Sept. 22, 1960; *Greenhills Journal,* Nov. 4 and Dec. 7, 1960.
44. *Forest Park Newsletter,* Mar. 19, 1960; Sept. 1963.

a fire department without incorporating as a village. Incorporation, while making possible additional services, would also mean higher taxes, a distasteful prospect in light of escalating school costs. To improve fire protection, all that was required was for the township trustees to create a fire district in the unincorporated area of Springfield Township which comprised Forest Park; this would enable voters in the district to vote taxes or bond levies for fire equipment but not for other uses. Forest Park residents could form a volunteer fire company to operate the equipment.[45]

The drive to start a Forest Park volunteer fire company began in October 1959, when the *Newsletter* issued a call for thirty men to begin training for the "future" company. The response was scarcely overwhelming; by December 17, only ten men had stepped forward, and in February the list included just six more. Nonetheless, the volunteers incorporated themselves as a fire company and the township trustees created a Forest Park Fire District. Next the Civic Association generated an enthusiastic and successful campaign to pass both a tax levy and a $24,000 bond issue, the chief theme of which was "vote the money or we pay higher insurance rates."[46]

The establishment of the volunteer fire company, according to the *Newsletter,* evoked a nostalgia for "the good old days" of eighteenth- and early nineteenth-century America, when "being a member of the local volunteer fire company was considered an honor."[47] To the Civic Association, the company's creation also seemed solid confirmation that the ideal of the small civic community of public-spirited individuals could be realized in mid-twentieth-century Forest Park.

But the glow of community satisfaction produced by the fire company's formation did not last. By 1959, many Forest Parkers' commitment to community without self-government had weakened considerably. As we have seen, by that date many Forest Park residents were concerned about the school and shopping center problems, which linked desirable conveniences with potential tax revenues.

45. Linda Gruenschlaeger, "Ohio Law and the Creation of the Forest Park Fire Department," typescript, n.d., LAC Files; *Forest Park Newsletter,* Dec. 17, 1959.
46. *Forest Park Newsletter,* Oct. 17 and Dec. 17, 1959; Feb. 13, 1960; Sept. and Nov. 1960; Jan. 1961; *Greenhills Journal*, May 24, 1957; July 15, Aug. 12, and Oct. 21, 1960; Jan. 13, 1961; *Cincinnati Post & Times-Star,* Aug. 2, 1960; Gruenschlaeger, "Ohio Law"; Joe L. Valent, "Forest Park Volunteer Fire Department," typescript, July 14, 1975, LAC Files.
47. *Forest Park Newsletter,* Dec. 17, 1959.

Expiration of the CCDC agreement with Warner-Kanter and dissolution of the developers' partnership contributed to a general sense of uneasiness about the future. To be sure, the Civic Association believed that satisfactory fire protection had been provided without incorporating Forest Park as a village. But now some residents raised other concerns which in their view called for some form of self-government in Forest Park. Even one of the staunchest early advocates of community without self-government, Eileen Kieffer, who in the late 1950s wrote a regular human interest column about Forest Park in the *Greenhills Journal,* began to call for local government in Forest Park. This could be achieved, she said, either by annexing the area to Greenhills or by incorporating it as a village.

Grievances about poor public services in Forest Park varied from observer to observer. In 1959, for example, Kieffer ran a series of stories in the *Greenhills Journal* about the "dog problem," reporting that "complaints about other people's dogs running loose are rampant." While the Civic Association shared Kieffer's concern about controlling dogs, it thought other kinds of predators deserved more attention. Its *Newsletter* first mentioned crime as a problem in September 1960, warning of "an alarming increase in the number of prowlers and attempted burglaries" and lamenting the county sheriff's inability to patrol Forest Park effectively.[48]

Other residents deemed additional public services unsatisfactory. Willard C. Pistler, for example, an architect who worked for a downtown Cincinnati firm but lived in Forest Park, compiled and publicized a long list of complaints about the shortcomings of life in Forest Park. He mentioned "thin" fire and police protection, insufficient playground and park space, and an unregulated once-a-week private garbage pickup and disposal service. He wondered, too, if county planning and zoning authorities could be trusted to protect Forest Park property values and doubted that the county and township could maintain roads adequately as Forest Park expanded. He admitted that the high tax rate in Greenhills ($40.56 per $1,000 valuation, compared with $35.76 in Mt. Healthy and $31.98 in Blue Ash) made Forest Parkers sensitive to the possible economic cost of incorporation. But he reported that, partly because neighboring

48. *Greenhills Journal,* Mar. 13 and 27, 1959; Apr. 24, May 8, and Nov. 6, 1959; Forest Civic Association, "Second Annual Report"; *Forest Park Newsletter,* Sept. 1960. Two new subdivisions opened in 1959: Hillcrest Acres, with homes in the $17,000-$20,000 range; and Vernondale, with homes in the $20,000-$27,000 category. *Greenhills Journal,* Feb. 12, 1960.

Springdale's recent incorporation provided a convenient local example, many Forest Parkers were seriously considering the idea.[49]

The growing demand for better public services led both Kanter and the Civic Association to investigate incorporation, albeit with caution initially. In January 1961, using Kanter Corporation funds, the Civic Association contracted with the Cincinnati Bureau of Governmental Research for "a study of the feasibility of different types of government for Forest Park." The bureau was to finish the work in three months and present the results to a "Civic Association meeting as soon thereafter as possible." In the meantime, Civic Association members visited officials of Cincinnati area incorporated suburbs, including Greenhills, Reading, St. Bernard, and Springdale, to get their advice on the pros and cons of incorporation.[50]

In March, however, the association's leadership suddenly abandoned its deliberate pace. On March 19, 1961, a special edition of the *Newsletter* announced that the association would start at once to circulate petitions asking the township trustees to set up an incorporation election. "The question," the publication explained,

> of whether we should incorporate, be annexed, or remain as we are has been asked many times in the past. Until now, the recommendation of the Civic Association Directors and Development Committee has been to stay as we are. . . . We now have reliable figures on probable [village] income and costs, and after careful consideration of these, the Directors and Development Committee of the Civic Association recommend that we incorporate as soon as possible.[51]

After recommending incorporation, and with Kanter's support, the association proceeded at maximum speed. In two hours on March 19, it collected the necessary two hundred signatures on incorporation petitions and the next day filed the papers with the township trustees, who set May 5 as the date for Forest Parkers to vote for or against incorporation. In the interim, the association held a special open meeting to discuss the election. Three days later, the *Newsletter* issued another special edition designed specifically to sell incorporation to Forest Park's college-educated residents, one or more of whom, the paper estimated, lived in the average Forest Park home.[52]

49. *Greenhills Journal*, Dec. 4, 1959; Jan. 15, 1960.
50. *Forest Park Newsletter*, Jan. 1961; Forest Park Civic Association, "Fourth Annual Report," May 15, 1961.
51. "Special Edition," *Forest Park Newsletter*, Mar. 19, 1961.
52. *Cincinnati Post & Times-Star*, Mar. 21, 1961; *Cincinnati Enquirer*, June 5, 1961; "Special Edition," *Forest Park Newsletter*, Apr. 3, 1961.

The most interesting section of this edition of the *Newsletter* sought to explain "Why the Rush?". Incorporation, it turned out, was being rushed not because Forest Park desperately needed better public services then, but because of impending "suburban imperialism." The threat came from Greenhills city officials, whose seemingly perpetual fiscal crisis forced them to skimp on city services to free funds for continual new school construction. In early spring of 1961, the Greenhills officials had decided to alleviate their problem by annexing a slice of Forest Park.[53] The slice they selected, not surprisingly, encompassed that portion of western Forest Park zoned industrial and included the land on which Union Central planned to construct its new headquarters. The Civic Association had temporarily blocked the annexation attempt by filing Forest Park's incorporation petition one day before Greenhills brought in its annexation request. Forest Park, the *Newsletter* explained, had to incorporate now, because Forest Park

> was originally planned as a well-balanced model community, with residential, business, and industrial development. The threat of annexation by Greenhills of a large industrial area . . . would effectively prevent realization of the original plan. If Forest Park incorporates now, the industrial area will remain part of Forest Park and broaden its tax base.[54]

Throughout April, the Civic Association continued its campaign for incorporation, stressing the importance of incorporation in realizing the plan to make Forest Park a balanced community. The discussion, however, failed to deal with the question of boundaries for the proposed incorporated area—a matter of critical importance in a place so preoccupied with establishing territorial community. The Civic Association petitions described boundaries which looked "irregular" to the Cincinnati Bureau of Governmental Research. The bureau's report, neglected in the rush of the incorporation campaign, pointed out some of the irregularities. Small parts of the proposed village, for instance, fell in the North West School District and part in the Princeton School District. This arrangement meant that village residents would not all have one set of elementary and secondary schools in common. The bureau also remarked, somewhat more emphatically, that on the north and west the corporate line intersected the intended route of the Circle Freeway at least three times,

53. *Forest Park Newsletter,* Apr. 3, 1961; *Cincinnati Enquirer,* June 5, 1961.
54. *Forest Park Newsletter,* Apr. 3, 1961.

leaving "remnants" of the new Forest Park cut off from the core of the community.[55]

The Bureau of Governmental Research did not comment on another interesting feature of the village map. The proposed southern boundary ran east along the Greenhills line until it reached Sheffield Road, where it could have been extended to enclose the unincorporated black subdivision of Hollydale, which lay between the white city of Greenhills on the west and the village of Woodlawn (by then largely black) and the city of Lincoln Height (all black) on the east. The proposed Forest Park boundary, however, turned abruptly northward at Sheffield and ran until it hit Springdale, thereby omitting Hollydale.[56]

The proposed boundaries, irregular or not, were those offered the voters. Discussion of the merits of incorporation centered on the concept of a model, balanced community and on economics, not on geography or race. The proposition proved attractive to Forest Park voters, who approved incorporation by a margin of 924 to 258, with the least enthusiastic precinct coming in at 69 percent in favor.

By an overwhelming vote, the experiment in civic community without self-government had ended. Even in the moment of independence, however, some reservations were expressed. While the Civic Association's *Newsletter* reported the election returns with satisfaction, it took time to remark on the horrors of two-party politics in local government. The smaller the governmental unit, said the *Newsletter,* the more "vicious" its party politics tended to be. Two weeks later, the ever-vigilant Kieffer noted in her *Greenhills Journal* column that thirty-four persons had announced their candidacy for nine seats in the new village governing council; she observed with concern that there now seemed to be more "bitterness and prejudice and wild rumor" in Forest Park "than ever before."[57]

Forest Park's incorporation upset the Hamilton County Budget Commission for different reasons. When Forest Park incorporated, the population of incorporated areas within the county rose to 81

55. *Forest Park Newsletter,* Apr. and May 1961; Cincinnati Bureau of Governmental Research, "A Study of the Proposed Village of Forest Park," typescript, Apr. 1961, Urban Studies Collection, Archival Collections of the Univ. of Cincinnati, pp. 1-2; *Forest Park Newsletter,* Apr. 3, 1961.
56. Cincinnati Bureau of Governmental Research, "A Study of the Proposed Village," 4; Berry to author, interview, May 16, 1976.
57. *Forest Park Newsletter,* June 1961; *Greenhills Journal,* May 19, 1961; *Cincinnati Post & Times-Star,* May 6, 1961.

percent of county population, leaving the population of unincorporated areas at 19 percent. State law allowed county governments to take up to 50 percent of the state's local government tax fund, so long as the county's unincorporated areas contained at least 20 percent of the population. The Hamilton County Budget Commission, which had been taking 29 percent of the local government fund, had been planning to increase its share of the fund to 50 percent. But with the new population figures, the county could take only 30 percent of the fund. Now, to recoup at least part of the revenue lost when Forest Park incorporated, one budget commissioner hoped to reduce the City of Cincinnati's portion of the fund. "The city has more money than it needs," the commissioner declared, "and I'm for cutting it down to where it belongs."[58]

Despite these various reservations, in 1961 Forest Park became a village. The incorporation affected others besides those who had engineered the incorporation drive, in response to Forest Park's own needs and to suburban struggles for community self-sufficiency. The incorporation intensified haggling between Cincinnati and Hamilton County over tax revenues, while strengthening Forest Park's hand in the suburban contest for amenities, tax revenues, and other development. The shape of the new village's internal politics was not yet clear, however. Kanter had provided unobtrusive financial support in the incorporation campaign, but he remained silent about any plans he might have had for making Forest Park a balanced community. Inevitably, incorporation would influence the style and practice of civic community. The advent of village government raised the specter of partisan politics, called into question the Civic Association's role as champion of the community ideal and defender of the public interest, and forced Kanter to deal with village authorities, rather than the CCDC and county officials, as he planned for Forest Park's future.

58. *Cincinnati Post & Times-Star,* June 10, 1961.

*[Forest Park has] no mixed land problems,
narrow rights-of-way, crowded housing,
blighted conditions, or slums. . . . With proper
citizen spirit, adequate development controls,
cooperation from developers, and a master
plan, Forest Park could develop into a model
community as originally envisaged.*
                    PAUL CHRISTIANSEN,
                    Planning Consultant, 1964

PLANNING A COMMUNITY OF LIMITED LIABILITY

The events of 1959 to 1961 concluded one experiment and started another. The end of CCDC supervision of Warner-Kanter's effort to build a civic community without self-government, the dissolution of the Warner-Kanter partnership, and Greenhills' attempt to broaden its tax duplicate by annexing a portion of Forest Park set the context within which incorporation occurred. But that incorporation itself established new relationships and started a new process of community development. Many of the participants remained the same, but the structure and rules of the game had changed. No one realized this more quickly than Joseph H. Kanter; in summer 1961, almost at the moment of incorporation, he moved to take control in molding Forest Park's future as a model community in village form.

Kanter could do little about the form of village government. State laws set down the number and type of officials to be elected, their terms of office, their mode of election, and their duties. Those laws, applicable to all new villages, assumed an essential similarity among such places. Though Forest Park was the most populous village in all of Hamilton County and the second largest in territory, it qualified for incorporation as a village under state law because its population density came to over 400 persons per square mile and its inhabitants in 1960 numbered 4,800. The population was only 200 short of the point at which any village became a city, another variety of municipal corporation with powers different from those of a village.

By state statute, before Forest Park could write its own charter, it had to organize a village government in accordance with the general state laws on that subject. Those laws stipulated that the new government should consist of a mayor, a six-person village council elected at large, a clerk, and a treasurer. The mayor presided over the council but could cast no veto. The village council not only enacted legislation but also exercised considerable executive authority through its committees. These were chaired by council members and filled out with appointed citizens.[1]

Forest Park's first election was held in July instead of the usual November, so that the new village could secure for its first budget a share of the state's local government fund, distributed in the fall. In the election, thirty-nine candidates vied for nine posts, with terms to run from July to November 1961. Three organizations—the Democrats, the Citizens for Forest Park, and a Good Government group— ran full or partial slates, while eleven persons ran as independents. Faced with an imposing array of names, the voters rejected Democrats and independents and selected Citizens and Good Government ticket members who had been active in community affairs before incorporation.

Each of the winners had been prominently associated with either the Civic or the Baseball Association, and two were holding offices in the Civic Association when elected to their village government posts. In addition, six successful candidates lived in the oldest area of the village, known in 1961 as the "C" section because each of its street names began with that letter of the alphabet. Citizens for Forest Park, with its "let's examine things carefully before we decide" platform, took the mayor's desk, three seats on the council, and the treasurer's job, while the Good Government group, which proposed to "do the necessary things quickly," carried two council seats and the clerk's office. A final council post went to an independent who ran on what the *Newsletter* called a conservative platform, bolstering what the paper referred to as an "unexpectedly strong conservative trend." Despite door-to-door campaigning and widespread literature distribution, however, just over half of the eligible voters turned out, a

1. Cincinnati Burea of Governmental Research, "A Study of the Proposed Village," pp. 4–6.

level of apathy the *Newsletter* found disgusting.[2] Nonetheless, Forest Park's new government rested in the hands of people inexperienced in village government and chosen by a minority of the voting-age population. Candidates picked were from the "establishment" section of the town and had records of visible civic involvement in the days before self-government, as well as an evident inclination to "examine things carefully" before making decisions.

The new officials had scarcely taken their seats when Joseph Kanter began to prod them into planning. Just eight days after the election, Kanter hosted a meeting with selected village officials and citizens. The agenda concerned not the immediate organization and operations of the village, but the future structure of Forest Park as a self-governing civic community and as a business enterprise. The Forest Park contingent consisted of Mayor Donald Gebhardt; Samuel Bryant, future chairman of the Forest Park Planning and Zoning Commission; and three citizens, among them Willard Pistler, the architect so concerned about local control over zoning. Whatever this group may have thought the meeting's goals were, Kanter viewed the session as the first step in educating village officials and residents about planning. For by this time, Kanter had worked out a fairly clear vision of how to make Forest Park a profitable undertaking. As he later put it, he wanted to "build a way of life" in Forest Park and to create "a community to last a thousand years."[3]

Kanter was no newcomer to the business of constructing a new town, although he knew less about Forest Park than his former partner. In July 1953, Kanter had married Nancy Reed, a talented composer and formerly a singer with the Hal McIntyre, Skitch Henderson, and Benny Goodman orchestras. After a European honeymoon, Kanter had returned to business, handling Warner-Kanter's non-Cincinnati interests and leaving the day-to-day development of Forest Park to Warner. Kanter had remained in the "new community" field, however, for he organized, planned, and managed development programs for the company's new-town projects in Greenbelt, Maryland, the New Deal venture which Warner-Kanter acquired in 1955, and in Fort Lauderdale, Florida, where the partners started a 10,000-acre planned community in 1957.[4]

2. *Cincinnati Enquirer,* July 10, 1961; *Greenhills Journal,* July 14, 1961; *Forest Park Newsletter,* July 1961.

3. Kanter to author, interview, July 5, 1975.

4. *Ibid.;* Forest Park, Inc., "Kanter Biography."

As a consequence of the division of responsibilities within the partnership, Kanter by 1959 was quite experienced in model community development. After taking over Forest Park, organizing his new holdings, and assisting with the incorporation drive, he hired as a consultant Justin Hartzog, the planner who had prepared the 1947 North Greenhills proposal for the federal government and the 1954 master plan for Forest Park. First, Kanter wanted to talk to Hartzog about the Forest Park shopping center promised in the 1954 master plan but not yet built and now a subject of increasing controversy.[5] He also wanted Hartzog's help in revising the master plan generally and in talking with village representatives about the changes required in the plan in light of new conditions.

By the time Kanter and Hartzog met with village officials in July 1961, the two men had reached tentative conclusions about the changes needed in the master plan. Certain facts seemed clear to them. First, the Tri-County Shopping Mall made the master plan's provision for a regional shopping center in the eastern portion of Forest Park unrealistic. Second, Union Central Life Insurance Company's move to Forest Park suggested broader possibilities for office construction. Third, the continuing concentration of industry and related housing in the Mill Creek Valley in northern Hamilton County virtually assured transportation and other public utility improvements which would benefit Forest Park; yet the village's relative isolation from the Mill Creek industrial belt would help keep Forest Park different from, and more prosperous than, the scruffy older industrial suburbs in Mill Creek Valley. Fourth, Circle Freeway interchanges planned west and north of the village would make Forest Park's western and northwestern sections particularly attractive to business, commerce, and light industry.[6]

From these premises flowed several planning conclusions and a major zoning problem. "Most" industry, Kanter and Hartzog decided, should be shifted to the western part of the village, and the amount of industrial land in the east should be reduced. The projected eastern shopping center should be scaled down in size, and its viability as a food and specialty shopping center should be enhanced by introducing nearby multi-family dwellings. The eastern part of Forest

5. "Sketch Plan. Proposed Shopping Center. Forest Park, Ohio," unsigned manuscript, July 24, 1961, Hartzog Papers.

6. [Lynn Lyon for Hartzog], "Forest Park," undated typescript [summer 1961], Hartzog Papers.

Park, however, was already zoned to conform with the old master plan's projections, and altering the zoning to accommodate the contemplated changes could be troublesome. In the past, zoning changes had to be secured on a piecemeal basis through the cumbersome, time-consuming process of amending the Hamilton County Zoning Code. But if a Forest Park Planning and Zoning Commission could be persuaded to assume zoning jurisdiction from Hamilton County and then be convinced that the whole village needed to be rezoned in accord with Kanter and Hartzog's new thinking, the changes might be made quickly and all at once.

It was this logic, combined with a sense of urgency about the need for zoning changes, which led Kanter to call the July 1961 meeting with the new Forest Park officials. During the session, which began in the morning at Kanter's office and stretched through a long lunch, the village representatives revealed their "conservative" bent. Although Kanter and Hartzog began by sketching the general history of planning and land use in the Forest Park area and explaining the changes they felt compelled to make in the master plan, most of the conversation dealt with zoning and the shopping center. At one point the new mayor indicated that he would like "tighter zoning" because it would "give us more control," to which Kanter responded that the "tighter I'm controlled, the less I'm interested in developing." At least twice during the session, a Kanter Corporation staff member asked how long it would take to do the rezoning and whether it could be done before the November elections. The question received no definitive response. Toward the end of the day, two of the Forest Parkers raised a "real question" about the practicability of the shopping center which Kanter and Hartzog now proposed. Kanter said he felt morally bound to fulfill the master plan's promise to put a center in the eastern sector where residential development was currently most intense, and he argued that securing "prime leases" would make it work. He also claimed that the Hamilton County Planning Commission's recent negative evaluation of the shopping center was based on the presumption of a local market limited to single-family development, instead of the multi-family units he and Hartzog now projected.[7]

Two days later, Kanter met with Hartzog, Hartzog's partner Lynn

7. JHK [Kanter] to LL [Lyon], "Notes—Meeting With FP Planning and Zoning Commission, 7/29/61," typescript, Aug. 2, 1961, Hartzog Papers; "Meeting of Kanter Corporation and Village of Forest Park, Ohio," unsigned manuscript, July 29, 1961, Hartzog Papers.

Lyon, and The Kanter Corporation's in-house planning group, to assess the proposed revision in light of the conference with Forest Park officials. They decided to continue moving in the general direction adopted before the meeting, although they expressed some apprehension that the villagers might turn down the apartment proposal, eastern industrial development, and the shopping center idea. Moreover, Kanter made it clear that he preferred a zoning code giving him maximum "flexibility," arguing, for example, in favor of zoning all residential sites to a 6,000-square-foot lot standard, in case the market for larger lots should decline and force him to go to a smaller size. Hartzog suggested that his proposal violated sound community planning principles. But in the end it was agreed that Hartzog would prepare maps reflecting the day's consensus, to serve as a basis for further discussions with the village leaders.[8]

A month later, Hartzog met once more with Kanter. The planner presented a sketch and a written rationale for thoroughfares and changes suggested in the eastern section. But the bulk of the discussion centered on what Hartzog should do next, on what schedule, and for how large a fee. Hartzog wanted more money to complete the work than Kanter initially had offered. And when Kanter told Hartzog that his work had to be done by September 15, Hartzog balked, saying that he could not meet that deadline. At one point, Hartzog suggested that Kanter postpone the master plan revision for the time being, because Hartzog lacked the time to put it in a form suitable for critical scrutiny. Kanter responded that he felt he had to make good on his commitment to present a plan to the village officials as soon as possible, and he stressed the need to secure a zoning ordinance and adoption of the plan while village leaders, though cool, seemed disposed to listen to him. He needed the plan by September 15 in order to expedite informal discussions in Forest Park before offering the plan for official consideration on December 15, 1961. Hartzog recognized Kanter's "dilemma," and agreed to do the best he could by providing "a guiding sketch for a master plan by September 15."[9]

The reasons for Kanter's urgency seem clear enough. Because of the Greenhills annexation threat, Forest Park had proceeded so

8. "Memorandum of Meeting, July 31, 1961," unsigned manuscript, Hartzog Papers.
9. "Record Memorandum, Aug. 28, 1961, Meeting in Office of J. H. Kanter," unsigned manuscript, Hartzog Papers.

rapidly with incorporation that its first election had been a special one in July, 1961. This meant that the entire set of officials chosen during the summer would face another election in November. If Kanter's plans for the village remained ambiguous throughout the fall, the master plan might become an inviting campaign issue for an ambitious candidate capable of capitalizing on citizens' latent distrust of the developer. Such campaign tactics would enormously complicate planning and zoning for both developer and village officials. Both officials and Kanter, then, had a stake in seeing that master plan revision and the November election took place in an atmosphere of mutual trust and accommodation.

Though the records do not show that Hartzog met his September 15 deadline or that Kanter kept in touch informally with incumbent council candidates, the fall election came and went without reference to the master plan. A total of thirteen candidates filed for six council seats, including all the incumbents but one. The Civic Association president resigned that post to run against the incumbent mayor, and the village treasurer also faced opposition. Only the incumbent ran for the clerk's post. The Civic Association's *Newsletter* all but ignored the campaign, and the voters reelected all the incumbents. A seat vacated by an incumbent who decided not to stand for reelection went to a candidate identified with the majority Citizens for Forest Park.[10] The first potential obstacle to the smooth and orderly resolution of the planning and zoning problem turned out to have been no obstacle at all.

With the election past, however, new conflicts arose between village officials and Kanter over Forest Park's future. By the end of November, the village council had appointed a planning and zoning commission, chaired by Samuel Bryant and composed of Mayor Donald Gebhardt, William Layton, George Lockwood, and Willard Pistler—the same men who had met with Kanter and his planning team in late July. By November, too, the commission had received the new Hartzog master plan map for formal review. The group had also begun to look for a planning consultant to review the new proposal. As part of the search the group asked Kanter to provide statistical data and background information relevant to the map, as well as assistance in paying the planning consultant. Kanter agreed to

10. *Forest Park Newsletter*, Spet. and Oct. 1961; *Forest Park Journal*, Nov. 17, 1961.

provide the statistical and other data but declined to help with the consultant's fee.[11]

The Hartzog master plan, which consisted only of a map (see Figure 6), reflected the agreements thrashed out in the summer 1961 meetings between Hartzog and the Kanter planning group. The map showed three nodes of non-residential activity in the village. The first, scheduled for earliest development, lay in the east. At its heart was a local shopping mall and office center, surrounded by multi-family housing and light industry on the northwest, north, and northeast; two-family housing on the east and south; a church to the southeast; and multi-family housing to the west. Single-family housing, much of it already in place, fanned out to the south, west, and north beyond the two- and multi-family units. The second node lay on the northern periphery of the village, just below the Circle Freeway, and included a local shopping center, a village civic center, and multi-family housing to the north and west of the non-residential hub. The last node lay on the western edge of the village around the Union Central site. Here were additional land for offices east, south, and southwest of Union Central; and a regional shopping center and light industry on the west between Union Central and Circle Freeway. Interspersed among these nodes sat single-family residential areas, six churches, five schools, and several playground and park sites.[12] Though the plan submitted to the commission late in 1961 lacked the philosophic rationale and statistics usual in master plans, Hartzog clearly had adhered to the original vision of creating a balanced community in which one could be born, grow up, and work, and which possessed the diverse land uses necessary to establish a solid tax base for a village.

Initial disagreements about the plan concerned procedural rather than substantive matters. Kanter clearly hoped for quick action for planning and zoning. At the planning commission's December 1961 meeting, a Kanter employee, Roger Bonta, claimed that Hartzog felt rather "insulted" that groups or individuals would question or delay adopting his scheme. A letter from Kanter regarding commercial and multi-family developments in the western area immediately aroused

11. *Forest Park Newsletter,* Sept. 1961; Forest Park Planning and Zoning Commission, "Minutes," Nov. 28, 1961, files of the Forest Park Planning and Zoning Commission, Forest Park Municipal Building.

12. Forest Park Master Plan, 1961, reprinted in Paul Christiansen, "Forest Park Master Plan Evaluation, 1962," typescript, files of the Forest Park Planning and Zoning Commission. Also see *Greenhills Journal,* May 4, 1962.

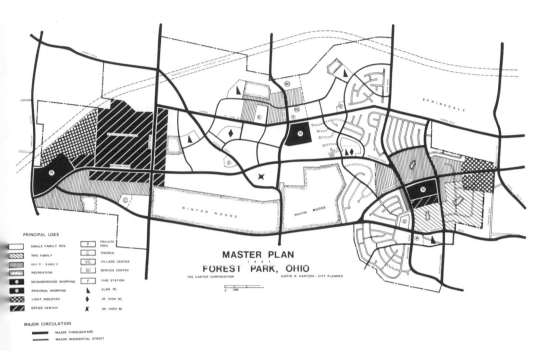

FIGURE 6. Kanter-Hartzog Master Plan, 1961. Reproduced by permission of The Kanter Corporation. Redrawn by Peggy Palange.

the Union Central representative's concern, and another Kanter letter laid out a proposal for garden-type apartments. The planning commission deferred action on both these requests, since both required rezoning of the land involved, and the village zoning ordinance was not yet finished. Village officials, however, remained in a cooperative mood, for early in January 1962, Mayor Gebhardt issued a statement calling for the adoption of a "realistic" master plan providing the most "effective use of our land"—a plan which would "attract industry and business for a balanced community" and establish a tax duplicate large enough to finance expanded village services.[13]

Meanwhile, development in the village continued, generating conflicts which complicated adoption of the proposed master plan. In spring 1962, Paul Christiansen, a professional city planner from Middletown, Ohio, was hired by the planning commission to evaluate the Hartzog 1961 master plan.[14] Before Christiansen finished his evaluation, however, Kanter had an opportunity to secure tenants for the local shopping center in the eastern portion of the village, though under conditions which led him to ask for an enlargement of the center from 10.7 to 27 acres. In June 1962, Kanter asked Hartzog to help him convince Christiansen, the planning commission, and the village council that a center of that size was viable. When Hartzog reviewed Kanter's proposal, however, he advised Christiansen that the eastern shopping center should not be expanded by more than 50 percent. Hartzog added that a center of larger proportions would indeed be desirable in the north-central village center shown on his 1961 master plan map.[15] Although Hartzog sent The Kanter Corporation a copy of his assessment, Kanter remained convinced that his own scheme would work. He took his proposal into the planning commission's June 26 meeting, where it was voted down unanimously.[16]

According to the *Newsletter,* public reaction to the vote "was generally one of dissatisfaction, very likely due to wishes for the

13. Forest Park Planning and Zoning Commission, "Minutes," Dec. 26, 1961; "Record Memorandum, Aug. 28, 1961, Meeting in Office of J. H. Kanter," unsigned manuscript, Hartzog Papers; *Forest Park Newsletter,* Jan. 1962.

14. *Forest Park Newsletter,* March, April, and May 1962.

15. Neil Stubbers [General Manager, Forest Park, The Kanter Corporation] to Hartzog, June 18, 1962, Hartzog Papers; Hartzog to Christiansen, June 25, 1962, Hartzog Papers.

16. Forest Park Planning and Zoning Commission, "Minutes," June 26, 1962.

biggest and best for Forest Park." The *Newsletter* itself, however, supported the planning commission, which had consulted the Hamilton County Regional Planning Commission, as well as Christiansen, before reaching its decision. The Forest Park Planning and Zoning Commission argued that the expansion merely projected an increase in "convenience" stores, without including additional types; that approval would mean abandoning the center proposed by Hartzog for north-central Forest Park; and that although it was prudent for Kanter to build shopping facilities after leases had been signed, the practice provided no insurance that original lease-holders might not later leave, forcing the developer to fill vacancies with second-class tenants.[17]

Kanter refused to give up, however. On September 13, 1962, he sent a long letter to the planning commission pointing out that such firms as Kroger, Super-X Drugs, Thriftway, Woolworth, and Central Trust, by their willingness to lease, had endorsed his reasoning about the wisdom of expanding the shopping center. If shut out of the village now, these companies might take other locations close enough to Forest Park to preclude their coming to the village at some future date. "We have a growing village now," Kanter wrote "and further growth is of prime importance to you as representatives of the village, and to me as the developer." While allowing that Christiansen's opinion was "unbiased and sincere," Kanter felt obliged "from a practical business viewpoint" to disagree with him, and Kanter closed by urging the planning commission and village council, on this point, to heed the developer rather than the planner.[18]

The disagreement over expansion of the shopping center pitted the developer and substantial numbers of citizens, pleading for growth and progress, against the planning commission and the council, who spoke for restraint. At almost the same time, however, another embroglio put the developer and planning commission together on one side and citizens' spokesmen on the other.

In May 1962, The Kanter Corporation sent a letter to the Forest Park Planning and Zoning Commission pointing out that "certain problems" might arise from the existence of an unnamed subdivision—presumably the black neighborhood of Hollydale—near Sheffield Road outside Forest Park. Adjacent to this subdivision was

17. *Forest Park Newsletter,* Aug. 1962.
18. Kanter to Members of Planning Commission [and] Members of Council, Sept. 13, 1962, files of the Forest Park Planning and Zoning Commission.

vacant land in Forest Park's extreme southeast corner below Sharon Road and between Waycross and Sheffield Roads (See Figure 6). "In order to prevent any encroachment from this subdivision," Kanter wanted to develop the vacant land at once, but Kanter and his advisers felt that "it would be impossible to sell these [Forest Park] lots to a builder and expect him to be able to build [houses] in the same price range as other areas of Forest Park." Kanter therefore sought planning commission approval of plans for the construction of homes on the vacant tract in a price range "equivalent to the adjacent subdivision on Sheffield Road."[19]

The proposal elicited no public interest until September 1962, when the *Newletter* devoted its front page to a list of "more frequently mentioned current problems" which the Civic Association expected to discuss in its first "Sound-Off Meeting" of the year. The list included, under the rubric "Property Devaluation," the Kanter proposal to build single-family homes in the $12,000–$14,000 range where they would "seriously threaten the value of the adjoining homes in the eastern side of the 'C' section." At the Civic Association's public meeting, lengthy discussion of the issue ended in a vote to oppose construction of any "low-priced" homes in that area.[20]

The Civic Association protest, in the end, forced Kanter to revise his overall plan for the area. In November, the Forest Park Planning and Zoning Commission heard the Civic Association's complaint but explained that it could influence the price of houses only indirectly, through zoning and building code regulations. The commission added that even requiring larger lots failed to guarantee construction of more costly homes. Moreover, Kanter' plat of the development showed lot sizes roughly the same as those in the adjacent "C" section, which averaged well above the minimum required by the zoning code. In short, there seemed to be no legal basis for changing the code, and such a change itself, even if possible, would not prevent the construction of "low-priced"homes.

The commission did, however, announce one step it planned to take to protect property values in the area. Hartzog's 1961 plan (Figure 6) showed Waycross Road as a primary thoroughfare cutting from the village's northwest commercial-industrial area through the southeast sector of the village and crossing Sheffield. That left the

19. Stubbers to Village of Forest Park Planning and Zoning Commission, May 29, 1962, files of Forest Park Planning and Zoning Commission.
20. *Forest Park Newsletter,* Sept. and Oct. 1962.

"C" section open to heavy traffic which was likely to depress property values and encourage low-income encroachments from the southeast. The commission now planned to make Waycross a dead end, and to use Sheffield and Southland as the primary south-north thoroughfare through the village. This would create a wall of traffic between Hollydale and Forest Park along Sheffield, make it impossible to enter the "C" section from the southeast, and reorient the neighborhood away from Sheffield and toward the north and west, in the direction of the Swim Club. The commission also noted that it was "worried" about the size and location of a school which the Greenhills-Forest Park Board of Education expected to construct in the area.[21]

The Planning and Zoning Commission's November meeting failed to mollify the "C" section protesters. In December, a Civic Association delegation met with the commission and a Kanter Corporation representative. Neil Stubbers, speaking for Kanter, said that the only way the village could control prices was by changing the zoning. Commission members observed that in this case such a revision would be indefensible if challenged by Kanter in court. The commission also announced that the school board had decided to put its proposed neighborhood elementary school just south of the Swim Club, instead of in the extreme southeast corner of the development.[22] The case seemed closed.

The disgruntled citizens, however, refused to give up. The next month, one resident wrote a letter to the *Newsletter* editor accusing village officials of acting as "rubber stamps" for the developer. The mayor and a member of the village government's Legal Committee met several times with Kanter in an effort to work out a compromise. In addition, 170 residents of "C" section petitioned the Planning and Zoning Commission to "up-zone" the Sheffield Road tract. At a subsequent public Planning and Zoning Commission meeting, the commissioners repeated their contentions that Kanter might take a rezoning to court and would probably win, and that enlarging lot sizes would not prevent builders from constructing cheaper houses on bigger lots. The commission also announced that 75 of 300 lots in the contested area would contain houses in the $18,000–$24,000 price range and reminded the petitioners of Kanter's pledge that any new construction would not devalue property in the area. With that, the

21. *Forest Park Newsletter*, Nov. 1962
22. *Forest Park Newsletter*, Dec. 1962.

commission washed its hands of the affair and suggested that the petitioners, who wanted Kanter's pledge in writing, should take their case directly to him.[23]

In the face of continuing pressure, Kanter tried to reassure the dissatisfied citizens. In December 1962, he had sent village council members a letter informing them that he planned to build some homes ranging in price from $17,000 to $23,000 in the Sheffield Road area, and asking both the council and the village to have "faith, trust and confidence in the developer."[24] Now, after discussing the situation with the mayor, Kanter went a step further. The January 1963 *Newsletter* carried a letter from him, pledging his "moral commitment" to develop Sheffield Road at an average house value of $18,000, a figure he described as consistent with the price of existing homes in the "C" section. At the same time, the Legal Committee member who had met with the mayor and Kanter vouched in the *Newsletter* for Kanter's sincerity. He also suggested that citizens pressure the school board to move the proposed elementary school site from the tract adjacent to the Swim Club to the southwest area of the neighborhood. Such a move, he contended, would not only save $10,000 in land costs, but would also facilitate the planning and "buffering" of the area.[25] The school, as it turned out, was never moved, but Waycross became a dead-end street at Sheffield, and the anticipated "encroachments" and devaluation in the "C" section never materialized.

Nonetheless, the anxiety which had accumulated over the Sheffield Road tract set a mood of discontent and brought out latent hostilities among various village subdivisions. In January 1963, a Kemper Heights resident wrote the *Newsletter* protesting the mayor's decision to permit a home beauty salon in this area. Such a salon, the writer claimed, would reduce the resale value of adjacent houses. He further wondered if the permit would have been issued if the home in question had been located in the "C" section, which since the first elections had received a disproportionate "share" of council seats and attention. The mayor responded testily. He called the letter an attempt to "raise sectionalism and factionalism in the Village," opening an "old wound." Before incorporation, the mayor noted, "there

23. *Forest Park Newsletter,* Jan. 1963; Forest Park Planning and Zoning Commission, "Minutes," Jan. 5, 1963.

24. Forest Park Council, "Minutes," Vol. I, Dec. 18, 1962, p. 120, files of the Forest Park Council, Forest Park Municipal Building.

25. *Forest Park Newsletter,* Jan. 1963.

were references to the various areas by name," but since then "we have attempted to conceive of our Village as a single cohesive area," in part by referring to the sections by letter rather than name. He suggested the writer put his considerable talents to constructive use in the village by "working toward its unification and advancement."[26]

This incident, and the disputes over enlarging the shopping center and developing the Sheffield Road tract, underscored the absence of a consensus in the village about how development should proceed and what its future form should be. Both the developer and the village officials seemed to have a clear sense of where the village's development should go, but the two views did not always coincide. Village citizens at times sided with one or the other and occasionally disagreed among themselves. These shifting alliances made the adoption of a master plan difficult, while the distrust and frustration generated by the shopping center, Sheffield Road, and beauty salon debates created an atmosphere of uncertainty about the outcome of the planning process. Christiansen's evaluation of Hartzog's 1961 master plan, released during summer 1962, intensified disagreements about the plan and contributed to growing doubts about the new town's prospects.

Chrisitansen's evaluation of what he called "the Kanter-Hartzog plan" opened by assessing the state of Forest Park at the time and underscoring just how far the village had to go to become a balanced community. He observed that the area had contained 100 persons in 1950; 1,080 in 1957; and 4,800 in 1960; with "optimistic" forecasts projecting a population of 45,000 in 1980. Christiansen, however, estimated that Forest Park would not grow so quickly; he predicted a population increase of 1,400 per year, to total 33,000 by 1980.

While Christiansen seemed unconcerned about the village's growth rate, other characteristics of Forest Park's demography clearly distressed him. He pointed to its low median age of 20.7; he noted that 43.1 percent of its population was below age 15 and 2.9 percent above 65, figures contrasting sharply with the national average of 30.4 and 8.9 percent respectively. He also cited the village's high rate of population turnover, which he attributed to regular lay-offs and job transfers in the Mill Creek Valley industries, where 35 percent of Forest Park's household heads worked. If that pattern persisted, the village could expect a continued demographic imbalance characterized by a disproportionately large number of young adults with children. Of the

26. *Forest Park Newsletter,* Jan. and Feb. 1963.

village's 3,705 acres (5.8 square miles), he added, 65 percent remained undeveloped and the rest was taken up almost entirely by residential developments, Winton Woods, and Union Central. Thus, Forest Park resembled a conventional bedroom suburb of the 1950s. It offered its inhabitants almost no places of employment, but worse still, it possessed no playgrounds or neighborhood parks except for one play area at Kemper Heights Elementary School, the only educational facility in the village, and baseball diamonds at West Sharon Road and Waycross Road leased to the Baseball Association on a year-to-year basis by The Kanter Corporation.[27]

Christiansen followed this unflattering description of the village's condition with a critical analysis of the Kanter-Hartzog plan. He recommended reducing the shopping center and office acreage and eliminating the industrial allocation in the village's eastern portion entirely. Forest Park, he felt, was too remote from Cincinnati and the path of Mill Creek industrial development ever to attract industry. He claimed that five more elementary schools were needed than the plan called for and suggested reserving space for two high schools instead of one. He viewed the village center as badly sited, because it sat on slopes with a 20 percent grade; he recommended moving the whole complex southward to a more central and level location. Three playgrounds planned were inadequate; two more neighborhood parks should be added and two others enlarged. He noted the absence of a facility for housing senior citizens. The thoroughfare plan was criticized for failing to distinguish between primary and secondary roads, for projecting the Waycross and Sheffield connector through rather than around an adjacent residential district, and for increasing the width of Hall Road between Kemper and the Circle Freeway to just 70 instead of 120 feet.[28]

Christiansen viewed more favorably the residential allocations in the Hartzog plan, and his commentary paid special attention to multi-family proposals. The plan set aside 404 acres for multi-family development, with 15 percent of residential land and 34 percent of all dwelling units in multi-family use. He labelled the latter percentage "far above average" and "optimistic." Nonetheless, he defended it:

> Cost revenue studies have long indicated that multi-family units pay for themselves and actually yield more dollars in tax revenue than they receive in return for municipal services. Inasmuch as the village has, and will most

27. Christiansen, "Forest Park Master Plan Evaluation, 1962," 1–10.
28. *Ibid.*, 26–31, 33–52.

likely continue to have, tax problems in the future, a high percentage of multi-family units as proposed in the Kanter-Hartzog plan appears not only feasible but also desirable.[29]

Christiansen's evaluation provoked heated controversy, with the initial fire coming from citizens and elected officials, not The Kanter Corporation. The report, including its recommendation that the Kanter-Hartzog plan be used merely as a basis for developing the village's official master plan,[30] was delivered to the Planning and Zoning Commission in July 1962. On August 27, the commission sponsored a public hearing on the report. The meeting attracted a crowd of 80 people, who peppered Christiansen and the commission with questions until 11:30 p.m., when the chairman ended the proceedings despite the willingness of some in the audience to talk longer. The discussion ranged over a wide variety of topics, including one suggestion that a hospital be built in northern Hamilton County, and produced a straw vote indicating that industrial development was preferred over multi-family housing.[31] But the general reaction to Christiansen's report was decidedly negative. Criticism centered on the large number of apartments regarded as appropriate, on the recommended reduction of industrial acreage, and on school-related matters.

Councilmember Donald English, whose comments the *Newsletter* later characterized as representative of "the general public reaction," sounded a deeper level of discontent. While touching on a broad spectrum of issues, English's remarks added up to a populist denunciation of urban planning professionals and their penchant for social engineering. Describing his views as a "layman's opinion," English attacked both the form and the substance of the evaluation. It read, he complained, too much "like a text book" and lacked "common sense," an element which he claimed the Planning and Zoning Commission could have obtained by resorting to a "layman's committee" rather than a "city-planning expert." English contended that the recommended reductions in industrial space reflected a misguided evaluation of the importance of railroad connections for modern industries. He objected to the large amount of space left in apartments, and the relatively small (one-quarter-acre) average residential

29. *Ibid.*, 32.
30. *Ibid.*, 53.
31. Forest Park Planning and Zoning Commission, "Minutes," June 26 and Aug. 27, 1962; *Forest Park Newsletter*, Sept. 1962.

lot size. English also claimed that the evaluation restricted shopping centers to less than marketable size, suggested that demand for office space in Forest Park remained strong despite similar development in surrounding areas, and argued that Christiansen had exaggerated the cost of installing utilities in the village as a whole.[32] In general, English seemed primarily interested in creating a community of detached homes for nuclear families who would enjoy a high level of services and amenities underwritten by taxes paid by business and industry. He appeared far less interested in any demographic, socioeconomic, and cultural "balance" which apartments might engender, no matter how cost-effective apartments might be from the standpoint of tax revenues and expenditures.

The planning commission's response to Christiansen's evaluation, issued on September 29, 1962, moved far enough in English's direction to alarm Kanter, but stopped short of following the councilman's suggestions to their logical conclusion. In a statement of philosophy, the commission declared that Forest Park should become a "city that is essentially suburban in character," with "ample parks and playgrounds and schools coupled with adequate, planned shopping facilities to serve our needs, plus an industrial, commercial, and office center" to provide "a sound tax base." The statement deplored both the "helter skelter growth" of nearby places like Brentwood, Evendale, and Lockland, and what it called the " 'dormitory suburb' philosophy," emphasizing instead the commission's desire to establish a "proper industrial-commercial balance" and to "strengthen and maintain the residential character of the living areas."[33]

The bulk of the planning commission's recommendations dealt with residential plans. Variety in single-family housing should be encouraged by allowing a range of lot sizes. The projected population should be reduced in proportion to the reduction in multi-family housing. The report admitted that apartments were needed to house unmarried residents, young and elderly couples, people subject to transfer, and "those who simply do not want to own property"; apartments would serve as a nucleus of trade for shopping centers and provide "living space for a certain segment of the work force required for our com-

32. *Forest Park Newsletter,* Sept. 1962.
33. Forest Park Planning and Zoning Commission, "Report on Forest Park Master Plan Evaluation and Recommendations for Future Action," Sept. 29, 1962, 3, files of the Forest Park Planning and Zoning Commission.

mercial, industrial and office-center areas." The commission, however, wanted to hold a tight rein on apartment development by requiring a complete review of each apartment project, from site development to construction type, before approving the building start; by restricting living units to two bedrooms or less; by limiting apartments to locations adjacent to or contiguous with commercial areas; and by prohibiting the "indiscriminate" construction of duplexes.[34]

The commission's non-residential land use recommendations came in three parts. The first concerned commercial and industrial areas. Two shopping centers of 10 acres each were proposed, one at Northland Road and the other at Hall and Kemper Roads (see Figures 6 and 8). No mention was made of the larger center to the west proposed by Hartzog and endorsed by Christiansen. The commission wanted to reduce the space reserved for office centers, expand industrial acreage in the west, and designate only a "reasonable number" of industrial sites in the east (an area the commission deemed unsuitable for industry). In its section on services and community facilities, the report argued that since a reduction in apartment construction meant a lower population, fewer park, playground, and school sites would be required than Christiansen had advocated, though more would be needed than Hartzog had proposed. In a final section, the commission suggested merging the village center with the Hall-Kemper shopping center, moving the municipal service and maintenance facility to a more central place on level ground, and making Hall and Kemper Roads major thoroughfares. In order "to discourage fast traffic through Forest Park" and avoid bisecting residential neighborhoods,[35] the commission would downgrade Waycross and restudy its connection with Sheffield Road.

The commission's report also included a unanimous recommendation that Paul Christiansen should be hired to "complete" the master plan, using the Hartzog plan, the Christiansen evaluation of that plan, and the guidelines and "supporting thinking" laid out by the commission as a basis for that work. In that same recommendation, the commission tied zoning to planning by recommending that Christiansen develop, in connection with his master plan, "the necessary supporting" zoning ordinances and subdivision regulations.[36] This stipulation meant that the village's entire western portion would not

34. *Ibid.*, 3–4.
35. *Ibid.*, 4–5.
36. *Ibid.*, 2.

be available for development by Kanter until after completion of the master plan and the zoning code.

The Kanter Corporation was not pleased with either the slow pace or the direction the planning process seemed to be taking. The village's hiring of Christiansen, after submitting him to a "security clearance" to alleviate suspicions about his past associations with Kanter,[37] suggested that village officials intended to use Christiansen as a foil against planning and zoning pressure from The Kanter Corporation.

That pressure came almost at once, when Kanter requested immediate rezoning of the western and northern part of Forest Park for residential, industrial, and commercial development. The zoning request was drawn directly from the 1961 Kanter-Hartzog plan and introduced nothing new. But an accompanying lecture which Kanter delivered on multi-family housing development drew on a Kanter consultant's analysis of post-World War II housing and demographic trends. The suburban single-family home market would drop, the consultant maintained, while demand for apartments in suburban locations would rise under dual stimuli—the baby boom and the rising tax burden on single-family homeowners around the rims of metropolitan areas.[38]

The planning commission referred the zoning request to Christiansen, who advised taking no action on it until after adoption of the new master plan, then scheduled for completion in summer 1963. Kanter refused to withdraw his request, indicating that he doubted the plan would be done on time. He argued that it was in neither the village's nor his own best interest to lose another building season. Kanter once again had good tenant prospects for his western shopping center, who, if lost, might locate elsewhere in the general vicinity and thereby reduce the village's chance of securing a regional, as opposed to a neighborhood, shopping facility. He needed the industrial zoning now, he added, because the unpredictability of industrial prospects made it necessary to have land available whenever a potential tenant expressed interest.[39]

37. Forest Park Council, "Minutes," Vol. I, Oct. 16, 1962, 110; *Forest Park Newsletter,* Nov. 1962.

38. Kanter to Forest Park Council and Planning and Zoning Commission, Nov. 15, 1962, files of Forest Park Planning and Zoning Commission.

39. Kanter to Forest Park Planning and Zoning Commission, Dec. 7, 1962, files of Forest Park Planning and Zoning Commission.

The commission, however, refused to alter its timetable. Between November 1962, when Kanter submitted his rezoning request, and July 1963, when Christiansen presented his draft of the new master plan, development took place only in areas previously rezoned. In November 1962, Marsh Supermarkets, with fifteen stores in western Ohio, opened a store in the eastern shopping center. In February 1963, the commission approved a site on the northeast corner of Northland and Waycross for an office building for a Kanter subsidiary, the Keystone Building and Loan Company. In April, a manufacturer of electrical lighting and motor equipment joined an industrial machine parts and plastics firm in the eastern industrial park. On June 15, the Union Central Life Insurance Company laid the cornerstone for its office building. And in July, Kanter unveiled plans for a 414-unit "Community Unit Plan" apartment complex, including a swimming pool, park, and parking space, to be built in the area of Waycross, Sharon and Southland Roads.[40]

By that July, public scrutiny of Christiansen's proposed master plan had begun. It showed Winton Road in six lanes and Winton, Kemper, and Sharon Roads extended into major thoroughfares (refer to Figure 6 for comparison). An elaborate civic center, with village hall, library, post office, shopping center, high school, swimming pool, baseball diamonds, and park and recreation area, was planned on both sides of the northern reaches of Hall. The plan allocated 14 percent of all dwelling units to three multi-family developments—one near the eastern shopping center where Marsh Supermarkets had located; another near the Winton, Hall, and Kemper Road intersection; and the third near the Waycross Road and Hamilton Avenue intersection on the west. Most of the industrial acreage was assigned to the extreme western portion of the village around Union Central, leaving a small area for industry in the east near establishments already in place.[41] Finally, Christiansen left the eastern shopping center untouched and projected a regional facility for the western edge of Forest Park, beyond Union Central and the industrial territory adjacent to it.

At a special August hearing on his rezoning request, Kanter commented on the 1963 Christiansen plan. "Basically," Kanter said, "we would like the old master plan left as intact as possible. The present residents of Forest Park were sold on Forest Park based on the

40. *Forest Park Newsletter*, Nov. 1962; Feb., Apr., June, and July 1963.
41. *Forest Park Newsletter*, July 1963.

present master plan," and "they seem to be well satisfied. . . ." Most complaints, he asserted, had been about the slow pace of development, and to counter that and "create a feeling of confidence" among the residents, "we have been pushing you to give us the go-ahead in the form of zoning and subdivision regulations." With a final appeal for quick action,[42] Kanter proceeded to list his specific objections to the Christiansen proposal.

He attacked the street plan first, maintaining that the proposed improvements would cost more to install and maintain than either the developer or the village could afford. Kanter also claimed that too much land had been set aside for public use. He asked for more office area north of the existing shopping center. And he took issue particularly with the industrial-residential balance suggested in the plan. More industrial area—as much as 155 acres—was needed in the east. While accepting the 14-percent ratio of apartments to total housing units, Kanter asked for more apartments north of Northland and west of Waycross; permission, he said, would keep a majority of the village's apartments in the east and allow lower-density multi-family development. Kanter also wanted more land in the original eastern shopping center tract used for apartments, and he requested zoning permission for duplex apartments.

Kanter concluded his response with an extraordinary suggestion that village officials give him a free hand in developing Forest Park. "Give us the opportunity to develop these items in accordance with the best judgment of our marketing analysis experts," he pleaded. "If we are successful, it will work to the advantage of the entire village."[43]

Planning commissioners, while unwilling to remove themselves from the planning process, felt inclined to compromise with Kanter. At a working session on September 10, 1963, the commission agreed, first, to treat the street plan as merely an indicator of the overall pattern, rather than as a blueprint for pavement widths or rights-of-way. The commissioners also agreed, albeit without unanimity, to amend the Christiansen proposal in several ways. They enlarged the industrial acreage in the east; designated additional land south of the existing shopping center for multi-family residential use, while pre-

42. Kanter to Samuel Bryant, Chairman, Forest Park Planning and Zoning Commission, Aug. 20, 1963, files of Forest Park and Zoning Planning Commission.
43. *Ibid.; Forest Park Newsletter,* Aug. 1963.

serving school and park areas; and assigned land east of the shopping center for offices rather than multi-family dwellings.[44]

The preliminary agreement on the amendments set off a minor furor. Two days after the September 10 meeting, Commissioner Daniel Meehan complained publicly in the *Greenhills-Forest Park Journal* that the commission was "giving in too much" to Kanter, who wanted to "overdevelop" both multi-family accommodations and industrial sites.[45]

With Meehan's charge in mind, the Civic Association's *Newsletter* urged all Forest Park residents to attend the public hearing on the plan. The main points of controversy, the paper indicated, would be a difference between the commission and Kanter over the exact size of the eastern industrial area, and the question of apartment construction. In short, the paper predicted, the session would be "far more exciting and educational than the [TV] studio wrestling match normally scheduled for Saturday afternoons."[46]

The meeting lasted two and a half hours, attracted over fifty people, and went just as the commission majority had planned. Chairman Bryant opened the gathering by explaining the items to be discussed and noting the commission's desire to assess public reaction to the plan before recommending it to the village council for adoption. Christiansen then presented the plan, after which Bryant called on The Kanter Corporation's representative.

The firm's lawyer, Sydnor Davis, began by addressing the street question (see Figures 6 and 8). Then he moved on to the more delicate question of land use. He requested, first, that the entire village east of Southland be allotted to industry and that the whole area bounded by Northland, Southland, Fresno, and Waycross be assigned to office use. Davis concluded by urging that all of the area south of the shopping center to Sharon be allocated for multi-family development; that the area east of the shopping center on Northland be designated commercial; and that an area in the Kenn, Waycross, and Northland section be reserved for apartments. No reference was made to parks, schools, or any other public facility.

---

44. Bryant to Members of the Planning Commission, [memo of understanding on] "Master Plan Public Hearing, September 21, 1963," files of Forest Park Planning and Zoning Commission.
45. *Greenhills-Forest Park Journal*, Sept. 12, 1963.
46. *Forest Park Newsletter*, Sept. 1963.

Surprisingly, during the ensuing discussion, no one objected to apartment construction. Finally, a commission member moved adoption of the plan, and amendment of the document began. First, the land east of Southland, but not the entire eastern portion of the village, was reserved for an industrial park. Second, all land south of the existing shopping center, except the park and school acreage, was devoted to multi-family housing. Third, an area east of the shopping center along Northland was designated for office instead of multi-family use. Fourth, collector street rights-of-way were narrowed from seventy to sixty feet. A fifth amendment changed the location of the Waycross-Hamilton Road intersection near Circle Freeway. Sixth, all pavement widths were deleted from the plan. Each amendment passed unanimously, although Commissioner Meehan was absent.[47] In the end, Kanter got less than he wanted in office and industrial space, though more than Christiansen had proposed, and secured major concessions on streets. If, as the *Newsletter* asserted, anti-apartment and anti-industry factions existed in the village, at this meeting they went unheard and unheeded.

The new plan, as amended, now went to the village council. There Councilmember Donald English, who had previously chided Christiansen for his "pessimistic" stance on industrial development while applauding the reduced size of the multi-family zone, introduced several new amendments. He suggested removing the reserve stipulation on the industrial area east of Southland Road and north of Sharon, thus turning almost the entire easternmost section into an industrial park and changing the area between Waycross and Southland from multi-family to office. The vote on each amendment was four to two in favor, with the two councilmembers who also served on the planning commission casting the dissenting ballots.[48] The council needed a three-fourths (five-to-one) majority to override a commission recommendation. So the plan was temporarily tabled, giving the commission a chance to consider the council's amendments.[49]

At the commission's next meeting, English's supporters had the votes. Both of the council's amendments passed by a margin of three to one, with Willard Pistler dissenting. (One other member, Mayor

47. Forest Park Planning and Zoning Commission, "Minutes of the Public Hearing, September 21, 1963," files of Forest Park Planning and Zoning Commission; *Forest Park News*, Oct. 4, 1963.

48. Forest Park Council, "Minutes," Vol. I, Sept. 21, 1963, 167; *Forest Park News*, Oct. 4, 1963.

49. *Forest Park News*, Oct. 4, 1963.

Gebhardt, was absent.) Pistler opposed the changes, he said, because they "contradict the advice of professional planners" and "represent naive wishful thinking regarding probable development." He acknowledged that he might be wrong but asserted that the "developer has not and does not evidence willingness to take risks or make commitments that would assure such development."[50] A supporter of the amendments countered with the argument that the east end was and always would be unsuitable for single-family dwellings and suggested that "a spirit of cooperation on the part of all village officials would add to the attractiveness of the area to potential buyers."[51]

The rest of the master plan, which dealt for the most part with community facilities, elicited surprisingly little interest and no strident public protest. Christiansen had placed a hospital, a garbage incinerator, village garage and storage yards, and a new water tower near the Winton and Waycross intersection; an old age home on Hall Road just below the Circle Freeway interchange; and three fire stations at sites in the east, central, and west portions of the village. Despite Kanter's earlier objections, Christiansen had yielded nothing on education and recreation space. The approved plan prescribed a senior high school, two junior highs, and eight new elementary schools, each located to function as a hub for its neighborhood. In addition, the plan called for nine neighborhood and three playfield parks besides Winton Woods, which Christiansen called a regional park. Finally, Christiansen proposed a roadside commercial area for drive-in restaurants, theaters, garages, motels, miniature golf courses, and other highway-oriented businesses, immediately north of the corporation line at the Hall Road-Circle Freeway interchange. He sketched in a cemetery just east of that complex but said nothing about churches, social centers, or meeting halls.[52]

As adopted by the planning commission and approved by the village council, the 1963 master plan expressed a compromise among citizens, village officials, and the developer about land use within the community. Though details were modified later, the plan provided the basic guidelines for Forest Park's development over the next decade. In one sense, the new 1963 plan represented a drastic change from the

50. Forest Park Planning and Zoning Commission, "Minutes," Sept. 24, 1963.
51. *Forest Park News,* Oct. 4, 1963.
52. Christiansen, "Comprehensive Master Plan for Forest Park, Ohio, 1964," files of the Forest Park Planning and Zoning Commission, 24–25, 32–33, 39–40.

scheme envisaged in 1956. Warner-Kanter originally had assigned approximately 1,400 acres to industrial, commercial, and municipal uses. In 1961, Hartzog had recommended cutting the industrial, commercial, and business total to 521 acres. The 1963 village plan increased the amount reserved for those purposes to 593 acres, an increase of 15 percent[53] but still well short of the non-municipal and non-residential land use allotment established in the mid-1950s.

In a larger sense, however, the 1963 plan struck a note of continuity, for it altered the proportions of the land use pattern without altering the basic structure. Christiansen himself made that point at the close of his final version of the new plan. From the outset, he noted, the developer had provided Forest Park with "many advantages," and as a result the village in 1963 had "no mixed land problems, narrow rights-of-way, crowded housing, blighted conditions, or slums. . . . With proper citizen spirit, adequate development controls, cooperation from developers, and a master plan, Forest Park could develop into a model community as originally envisaged."[54]

Christiansen was accurate in his assessment of the 1963 plan's relation to the CCDC and Warner-Kanter's original conception. From the outset, these two prime movers had built Forest Park for that enlarged, upwardly-mobile, and transient middle class which they had expected to emerge after World War II. The 1963 plan, with its emphasis on balanced land use and comprehensive public services and facilities, reaffirmed that market orientation. Kanter, Hartzog, Christiansen, village officials, and citizen activists all saw Forest Park as a community of limited liability. There one could, if one desired, be born and raised, work, act out the role of citizen, and die. But few Forest Parkers actually thought of living out their lives in Forest Park. These socially- and geographically-mobile middle-class people had loyalties and ties to non-territorial communities, as well as to their residential locality, and they changed addresses routinely in response to changing job opportunities and family life cycles. Therefore, a community such as Forest Park was primarily important as a place these people could move into and out of with a minimum of social and psychological disruption and a maximum of material comfort.

It was precisely the general agreement on the nature of community in Forest Park which accounted for the nature of the fight over the master plan. The idea that Forest Park was a community of limited

53. *Forest Park Newsletter,* Mar. 1964.
54. Christiansen, "Comprehensive Master Plan, 1964," 33.

liability led to a quest for enduring and stable property values, not an enduring and stable population. The problem was how to make the place economically viable for three parties simultaneously: the developer, who owned the undeveloped land; the residents, who bought and sold real estate or rented there; and the village government, which needed a tax base sufficient to provide a level of services attractive to middle-class people, employers of middle-class people, and merchants who catered to middle-class tastes. It was inevitable, given these interest groups, that the planning process would be marked by disagreements over the proper balance of business, industrial, and residential land use, and not over the proper socio-economic, racial, religious, or ethnic mix in Forest Park's population. The same configurations doomed Kanter's hopes for significant multi-family development; Forest Park residents feared that too many apartments might bring in large numbers of people deemed "undesirable" not because they were transient but because of their presumed disinterest in maintaining stable property values. And the concerns which dominated the three key interest groups in Forest Park made it easy, if not inevitable, for participants in the planning process to ignore entirely the role the village could have played as an agent of social cohesion and of social and economic justice within the metropolis by leaving Forest Park more open to every class and type of resident of the metropolis seeking a better quality of life.

This is not to say that the making of the 1963 plan occurred without reference to class, race, or the larger metropolitan context. Implicit in the process and the resulting plan were assumptions about the socioeconomic and racial composition appropriate for Forest Park's population and about the village's relationship to the larger metropolis. Those assumptions underlay the so-called "step up" theory[55] of metropolitan growth prevalent in mid-twentieth-century America, which associated upward socioeconomic mobility with outward geographical mobility. According to these assumptions, the poor and the black lived within the confines of the inner metropolis; the white working class resided in the next band of neighborhoods outward; and the middle and upper classes commanded more affluent separate communities, some still within the big city but most on the periphery of the metropolitan area. That set of assumptions about the appropriate metropolitan geography provided a variety of residential choices

---

55. The phrase is Lawrence Tucker's. Tucker to author, interview, Aug. 12, 1976.

for the presumably autonomous individuals who made up the communities of limited liability within the metropolis as a whole. It also freed Forest Parkers involved in the 1963 conflict over the village plan from worrying about the future of the metropolis. They had merely to confront the problem of adjusting Forest Park's land use pattern to fit the requirements of a suburban community of limited liability. Their resolution of that problem considered the creation neither of an "elite" nor of a "mixed" suburb tied to the city, but rather of an autonomous place quite different and, for planning purposes, quite separate from the city.

The population of Forest Park is far more homogeneous than most communities. There is much less difference in age, income, education and background. There are no organized interests, if you exclude the man who owns all the vacant lots. Partisan politics in Village government has been firmly rejected by the voters. Council can base its decisions on what it thinks is good for the Village and a majority of the residents want. . . . This makes for a more responsible, responsive and efficient government. We hope it stays this way.

The [Forest Park] *Village Voice*
September 1967

DEVELOPMENTAL POLITICS[1]
IN A NEW TOWN, 1963–1970

The village council's adoption of Forest Park's new master plan in September 1963 established a broad consensus on a blueprint for Forest Park's future as a community of limited liability; that grand consensus stood unchallenged for almost a decade. Yet disagreements over village development persisted. The issue was not what the village should become in the long run, but who—developer, village government, homeowners, or businessmen—would pay most in the short run to get what everyone professed to want. For just below the surface of rhetoric about the joys of building a balanced model community lay an abiding concern for municipal revenues and property values.

For a time, the atmosphere was clouded by an acrid dispute over the appropriate political mechanisms for resolving key issues. That

1. See Milton Rakove, *The Changing Patterns of Suburban Politics in Cook County, Illinois* (Chicago: Center for Research in Urban Government, Loyola Univ., 1965), and Rakove, *Don't Make No Waves, Don't Back No Losers: An Insider's Analysis of the Daley Machine* (Bloomington: Indiana Univ. Press, 1975), 234–56, for discussions of politics in both "development" and "establishment" suburbs.

contest initially pitted defenders of the two-party system in local politics against advocates of nonpartisanship. But ultimately a cooperative relationship emerged, under which the developer, village officials, and school officials took the initiative in formulating and securing adoption of measures which they felt promoted community welfare.

During Forest Park's first two years as a village, community politics centered on the new master plan. Yet while the village elections of November 1963 occurred in an atmosphere of rising factional hostility, neither the master plan nor any other particular issue dominated the campaigns. When incumbent mayoral candidate Donald Gebhardt withdrew late in the campaign, his challenger, Donald English, took the mayor's seat by default. Unlike Gebhardt, who had belonged to the nonpartisan Citizens for Forest Park, English was a partisan, conservative Republican precinct leader and chairman of a local American Legion post's Americanism Committee. An industrial engineer with Procter and Gamble, as a council member English had been a staunch proponent of more industrial development, an outspoken critic of multifamily housing, and a leading supporter of stricter enforcement of village ordinances. While Citizens for Forest Park retained its majority on the council, a candidate associated with English polled the largest vote, and another non-incumbent member of the English faction, Loraine Blackburn, ousted the sitting clerk-treasurer.[2]

The *Newsletter* interpreted the election results as a sign that Forest Park was headed for trouble and suggested that incorporation had abruptly created new and dangerous channels for conflict. This analysis was bolstered by the Civic Association's collapse in November 1963. The monthly *Newsletter,* now run independently, felt that the association's early vitality and the community's cohesiveness had stemmed from residents' fears about the machinations of "outsiders." Somewhat nostagically, the *Newsletter* remarked, "We used to talk about the developer, 'Green Hillsians,' and others as if they were the aborigines at whose expense all progress in Forest Park must be made." Then came incorporation, and the 1963 election, in which "honest-to-goodness party factions" participated, "each claiming to know what is best for the community." That factionalism signaled the coming of "more worldliness—more sophistication—more apathy"

2. *Forest Park Newsletter,* Aug. Sept., Oct., and Nov. 1963; *Greenhills-Forest Park Journal,* Aug. 29, 1963.

and perhaps even "the development of the two-party system." The *Newsletter* felt this meant the loss of Forest Park's uniqueness[3] as a cohesive civic community governed by a rationally-determined consensus.

During the last week of the 1963 campaign, the English faction raised a new issue which was to become a major source of contention in village politics. Too late for either Citizens for Forest Park or the *Newsletter* to reply, English and his group circulated literature blaming the slow pace of industrial development on the incumbent council. Soon after the election, however, the *Newsletter* addressed this question. The initial treatment was calculated to eliminate factionalism, stifle partisanship, and reunify the community, by turning the attack away from Citizens for Forest Park and redirecting it toward The Kanter Corporation. The paper explained:

> The Village can zone the land. It has done that. The Village can hold the tax rate down. It has done that. The Village can lean over backward to make the area attractive to industry. It has done that. But the Village cannot sell or lease the land. Only the developer can do that.[4]

In subsequent issues, the *Newsletter* elaborated its case against the developer.[5] But Kanter now possessed formidable weapons with which to defend himself in the public opinion arena. In summer 1963, after initiating informal discussion about Christiansen's master plan proposals, and while a tight mayoral contest between Gebhardt and English still seemed likely, The Kanter Corporation had announced its intention to launch a new publication, the *Forest Park News*. The *News* would be distributed free to all village residents, to real estate firms, and to prospective industrial and commercial clients. The paper also would be "loaded with pictures and news of people and events in Forest Park," and would print all letters sent to the editor.[6] The editorial policy would be "nonpartisan," a characterization which went unquestioned during the campaign.

To counter the assault on his industrial development record, in January 1964 Kanter announced the formation of a new corporation,

3. *Forest Park Newsletter*, Nov. 1963. For a useful sociological exposition of the defended neighborhood as community, see Gerald D. Suttles, *The Social Construction of Communities* (Chicago: Univ. of Chicago Press, 1972), especially pp. 235–68.

4. *Forest Park Newsletter*, Nov. 1963.

5. *Forest Park Newsletter*, Mar. 1964. Also see, in the same issue, an outline history of the shopping center. The implication is that the developer's indecisiveness held back inception of the project.

6. *Forest Park Newsletter*, June 1963; *Forest Park News*, June 28, 1963.

99

Forest Park, Inc., which had been "organized to develop Forest Park." Its president, George M. Lockwood, lived in the village and had been one of the first members of its Planning and Zoning Commission. His leadership of the new firm would release Kanter to devote his time to "philanthropic and financial interests." The *News* described Lockwood as an individual who had been "associated with the development of Forest Park from its inception and shared in the dreams of its growth. Forest Park is close to his heart and will receive his infinite personal attention." Lockwood was expected to place "major emphasis on industrial and commercial development in addition to handling residential development,"[7] just the posture advocated by English.

Kanter's next step to contain the anti-developer thrust of the new village politics took place shortly after Lockwood's appointment. In January 1964, Lockwood met with the village planning commission to discuss the zoning ordinance which Christiansen has prepared for the village. For the first time, a Kanter representative moved away from Kanter's heretofore invariable demand for a wide margin of flexibility in developing Forest Park. The new position reflected both Kanter's satisfaction with the master plan and his fear that in the future anti-developer feelings might lead village officials to deviate markedly from that document. Lockwood requested that land use and zoning regulations be merged into "one plan," because, as he put it, "you cannot legally bind subsequent Planning Commission [sic] and Councils to re-zone as you would re-zone. We cannot . . . ," he added for emphasis, "afford the delays that may be caused by re-zoning and the chance that people may change their minds and may not feel good the day a re-zoning is voted upon."[8]

Kanter's efforts to neutralize anti-developer sentiment received an unexpected boost when an extraordinary series of controversies pitted Mayor English against the village council and made English, rather than the developer, the most prominent figure in Forest Park affairs. English wanted to be an activist chief executive, molding and leading public opinion and formulating policy in community development. The village form of government, however, prescribed a more restricted role. It gave the mayor merely administrative powers, and

7. *Forest Park News,* Jan. 10, 1964.
8. George M. Lockwood to Forest Park Planning and Zoning Commission, Jan. 24, 1964, files of Forest Park Planning and Zoning Commission.

accorded the council, over which he presided, full legislative authority. The mayor could not vote in the council, except to break a tie, nor veto council ordinances. To exercise the influence he sought, therefore, English tried to build public support for his views by writing a regular column in the *Forest Park News* and by participating quite aggressively in council deliberations. The council, for its part, not only resented English's imperial ambitions for the office of mayor, but also jealously guarded what it viewed as its prerogatives in administrative matters.

The feud between the mayor and the council broke out publicly during February and March 1964, in a dispute over the mayor's allegedly lax enforcement of a "mud" ordinance designed to keep the developer and builders from dirtying and damaging streets and sidewalks.[9] In one exchange on the issue, the mayor indicated that he had requested, but not yet received, a legal opinion about its enforceability; the impression left was that he had decided not to enforce the law until he received the legal opinion. Council member Philip White promptly introduced, and the council adopted, a resolution calling for a council investigation of the mayor and police for their refusal to enforce council legislation.[10] The mayor, however, refused to cooperate and declined an invitation to present his case, on the grounds that the request constituted an unwarranted and illegal legislative interference with the executive branch. He added that the absence of arrests under the mud ordinance was due to a preventive policy of inspection and education.[11]

These events dismayed the *Newsletter,* which declared both sides guilty of petty bickering. In its April issue, however, the paper changed its tune, deploring the evaporation of Forest Park's "small town" atmosphere of trust and cooperation and the intrusion of "politics" into village affairs. It blamed English for the mud ordinance flap, moreover, and accused him of trying to usurp the legitimate legislative functions of the council. The mayor was advised to exhibit more "humility and cooperation in public office," and it was suggested that he undertake "a careful reading of the state statutes

9. Forest Park Council, "Minutes," Vol. II, Feb. 4, 1964, 2; Forest Park Ordinances, Ordinance No. 6-1964, files of Forest Park Clerk of Council, Forest Park Municipal Building.
10. Forest Park Council, "Minutes," Vol. I, Mar. 3, 1964, 13.
11. Forest Park Council, "Minutes," Vol. II, Apr. 7, 1964, 20–21; *Forest Park Newsletter,* Apr. 1964.

pertaining to the duties of the Mayor in a village government, followed by a faithful and complete performance of those duties."[12] Whether at the *Newsletter's* bidding or to help village officials present a united front during the spring school-levy campaign, English terminated the mud ordinance fight with a show of grace. At the April 21 council meeting, he apologized for his misleading statements about the law, and the council reciprocated by closing its investigation.[13]

Peace in village hall, however, lasted only until July 1964, when the 1965 budget came up for discussion. The council got some fiscal relief when Hamilton County, as part of a movement to improve suburban sewer management, agreed to maintain and service old and new sewers in Forest Park.[14] The council itself placed a $310,000 levy on the fall ballot for a new municipal building, to house the police and fire departments and replace the makeshift quarters rented since 1961 from The Kanter Corporation for $1 per year. The measure seemed likely to pass. If it failed, fire insurance would increase an average of $6 per year per house, while the bond issue, which the taxpayers could deduct from their federal income taxes, would cost only $8.[15] But even with those two new income sources, the budget provided no money to hire more police, to increase police salaries to levels competitive with those in other suburban municipalities,[16] or to purchase more fire equipment. These questions could not be ignored, because English was determined to add at least one patrolman to the police force, even if it meant keeping salaries down. When some council members questioned the wisdom of the mayor's position, he issued a blast in a local paper, asking why the council had to spend an hour and a half debating such an obviously desirable proposition, and noting that "burglaries were taking place, while council still wondered if better police protection is really needed." English asked Forest Parkers to "draw your own conclusions."[17]

Having been elected on a platform of no tax increases, the council majority was reluctant to endanger passage of the bond issue by

12. *Forest Park Newsletter,* Mar. and Apr. 1964.

13. Forest Park Council, "Minutes," Vol. II, Apr. 21, 1964, 24.

14. *Cincinnati Post and Times-Star,* Aug. 7 and 10, 1963; *Forest Park Newsletter,* Aug. 1963; Hamilton County Commissioners, "Minutes," Vol. 144, Jan. 7-Dec. 30, 1963, 535, 882, files of the Hamilton County Commissioners, Hamilton County Courthouse, Cincinnati, Ohio.

15. *Forest Park Newsletter,* Oct. 1961; Jan. Feb. 1962; Apr. and Oct. 1964.

16. Forest Park Council, "Minutes," Vol. II, July 21, 1964, 41–43.

17. *Ibid.; Greenhills-Forest Park Journal,* July 30, 1964.

raising taxes. But the group also wished to avoid taking a weak stance on "law and order." In an effort to wriggle out of this tight spot, the council adopted a budget increasing police and fire expenditures about equally. One additional patrolman and a raise in police salaries were adopted, as well as increased funds for fire department equipment and a life squad. The money was to come from an increase in Forest Park's share of the state's local government fund. If the increase did not materialize, funds could be raised in a last-minute tax hike.[18]

As it turned out, the council did not have to raise taxes in order to cover the 1965 budget increases, but before that became apparent, the mayor-council feud broke out again. In 1964, Mayor English served as chairman of the campaign planning committee of the Hamilton County Citizens for Barry Goldwater, the Republican nominee for president of the United States. About the same time, English nominated for a seat on the Forest Park Recreation Commission a woman who managed the Goldwater group's finances. Twice the council refused to approve her appointment to the commission, preferring, instead, its own candidate, a man who had been active in the Baseball Association.

During summer and fall 1964, the mayor's regular column in the *News* ignored the disagreement over the Recreation Commission post. In keeping with the Goldwater campaign's emphasis on law and order, English repeatedly broached the issue of village law enforcement. Citing a *U.S. News and World Report* article about "crime running wild" in the United States, English observed that the question of law enforcement recently had been the subject of much local debate. Now he asked whether people wanted "total enforcement" or "some lesser degree of enforcement" of local laws. Should a traffic violator, he asked, be merely warned on the first offense, or arrested? Should the mayor publicize a pending crackdown before carrying it out? And what, he wanted to know, should he do about the teen-age curfew ordinance, a law enacted in 1961 but never enforced? Did voters want rigid enforcement, none, or a "compromise?"[19]

English's law-and-order campaign inspired no noticeable reaction. Next English turned to the issue of free speech and free use of private property in Forest Park. In an October 16 article, he pointed out that the council had passed a law inhibiting free expression in the support

18. Forest Park Council, "Minutes," Vol. II, July 21, 1964, 41–43.
19. *Forest Park News,* Aug. 21, 1964.

of the candidate of one's choice, by requiring property owners to purchase a $5.00 permit before displaying a political yard sign or poster. English asked if it bothered readers "that your rights to use your property in Forest Park are rapidly being taken away?".[20] Two council members, Philip White and John R. Lesick, objected vigorously to English's interpretation of the sign ordinance, and particularly to his reference to the erosion of property rights in the village. Lesick also suggested that the *News* might exercise tighter editorial supervision over its columnists. Eileen Kieffer, a co-editor of the paper, took this remark as a charge of irresponsible journalism, equivalent to her calling Lesick a crook lawyer or White an unscrupulous salesman. Kieffer also protested in print against descriptions of the *News* as the "mayor's paper"; reminded Lesick and White that George Lockwood of Forest Park, Inc., not English, published the paper; and reasserted the paper's commitment to "write the news as honestly as we can and let the chips fall where they may—even when it involves the developer."[21]

Lesick responded with a letter to the editor in December 1964, repeating his charge that the *News* had abdicated its "civic responsibility" by publishing English's article without checking the facts. But Lesick did not stop there. "Perhaps," he speculated,

> the editors agreed with the Mayor's statement. And if so, the reason would not be difficult to see because the editors are avid supporters, politically, of the Mayor and one editor (Ed. Note!: For our readers' information, that one editor is Eileen Kieffer) is the wife of the Mayor's past political campaign manager.[22]

Despite the controversy between English and the council during autumn 1964, local voters approved the $310,000 municipal building levy. Goldwater also ran well in Forest Park, carrying 60 percent in the November election, compared with 52 percent in the Hamilton County suburbs generally, 38 percent in Cincinnati proper, and 38 percent nationwide.[23] But the election day consensus did not signal the opening of an era of good feelings in the village. The last precinct had scarcely been polled when another skirmish over the police broke out between the mayor and council.

20. *Forest Park News,* Oct. 16, 1964.
21. *Forest Park News,* Nov. 13, 1964.
22. *Forest Park News,* Dec. 11, 1964.
23. Hamilton County Board of Elections, "Official Results, General Election, 1964"; *Forest Park Newsletter,* Nov. 1964; Theodore H. White, *The Making of the President, 1964* (New York: Atheneum, 1965), 380.

Late in 1964, one Forest Park patrolman threatened to quit and another submitted a "proposed" letter of resignation cataloging a series of complaints about the chief, his colleagues, and the operation of the police department. Mayor English asked the council's Public Safety Committee to determine why policemen would consider resigning. The committee conducted an investigation and compiled a three-page summary of its findings, along with twelve recommendations for improving the department.[24] At the council sessions where the report was considered, the committee's new chairman, Philip White, asked the mayor to accept all twelve recommendations. English refused, instead taking the occasion to offer his "impressions" of other recent council actions.[25]

The mayor began by observing that debate in the November 17 council meeting included remarks about "newspaper ownership by local politicians and . . . bias on the part of certain publications." The mayor wanted to make the record "complete on this score. The politically owned opinion sheet," he charged, was not the *News* but the *Newsletter,* which he called a mouthpiece for the council majority, "negative—irresponsible—or *at least* incorrect." He claimed the paper put out "misleading statements" about the school bond issue, made an "incorrect proclamation of a tax increase for operating purposes," and wrongly stated that money saved on construction of the municipal building could be used for streets and other expenses. The mayor called the latter idea "a diversion of funds . . . forbidden by law."[26]

Next English turned to the new zoning ordinance and one recent instance of rezoning. He objected to the council's designating itself as the Zoning Board of Appeals, a step he labeled legal but illogical. He doubted that the council could "impartially judge appeals from its own handiwork." He also disliked zoning code provisions regulating front yard fences, walls, and hedges, and he remained unconvinced that "strict conformity to the arbitrary will of government is conducive to the creation of an attractive and free community." And he denounced most strenuously the "impulsive" rezoning of the "potentially rich western industrial zone to residential." In conclusion, the mayor suggested that "if the Council would devote as much time and energy to constructive activities as it does to charges and investi-

24. Forest Park Council, "Minutes," Vol. II, Feb. 2, 1965, 98–99.
25. *Ibid.,* 99–102A.
26. *Ibid.,* 102A.

gations and to restrictive legislation . . . we could look forward to a period of real progress."[27]

The mayor's statement seems inappropriate in the context of a council meeting preoccupied with police trouble. But it may seem less inappropriate in a political context of rising partisan competition. Through eight long years of the Eisenhower administration, the Hamilton County Democratic Party had struggled to survive, in a county notorious for its strongly entrenched Republican organization. In 1962, Democratic Governor Michael V. DiSalle had been defeated by James A. Rhodes, a durable Republican politician who advocated encouraging industrial development to provide jobs, holding the line on property and corporate taxes, avoiding an income tax, and launching public works construction projects financed by revenue bonds. After this defeat, the local Democrats, lacking both patronage and moral support from the state and national capitols and the county courthouse, could expect little but the crumbs traditionally accorded the minority by the majority in areas dominated by one political party. Throughout the 1950s, then, the suburban Democratic organizations languished.

John F. Kennedy's presidential nomination and subsequent election in 1960, however, had a dramatic effect on the local Democratic party. Kennedy's primary and general election campaigns demonstrated that bright young "outsiders," with well-planned, energetic grassroots campaigns, could defeat seemingly impregnable incumbent political organizations. The subsequent invigoration of the Hamilton County Democrats, however, first produced not an assault on the Republican machine, but an intra-party fight for control of the county organization. One side was composed of the regulars, led by John A. "Socko" Wiethe, Hamilton County Democratic Party chairman. The other side consisted of a group of former leaders in the local Citizens for Kennedy Committee. These insurgents rallied around John J. Gilligan, an articulate young former college English instructor and future governor of Ohio who began his political career on the Cincinnati City Council. One part of the dissidents' strategy to unseat Wiethe involved organizing areas where the party had long been dormant. These efforts, although not immediately successful in challenging Wiethe, revived grassroots interest in long-neglected suburban and city Democratic precinct posts and clubs.[28]

27. *Ibid.*
28. This account of local Democratic politics is based on the author's informal "inter-

In the early 1960s the Democrats had maintained an organization in Forest Park, though it had been scarcely visible in village affairs. In the spring 1964 primaries, however, the Democrats ran candidates for precinct executive in each Forest Park precinct. Among these candidates was Philip White. At its December 1964 meeting, moreover, the Democratic club decided to shift its attention from county, state, and national affairs to village concerns. The first goal was to elect Democrats to the village council in fall 1965. The Democrats would also work to establish a charter commission to determine the village's form of government once it became a city, and try to insure that Forest Park developed along the lines proposed by the village's current planning commission. In view of the fight between English and the commission in fall and winter 1963 over zoning and industrial development,[29] the latter commitment was particularly interesting.

In this context, the mayor's statement at the council meeting of February 2, 1965, seems like the second move in the fall 1965 village election campaigns. The mayor, the speech suggested, intended to play a leading role in that campaign, and his remarks, in both what was said and what was left unsaid, declared his policy. English posed, in effect, as a local James Rhodes. He stressed progress but protested higher taxes. He supported planning when it promised industrial development but opposed government restrictions on the rights of homeowners. In zoning, he preferred giving the developer maximum leeway in attracting business and industry to Forest Park, in order to broaden the revenue base and let single-family homeowners enjoy maximum municipal services and school facilities and a low tax rate. He also favored minimum residential zoning regulations, to permit homeowners the freedom to use their property as they saw fit.

The side opposing English, consisting of the planning commission, the council majority, the *Newsletter,* and, apparently, the Democrats, shared the general desire for a community with a balanced land-use pattern and revenue mix. But this faction did not trust the developer and homeowners, without strict local government surveillance, to place quality, "proper" balance, and aesthetic value above short-term economic gain in shaping Forest Park's future.

Thus, with the lines of conflict clearly drawn, the Republicans, late in February 1965, fielded a slate of candidates for the fall election.

---

views" with many of the leading participants and their supporters, conducted after steering committee meetings and other political functions.

29. *Forest Park News,* May 29, 1964; Dec. 11, 1964.

Their ticket consisted of three incumbent councilmembers, Lesick, the incumbent clerk Loraine Blackburn, and Mayor English.[30]

Nothing took place before the election to dispel the growing impression that both English's Republicans and Forest Park, Inc., whether formally allied or not, placed too high a priority on industrial development. While everyone recognized that more industry meant a broader tax base, more municipal services, and lower property taxes for homeowners, many also feared that looser restrictions on industry might attract "offensive" manufacturing and so reduce residential property values. For them, stable or appreciating housing prices were more important than low taxes purchased by admitting industries detrimental to their image of Forest Park as a nice place for middle-class people to live.

The popularity of this "nonpartisan" attitude ultimately helped prevent the emergence of a pattern of local politics organized around the two major national parties, after several events in spring and summer 1965 suggested the wisdom of the position. The planning commission and the council twice resisted developer efforts to "spot-zone" small residential tracts to permit construction of service stations at locations which village officials deemed unadvisable. The council also denied a variance on the sign ordinance to enable The Kanter Corporation to display more and larger advertisements in the village. A more serious fight erupted over an attempt to introduce a new industrial zoning category. Manufacturing plants would be allowed on two-acre plots, with larger setbacks and clearances required when the site abutted office areas. J. Stuart Mill of Union Central interpreted the move as a threat to the residential zoning next to his company's office building, describing the new zoning as so "permissive" it might admit something as repulsive as a large trucking company. The measure passed, nonetheless, and shortly thereafter the mayor advocated industrial zoning for the area east of Union Central.[31]

The Village Voice, a monthly newspaper created by the Forest Park Women's Club to replace the *Newsletter,* which had ceased publication in 1964, found the move toward industrialization frustrating. In its July 1965 issue, the new paper contrasted the impotence of the small homeowner with the power of the developer, who could afford

30. *Greenhills-Forest Park Journal,* Feb. 25, 1965.
31. *The Village Voice,* May and July 1965; Forest Park Council, "Minutes," Vol. II, July 6, 1965, 132; *Forest Park News,* Aug. 6 and Sept. 3, 1965.

to send a "local manager or attorney" to lobby the council and, if that failed, use his newspaper as he pleased to make "a hero or a goat out of any Village official."

Next the paper focused on Mayor English. In a signed article, Charles Dawson linked the mayor and the developer in an unholy alliance, pointing to English's regular column in the *News*. If "you are wondering," he wrote, "who is the developer's rubber stamp in the Village government, you will find the answer in the back issues of the developer's newspaper. See whose name and picture appear most often. Check his voting record on questions affecting the developer's interests. As nearly as we can ascertain, he has voted against the developer only once. Draw your own conclusions."[32]

The mayor was not amused. He retaliated in an article run by *The Village Voice* in August. English started sweetly enough, praising the Forest Park Women's Club as the leading civic organization in the village. But he concluded with an acid question. "I wonder, then, with this proud background of community service," he asked, "how long the membership is going to tolerate the publication of the vicious scandal sheet known as *The Village Voice*," a paper filled with "false, slanderous . . . destructive, venomous, and malicious material."[33]

That exchange heralded the opening of the fall campaign, one of the liveliest and most significant political contests in the history of Forest Park. In August 1965, Democrat Philip White announced his candidacy for mayor as an independent, and his filing petitions contained the names of three incumbent Republican councilmen who, just a few months before, had entered the local GOP primary with English. The mayor, claiming that his former allies had "betrayed the party," persuaded the Forest Park Republican Central Committee, which he chaired, to withdraw the GOP endorsement from the three "independents" and to support other Republican candidates. Thus the 1965 campaign, instead of ushering in conventional partisan politics, pitted an independent slate dominated by Republicans with Baseball or Civic Association backgrounds, but headed by White, a Democrat; against a "regular" ticket composed of two Republican precinct executives and another man identified with the Jaycees.[34] The Republicans who joined with White, moreover, denied that, during the

---

32. *The Village Voice*, July 1965.
33. *The Village Voice*, Aug. 1965.
34. *The Village Voice*, Aug. Sept., and Oct. 1965; *Forest Park News*, Oct. 29, 1965; *Greenhills-Forest Park Journal*, Aug. 26 and Sept. 9, 1965.

spring primary, they had pledged to support a Republican ticket in local elections; they came out "strongly opposed" to partisan politics.

English responded to this sudden political realignment by attacking the "so-called 'independents' group" as "a strictly local clique which has always attempted to control everything in Forest Park." He described the clique as undemocratic, because its organization was assembled through a "buddy system" of appointment rather than by elections at the precinct level. He said it was formed out of fear that "the people" would take over village affairs. English argued that one-party control went back to the first election after incorporation, when three slates, one Democratic and two independent, entered the lists. The winning independent group, he contended, made up the governing clique. It was, he alleged, once known as the "Original 112," all of whose members came "from one area of Forest Park," clearly the original "C" section. The clique controlled 67 percent of the seats in the first council, by English's reckoning, 85 percent in the second, and 100 percent in the third, although by that time it had recruited candidates from other sections besides the old neighborhood.[35]

Despite English's counterattack, the independents swept to victory in fall 1965. White defeated English for mayor by an "unprecedented" two-to-one margin, a showing almost matched by all three council candidates who ran with White. A "regular" Republican from the English slate took White's vacated council seat. Columnist Dawson characterized White's victory as a repudiation of English's attempt to insert partisan politics into Forest Park elections, and English issued a terse statement congratulating the winners.[36]

Other developments soon bolstered the trend toward nonpartisanship. In January 1966, English announced his intention to enter the Republican primary for state representative in the 73rd House district. Less than a month later, however, "in the interest of unity and harmony within the Republican Party," he withdrew from the race. Subsequently he devoted most of his energies to carving out a suc-

35. *Greenhills-Forest Park Journal,* Sept. 23 and Oct. 21, 1965. Also see *The Village Voice,* Feb. 1967 for a similar analysis.

36. *The Village Voice,* Oct., Nov. and Dec. 1965; *Forest Park News,* Oct. 29 and Dec. 10, 1965; *Greenhills-Forest Park Journal,* Nov. 4 and 18, 1965.

cessful career in suburban real estate.[37] On the whole, Democrats, too, seemed oblivious to local concerns. In January, the Forest Park Democratic Club heard John Wiethe speak, not on the prospects and methods for electing suburban Democrats to local offices, but on the operation of the Coleman system of vote tabulation.[38]

Nonpartisan politics dominated Forest Park through 1969, when the village became a city and adopted a city charter which institutionalized nonpartisanship in local politics and government. Surprisingly, the bitter 1965 contest was followed by a series of virtually uncontentious local campaigns. In 1967, in an "election" all but ignored by the local press,[39] all incumbent officeholders ran unopposed. The 1969 contest proved only slightly more lively. Though it attracted twelve candidates for seven council seats, all limited their public discussion of the "issues" to pronouncements about the importance of getting the new form of city government off to a good start.[40]

The diminution in political conflict between December 1965 and December 1969 stemmed from a number of factors. First, the national economic boom of the late 1960s had created an atmosphere in which growth seemed so likely that everyone agreed that in Forest Park high-quality development should have top priority. The Kanter Corporation fostered that notion in various ways. In January 1965, Kanter himself announced plans for an "office and research park" around two new buildings at Northland and Waycross Roads. He intended to attract "research-oriented companies" to the campus-like setting in part by proposing "working arrangements" with the University of Cincinnati "for the use of its research facilities."[41] And in January 1966, The Kanter Corporation proudly announced plans for "country club living in a vast apartment colony," featuring town house and "garden type stylings" in fifty projected buildings designed to complement the single-family "prestige addresses . . . built over the years" in Forest Park.[42]

---

37. *Greenhills-Forest Park Journal,* Jan. 27 and Feb. 10, 1966; *Forest Park News,* Apr. 1, 1966.

38. *The Village Voice, Jan. 1966.*

39. *The Village Voice,* Sept. and Oct. 1967; *Forest Park News,* Oct. 16, 1967.

40. *Forest Park News,* Oct. 28, 1969. Also see the candidates' biographical sketches and position statements in *Forest Park News,* Oct. 14, 1969.

41. *Cincinnati Enquirer,* Jan. 8, 1966.

42. *Cincinnati Post and Times-Star,* Jan. 8, 1966.

The bullish outlook cultivated so assiduously by The Kanter Corporation in the mid-1960s helped reduce tensions and divisions in the village. Given the expectation of growth and prosperity, village officials could pursue the ever-popular low-tax policy, confident that a broadened tax base would generate the tax duplicate needed to pay for the most urgently needed services. The developer, too, could relax, more assured than in the past that the model community would generate profits, without squeezing the maximum possible gain out of each lot. And homeowners could look forward to stable or rising resale values, without relentlessly and suspiciously scrutinizing each move by the developer or village officials.

At the same time, persisting conflict with the village of Springdale helped unite Forest Park residents and turn their attention away from internal differences. In late 1964, Springdale had launched an effort to annex 340 acres of prime commercial, business, and industrial territory around the site of a proposed Circle Freeway interchange. Twice in 1965 Springfield Township voters trooped to the polls to vote for or against the annexation. The first vote proved affirmative, but on a technicality, the Hamilton County prosecutor ruled the election invalid. Springdale appealed the ruling to common pleas court, but before the decision was rendered, the second election reversed the initial favorable judgment. With the matter still in judicial limbo, Forest Park in 1966 petitioned to annex the same plot of land, and in July 1967, the coveted territory became part of Forest Park.[43]

Growing concern in Hamilton County and the Cincinnati metropolitan area generally over the "fragmented metropolis" question also contributed to Forest Park's sense of being a village under siege and of the need for unity, to establish and maintain village autonomy and right of self-determination. By the late 1960s, the proliferation of local governmental units had turned Hamilton County into a patchwork quilt of overlapping jurisdictions consisting of thirty-seven municipalities, twelve townships, eighteen local fire districts, a park district, a library district, a health district, a sewer district, a housing authority, and the Mill Creek Valley Conservancy District, in addition to county government itself. Those with a more cosmopolitan attitude toward local government believed that, if all these jurisdictions could

43. *Forest Park Newsletter,* Oct. 1964; *The Village Voice,* Apr. 1965; *Forest Park News,* Sept. 3 and Dec. 10, 1965; Oct. 28, 1966; and July 24, 1967; *Cincinnati Post and Times-Star,* Oct. 28, 1966; Hamilton County Commissioners, "Minutes," Vol. 150, Apr. 26, 1967, 776-79.

be coordinated and centralized, governmental activities could be made more efficient. The result was an effort, unsuccessful in the end, to increase the powers of the Hamilton County Commissioners. That move alarmed suburban exponents of community control,[44] and localists also blanched at the multiplication of regional special-purpose government agencies. By 1969, these included the Ohio-Kentucky-Indiana Regional Planning Authority, Ohio River Valley Sanitation Commission, Southwestern Ohio-Northern Kentucky-Southeastern Indiana Air Pollution Control Commission, and the Central Ohio River Valley (health) Association. The mere existence of such entities fed the general fear of big-government interference in the affairs of Forest Park.[45]

The new mayor elected in fall 1965 himself contributed significantly to the political cohesion which marked Forest Park in the last half of the 1960s. Philip White brought to his four years in the mayor's office superb credentials for governing by consensus. He was, at the time of his election, 38 years old, an eight-year resident of the village, and a family man with four children aged 9, 11, 14, and 15. A former district sales manager of Great Lakes Carbon Company and ex-owner of Modern Folding Door of Cincinnati, Inc., White now owned the Forest Park Pony Keg—Cincinnati vernacular for a carry-out shop for beer, wine and snacks. Thus, he possessed the business experience necessary to understand both the independent entrepreneurs and the "organization" people in the village. He had, moreover, an extraordinary history of community leadership. He had been a director of the defunct Civic Association, a charter member in the Toastmasters Club, and a board member at the Swim Club. He had been one of the organizers of the Baseball Association and had labored as coach, manager, umpire, and member of the board of directors. A council member since village incorporation, he had served on all of the council's committees, had chaired the Finance and Public Safety Committees, and had served on the Planning and Zoning Commission before his election as mayor.[46]

White began his tenure quietly but auspiciously. In January 1966, as one of the first acts of his administration, he joined with the Women's Club in lobbying the Public Library of Cincinnati and Hamilton County to locate a projected north suburban branch in

44. *The Village Voice*, Oct. 27, 1967; *Greenhills-Forest Park Journal*, Nov. 16, 1967.
45. *Ibid.; Forest Park News*, Nov. 25, 1969.
46. *Cincinnati Post and Times-Star*, Nov. 11, 1965.

Forest Park, rather than in Springdale or elsewhere. By August 1966, the plum, a $250,000 building on Waycross and Sharon, was in the bag; dedication ceremonies for Parkdale Branch, as it was dubbed in an obvious effort to appease the losers in the most recent Forest Park-Springdale contest, took place two years later.[47] Consisting of 11,000 square feet, with space for 60,000 books, Parkdale was the largest and most elegant suburban branch in the system.[48] Final costs for the building, including air-conditioning, parking for fifty automobiles, and ramps for patrons in wheel chairs, came to $300,000.

The mayor also worked with the council to strengthen the police department. During 1966, the chief and two officers resigned, and the new administration not only found replacements but added three more full-time and two part-time officers, plus a sergeant. Together the new employees received 480 hours of special training at the police academy in nearby Norwood, the Hamilton County Patrol headquarters, and the Bureau of Criminal Investigation in London, Ohio. At the same time, White encouraged development of new methods of reporting, filing, record-keeping, and communications, as well as better patrol and dog-control techniques.[49] White capped the law enforcement campaign by establishing a Mayor's Youth Commission, headed by an Episcopal priest, to stem an alarming increase in teenage vandalism and find constructive leisure pursuits for the village's adolescents.[50]

White and the council also tried to rationalize and professionalize the housekeeping aspects of village government. They shifted street lighting from a special assessment to a uniform basis by permitting homeowners on a block, by majority petition, to keep their street dark while requiring all homeowners, whether their streets were lit or not, to pay the same tax.[51] White made a special effort to improve the efficiency of the village's Building Department through internal ad-

47. *The Village Voice,* Oct. 1965, Jan. and Aug. 1966; *Forest Park News,* Sept. 30, 1969.

48. *Cincinnati Enquirer,* May 21, 1967; *Cincinnati Post and Times-Star,* Apr. 3, 1968.

49. "Mayor's Annual Report," *Forest Park News,* Feb. 3, 1967; Forest Park Council, "Minutes," Vol. III, Sept. 20, 1966, 29.

50. "Mayor's Annual Report," *Forest Park News,* Feb. 3, 1967; Forest Park Council, "Minutes," Vol. III, Mar. 21, 1967, 118; *The Village Voice,* June 1967.

51. Forest Park Council, "Minutes," Vol. III, July 19, 1966, 58. Under the previous arrangement, homeowners had to agree to pay the assessment and petition the council to install the lights. See *Forest Park Newsletter,* July 1963.

ministrative reform.[52] And in 1968 the council took "the big step" toward bureaucratic modernization by hiring a professional adminis- trator to supervise the Public Works, Engineering, and Building De- partments.[53] The council and White fared less well with street maintenance. They estimated that effectively resurfacing the village's seventy miles of streets on a ten-year base plan would require a new 3.5-mill tax levy. Leery of inciting a taxpayer's revolt, they resorted instead to "surface treatment" with tar and black top, a combination which, they noted apologetically, "bleeds" and "sticks" to tires and footwear, creating an "inconvenience" which nevertheless seemed more tolerable than a tax hike.[54]

During the four-year reign of the consensus council, recreation was the most controversial issue in village politics. In 1966, the council placed on the fall ballot a .5-mill levy to hire a professional recreation staff, and a $400,000 bond issue for land purchase and development.[55] Proponents also hoped that passage of the bond issue and tax levy would enable the village to secure $200,000 in federal funds to build a municipal swimming pool, purchase additional land, or pay off the bonds, allowing the millage to be reduced. While the proposed 35 acres seemed excessive, the council and the Recreation Commission, using a "rational" approach characteristic of the White era in village government, had reasoned that it made sense, before prices rose, to acquire more land than was immediately needed. The voters, how- ever, rejected both the operating levy and the bond issue.[56]

Rebuffed at the polls, recreation proponents lowered their sights and tried once more in 1967. This time the council placed on the ballot a five-year, .5-mill levy, expected to yield about $125,000, exclusively for playfield acquisition. Program development, operation, and maintenance would be left to volunteers. Voters approved this mod- est proposal, and the following year the council obtained $100,000 in federal matching funds and purchased 28 acres for $200,000.[57]

52. "Mayor's Annual Report," *Forest Park News,* Feb. 3, 1967.
53. "Mayor's Annual Report," *Forest Park News,* Feb. 4, 1969.
54. *The Village Voice,* Sept. 1966.
55. Forest Park Council, "Minutes," Vol. II, July 6, 1965, 132; Vol. III, July 5, 1966, 53; *The Village Voice,* Aug. 1966.
56. *The Village Voice,* Mar., Sept., and Nov., 1966; *Forest Park News,* Sept. 16, 1966.
57. *The Village Voice,* Oct. 1967; *Forest Park News,* Oct. 16 and Nov. 13, 1967; *Greenhills-Forest Park Journal,* Feb. 6 and 20, 1969.

The council and the Planning and Zoning Commission also took a rational and systematic approach to land use. Given the controversy which had surrounded adoption of the 1963 village master plan and zoning decisions during the English administration, land use issues created surprisingly little discord.[58] The key to peace in the planning and zoning arena was, in the words of the master plan, "good liaison" between the developer and village officials.[59]

At a regular council meeting in January 1966, the planning commission reported on talks it had held with The Kanter Corporation about the feasibility of a non-profit "community improvement corporation" to finance industrial growth. To begin with, the Cincinnati CIC was to act as an agent for the City of Forest Park to attract industry by raising capital for the improvement of industrial sites through tax-free land sales.[60] After ascertaining the legality of the joint venture, Forest Park entered the arrangement.[61] However, not long after, in March 1967, Forest Park withdrew to set up its own non-profit CIC. "Liaison" figured prominently in this maneuver, for the president of the new corporation was Mayor Philip White, and the vice-president was Richard Shenk, an assistant to Joseph Kanter of The Kanter Corporation.[62]

Meanwhile, the question of rezoning the area west of Union Central for industry had reappeared. By August 1966, The Kanter Corporation had completed plans for an industrial park on that site; and in November the plans, already approved by the Hamilton County Regional Planning Commission, were presented to the Forest Park Planning and Zoning Commission. The proposal created the new zoning category of "industrial park" and rezoned the western part of the village from residential to the new classification. The project breezed through the planning commission without protest,[63] and on April 4, 1967, the council held a public hearing on the proposal. A sparse crowd turned out for the discussion, and the council approved the change without a dissenting vote.[64] *The Village Voice* made a

58. *The Village Voice,* Mar. and July, 1966; *Greenhills-Forest Park Journal,* Mar. 10, 1966; *Forest Park News,* Sept. 16, 1969.

59. *The Village Voice,* Mar. 1966.

60. Forest Park Council, "Minutes," Vol. III, Jan. 18, 1966, 8.

61. *Cincinnati Post and Times-Star,* Apr. 18, 1966; Forest Park Council, "Minutes," Vol. III, Mar. 15, 1966, 24; Aug. 2, 1966, 62; Aug. 16, 1966, 68.

62. *Forest Park News,* Mar. 31, 1967.

63. Forest Park Planning Commission, "Minutes," Nov. 22, 1966; Feb. 28, 1967.

64. Forest Park Council, "Minutes," Vol. IV, Apr. 4, 1967, 120 and 123.

matter-of-fact, one-sentence report of the change in its May issue. Thus quietly terminated discussion of a question once so controversial that it had helped precipitate the political crisis of 1965.[65]

By contrast, two other Kanter-initiated changes in the land use pattern did run into stiff opposition from both citizens and some elected officials. Both proposals, however, shared one justification: they would render less expensive the schools contemplated in the master plan and deemed essential by the school superintendent, the school board, and the child-oriented majority of residents. The ultimate passage of both proposals indicated that "liaison" had involved school officials as well as village leaders and Kanter representatives.

The Kanter Corporation's first proposal suggested relocating the shopping center proposed for the west side of Hall-Winton Road to the southeast corner of the intersection of Hall-Winton and Kemper Roads, near the civic center (see Figure 6). The change would also modify the configuration, but not expand the area, of multi-family housing; eliminate a proposed seven-acre park; and move the village incinerator and municipal garage.[66] The planning commission, after conferring with a planning consultant paid jointly by the village and The Kanter Corporation, unanimously approved the proposal.[67]

In the subsequent council hearing, moreover, it became clear that educational aims would also be furthered by the proposed change. The 1963 master plan called for a new senior high school, with extensive recreational facilities for community as well as school use, to be located in the civic center area. The school board now objected to the plan's placement of a shopping center next to the school site, because the center "created a problem of student control." Discussion also revealed that although the planner, Recreation Commission, and school officials endorsed the change, support by the "experts" had failed to dispel popular suspicion.[68] When the council voted, the proposal passed by a narrow three-to-two vote.[69]

The second school-related Kanter proposal met more stubborn resistance, partly because it expanded the space allotted to apartments, the *bête noire* of suburban homeowners everywhere. In this measure, the developer asked for rezoning of the area surrounding

65. *The Village Voice*, May 1967.
66. Forest Park Council, "Minutes," Vol. III, May 17, 1966, 38.
67. *Ibid.*; *The Village Voice*, Mar. and May 1966.
68. *Ibid.*, June 1966.
69. Forest Park Council, "Minutes," Vol. III, May 17, 1966, 38–39; *The Village Voice*, June and July 1966.

the intersection of Waycross and Northland Roads, in the eastern part of the village. The Kanter Corporation wanted to divide a plot zoned residential into three parcels—a .5-acre highway service and commercial district, a 1.3-acre office district, and a 7.8-acre multi-family residential project.[70] Once more a school board action had initiated the move. In this case, the board, judging that the master plan site for a junior high school was too small, wanted the school placed on 20 acres between Northland and Waycross. The developer offered to sell the land to the board for a favorable price, $160,000, provided that the school board omit the Northland frontage and 400 feet of the Waycross frontage, and provided that the village rezone the frontage in three parcels as requested. The rationale for the deal was simple. A higher return would accrue to The Kanter Corporation from apartments and commercial frontage and enable the firm to sell the school site at a more reasonable price while realizing substantially the same profit as if the entire tract were used, as proposed in the master plan, for single-family residential construction.[71]

Public hearings on this proposal were long, attracted as many as 25 participants, and produced various objections to the proposed alteration of the master plan. Nevertheless, the planning commission approved the document and sent it on for council consideration.[72] At the council hearing, according to *The Village Voice*, "the public outtalked the Councilmen by a considerable margin, and that is not easy." The council stalled until it heard a formal opinion from its planning consultant. Finally, at what *The Village Voice* called a "highly unpublicized" special meeting, council approved the proposal, though only after Mayor White broke a three-to-three deadlock on the question.[73]

For the second time in a year, though by the slimmest of margins, "liaison" among the developer, school board, and key village officials led to a decision encouraging balanced, as opposed to strictly residential, development for Forest Park. This "integration" was judged most likely to produce maximum profits for the developer and the strongest possible tax base for the hard-pressed school district and village government. The decision, though altering the master plan in detail, conformed to its original spirit. Too, the approval reinforced

70. Forest Park Council, "Minutes," Vol. III, Aug. 16, 1966, 66–67.

71. *The Village Voice,* Oct. 1966.

72. Forest Park Council, "Minutes," Vol. III, Aug. 16, 1966, 66–67; *The Village Voice,* Oct. 1966.

73. *The Village Voice,* Oct. and Nov. 1966.

the tendency define Forest Park as a community of limited liability—simply one of a series of interchangeable locations across metropolitan America through which the mobile middle classes could move with a minimum of inconvenience and cost. Before the end of White's tenure, the village moved farther along this path by establishing a new form of government based on this same set of values.

From Forest Park's beginning, local officials knew that Forest Park could not retain its village status for long. Ohio law required any village to become a city whenever it had, according to the federal decennial census, 5,000 inhabitants; or whenever the village tabulated 5,000 registered voters, which might occur between censuses. The new city government, however, might take one of several forms. The new city could take on a structure and set of rules and procedures provided by general state laws. Or, under "home rule," the city could write a charter laying out its own plan of government. The "home-rule" charter provisions could not, of course, conflict with the laws of the state, and the basic form of city government had to be either the commission, the city manager, or the federal type.[74] Beyond this, the city government could take whatever form local authorities deemed appropriate.

The growth of Forest Park, an article of virtually everyone's faith, meant that someday soon decisions about the form of city government would have to be faced.[75] In the November 1967 elections[76] the voters endorsed the formation of a Charter Commission to write a "home rule" charter and selected fifteen commissioners from a list of eighteen candidates.[77]

The Charter Commission lost no time in getting started on its task. At its first meeting, just two weeks after the election, the group determined to place a charter on the ballot in November 1968. To meet that deadline, the commission scheduled sessions twice a month. It was hoped that the group could decide on the city's form of government by February, after which each meeting could take up one section of the charter. On that schedule, the draft charter could be sent in July to a recognized authority on Ohio municipal government, who would review it from a technical standpoint; it could be printed in

74. *Forest Park Newsletter*, Dec. 1964.
75. *Forest Park Newsletter*, Aug. 1962 and Dec. 1964; *Forest Park News*, Feb. 19, 1965.
76. "Mayor's Annual Report," *Forest Park News*, Feb. 3, 1967; *The Village Voice*, Mar., Aug. and Dec. 1966; Sept. 1967.
77. *Forest Park News*, Oct. 16 and Nov. 13, 1967.

August; and in September it could be distributed to each registered voter, well in advance of the election.[78]

Charter Commission deliberations moved quickly. By February 1, 1968, the body had "dismissed" the commission form of government, a mode it regarded as "rapidly disappearing," and rejected the weak-mayor type as inexpensive but useful only for villages. The group seemed most favorably inclined toward the manager-council system, the "most efficient form of government since it operates much like a typical [business] corporation." The issue was far from settled, however. A test vote in January showed nine commission members for the manager-council form and five for the strong mayor-council type.[79] This question remained a point of contention in subsequent proceedings on the charter.

Although both Mayor White and Council Member Edwin F. Sullivan preferred the strong-mayor form, their views carried little weight with some commissioners because of the suspicion that White and Sullivan harbored personal ambitions to become that strong mayor. But the commission listened more seriously to another strong-mayor advocate, Union Central. With a strong mayor, argued the Union Central president, the "people" could "best control the cost of government, the efficiency of government and the nature of government." Some commissioners cynically reasoned that Union Central wanted a strong mayor on the theory that the company could more easily influence one mayor than seven council members. In the end, the commission struck a bargain. Union Central pledged to support a manager-council charter, if the document mandated a popular vote on any tax upon the "earnings or income of any person, business, or corporation" within the city.[80]

This compromise, along with other features of the document, gave Forest Park a government eminently suited to a suburban community of limited liability. The charter reduced the mayor to a figurehead and placed administration in the hands of a city manager, although the council retained the right to approve the appointment of department heads. The charter required a two-thirds vote of the seven-person council to appoint or remove a city manager from office, and any

78. *The Village Voice*, Dec. 1967. Forest Park Charter Commission, *Charter of the Municipality of Forest Park, Ohio* (n.p., [1968]), inside front cover.
79. *Greenhills-Forest Park Journal*, Jan. 4 and Feb. 1, 1968.
80. *Greenhills-Forest Park Journal*, June 6, 1968; Charles E. Dawson to author, Dec. 5, 1976; Forest Park Charter Commission, *Charter of the Municipality*, 17.

manager with six months' service who was threatened by removal had the right to a public hearing before the final vote. The charter, in addition, established a merit civil service system; banished partisanship in elections; set four-year staggered terms and at-large elections for council positions; gave the council the power to appoint either outsiders or its members, or both, to "independent" boards and commissions; created a planning and zoning commission charged with maintaining and amending the master plan and handling zoning issues; and set up a capital-improvements reserve fund which, once created, could not be used for any other purpose. And while the charter permitted legislation by initiative and referendum, and the recall of elected officials, it did so only to the extent required by state law.[81]

The charter, in effect, set up a governmental structure dominated by city government professionals, limited their taxing powers, and bound them to a master plan outlining what the community should become. The requirement of nonpartisanship handed incumbents a significant advantage in elections, thereby protecting the activist political "establishment" from the kind of politics in which old residents and special interests, because of connections, special knowledge of social conditions, or raw political or economic power, could exercise a sudden or disproportionate influence. The charter, in short, envisaged a municipal and community structure through which the mobile middle classes could pass with a minimum of strain; under the charter, it would be difficult for a new set of officials to break with the fundamental concept of a balanced community.

In the November 1968 election, Forest Park voters approved the work of the Charter Commission by an overwhelming margin. The November 1969 city election then became a contest to decide who would inaugurate the home-rule charter. Mayor White dropped out of politics, and twelve candidates competed for the seven council seats. Seven incumbents (though three were "newcomers" who had been appointed to fill vacancies created by job transfers and resignations) ran together on one slate. The incumbent slate contained at least two Republican stalwarts; three Catholics, two of them "newcomers"; and one who had been active in the Jaycees, a group previously not associated with the Forest Park "establishment." Five of the candidates carried Baseball and/or Civic Association credentials, and the

81. Forest Park Charter Commission, *Charter of the Municipality,* 5, 8–18, 22–24.

other, Loraine Blackburn, not only held an office in the local GOP but also was "connected" to the Baseball Association through her husband, a past president of that group.[82]

The other five contestants ran separate campaigns, and all, except for one five-year member of the Baseball Association's board of directors, lacked the credentials traditional for success. Nonetheless, to the surprise of most observers, two of this group, including the Baseball Association board member, won. Interestingly, both shared a background in public safety. One had worked for four years as a Forest Park policeman, and the other had been an organizer and president of the volunteer fire company. These men's victory signaled continuing voter concern with "law and order" issues and the opening of another potential power base and avenue of advance in local politics and civic life.[83]

Within a month after the election, the new council was organized. Although Loraine Blackburn had run well ahead of all other candidates in the election, her colleagues chose Sullivan, who had finished last among the winners but had long council tenure, as mayor. On the recommendation of outgoing Mayor Philip White, the council named the incumbent village administrator, Alvin M. Tomb, as acting city manager. And in one of the council's first legislative actions, Forest Park became the twenty-second municipality in Hamilton County to become its own township. From now on, Forest Park Township, rather than Springfield Township, would receive the .08-mill local government tax collected in Forest Park and distributed annually by the state to its township government.

Though Forest Park may not have been, as its new mayor said in 1969, "the greatest city in existence," since incorporation as a village in 1961 in had come a long way toward installing the physical plant and governmental machinery of a viable suburban community of limited liability. The government was housed in a new municipal building complete with community room (see Figure 7), and the city had a post office and a branch library under construction. The police force, which with twelve employees was well short of the number standard for a city this size, was one of the few departments in the state whose youth work qualified for a subsidy from the Ohio Youth Commission. The force was also free of the bickering which had long

82. *Greenhills-Forest Park Journal,* June 6, 1968; *Forest Park News,* Oct. 14 and 18, 1969.
83. *Forest Park News,* Oct. 14, 1969.

FIGURE 7. View east across Winton Road, 1969. The partially completed "J" section can be seen in the left foreground. Just above it is the Municipal Building at the corner of Winton and Waycross; that site also contains the Greenhills-Forest Park School District headquarters and Forest Park High School (largest of the three structures). South on Winton Road, in the picture's right center, stands the storage tank of the Cincinnati Water Works. Reproduced with permission of The Kanter Corporation.

plagued it. Judging from the mayor's reports, the 38-person volunteer fire department kept pace with the police in equipment and performance. By the end of the 1960s, the Recreation Commission was boasting of a diversified program of organized activities for boys and girls.[84] In both 1967 and 1969, voters approved capital expenditure bond issues and operating levies for schools, keeping the district's perfect record of approving educational taxes. In 1968 alone, three new schools, including a junior high-senior high building, opened in Forest Park.[85]

Others beyond the village government agencies, of course, played a part in rounding out the physical plant. In 1968, for example, workers completed the Hall-Winton interchange off I-275, the Circle Freeway, as well as the stretch of that expressway which passed through the city.[86] Even the persistently bothersome problems of sewer planning, inspection, and maintenance seemed settled by the end of the 1960s, with the creation of the Metropolitan Sewer District and the distribution of responsibilities among the district, the county, municipalities, and developers,[87] although the continued use of drainage ditches for storm sewers remained a point of contention. To be sure, in the 1960s, the village ignored those who wanted neighborhood parks and green spaces, but Kanter had helped matters by continuing his early practice of donating otherwise useless land for park purposes.[88]

On the other hand, Forest Park had no hospital, no Health Department, and no public health program. And other features of city government familiar elsewhere, such as human relations commissions to alleviate discrimination against minorities or special facilities for the poor and the elderly, seemed unnecessary in Forest Park in the 1960s.

Despite the accomplishments of a decade, Alvin M. Tomb was worried about the city's fiscal condition. Tomb was an engineer who had been supervisor of the village's public works, engineering, and

84. *The Village Voice*, Oct. 1966, Apr. 1967; *Forest Park News*, Dec. 10, 1965; July 24, 1967; and Feb. 4, 1969; *Greenhills-Forest Park Journal*, July 24, 1969.

85. *Greenhills-Forest Park Journal*, May 4, 1967; May 23, 1968; *Forest Park News*, Feb. 4 and May 20, 1969.

86. *Forest Park News*, Feb. 4, 1969.

87. See "Forest Park" file, files of the Hamilton County Commissioners; Forest Park Council, "Minutes," Vol. I, Mar. 5, 1963, 1; Vol. III, Aug. 15, 1967, 145; Vol. IV, Feb. 5, 1968, 6.

88. *The Village Voice*, Aug. and Nov. 1966; Oct. and Dec. 1967.

building operations, and who became Forest Park's first city manager. In 1969 Forest Park received just 9 percent of the real estate taxes assessed on territory within its corporate limits. The rest went to school districts (76.5 percent) and to the state and county (14.5 percent). That distribution of public funds had always hampered village improvement, but in 1970 the situation looked worse because service costs were increasing while, as money became tighter, the growth rate declined. Tomb had expected a population of 16,000 by 1970, but census takers counted just 15,094. And the number of building permits issued by local officials dropped from 307 in 1969, to 30 in 1970.[89]

Nonetheless, prominent local observers were optimistic about Forest Park's future as a white-collar community of limited liability. Retiring Mayor Philip White and the *Forest Park News* looked back with nostalgia and satisfaction on his career in village politics. Elected to the village council in 1961 on the Baseball Association slate, White had survived, as he put it, the "stormy battles that were routine in those early days of incrporation" and helped develop, the paper said, a "spirit of cooperation" which had become "the hallmark of Forest Park politics." The owner of one Forest Park pony keg, White was considering opening a supper club or another pony keg, or joining the same local real estate firm selected by Donald English when he ceased to be mayor. English had now moved on to a larger metropolitan firm which also handled Forest Park property. Mayor Sullivan, of course, was bullish on Forest Park's future, stating his belief that it would be able to make its claim as the "greatest city in existence . . . ten, twenty-five, fifty years from now." Judge Lyle Castel of Hamilton County Common Pleas Court, who swore in the new city officials, would not go that far. But he agreed that the "future of Forest Park is a bright one with these fine citizens at the helm."[90]

89. *Cincinnati Post and Times-Star,* Dec. 4, 1968; *Greenhills-Forest Park Journal,* Jan. 23, 1969; *Cincinnati Enquirer,* June 18, 1970.
90. *Cincinnati Enquirer,* Dec. 2, 1969; *Forest Park News,* Jan. 20 and Feb. 3, 1970; "Mayor's Annual Message," Forest Park Council, "Minutes," Vol. IV, Feb. 1970, 2.

*Our coming generation, your children, needs
to acquire the sense of localized community
and to feel personal responsibility for ruling
that community. This used to be characteristic
of nearly all Americans . . ., and a lacking in
this sense leads to social irresponsibility in
today's contracted and disordered world.*
    The [Forest Park] *Village Voice*,
    July 1966

VILLAGE SOCIETY IN THE 1960S:
TOWARD A COMMUNITY OF ADVOCACY

Forest Park existed as a village for almost a decade, in that period making substantial steps toward becoming a "balanced" community. To be sure, business and industrial growth took place slowly, but people came in profusion. Forest Park's population jumped by 80.9 percent between 1960 and 1970, going from 8,405 to 15,174, while Cincinnati's suburbs as a group increased by 30.4 percent. Neighboring Greenhills' count rose by 12.7 percent, while Cincinnati's fell by 10 percent.[1]

The new Forest Parkers came to and helped make the community a different place from that which Kanter had taken over in 1959. Not only had the socioeconomic and demographic structure altered perceptibly by 1970, but so had the tone and structure of village voluntary organizations. There was in 1970 no general association based upon a civic community ethos. Those who talked about civic community assumed that the residents' participation in special interest "community" groups would weld village society into a unit sufficiently cohesive for the advancement of the community welfare.

1. The population and housing statistics in this chapter are taken from the *U.S. Census of Population and Housing, Cincinnati and Adjacent Areas, Census Tracts,* 1950, 1960, and 1970 and from the manuscript census data in the Urban Studies Collection, Archival Collections of the University of Cincinnati. Lyle Koehler, research assistant on this project, compiled the figures.

Forest Park in 1960, judging by the population in its census tracts,[2] was a young, fertile, transient, white, middle-class community. The median age for females and males stood at 24.4 and 19.5 respectively; 67.8 percent of its females and 68.1 percent of its males fell between the ages of five and forty-four. Just under a third of each sex was between five and nineteen. Those figures placed more individuals of both sexes in the ages when couples most commonly have children, and three-quarters of all Forest Park's males and females over 14 were married. Only one-fourth of the married women appeared in the census as searching for or holding a job outside the home, despite the fact that the median years of schooling attained by all persons over 25 in Forest Park came to 12.4. Forest Parkers, then, were a well-educated and, presumably, eminently employable lot.

As Forest Park was a new town in 1960, of course its residents were transient, only 24.7 percent having lived in the same dwelling for five or more years. Just under half (46.5 percent) of the recent arrivals had moved to Forest Park from within the Cincinnati metropolitan area.[3] The population increase had little to do with either the great 1950s migration of southern blacks to northern cities or the flight from Cincinnati's central-city low-income districts. In 1960, blacks comprised .5 percent of the census tract's population, but none at all lived in Forest Park proper. With unemployment rates for the total work force at 2.6 percent among males and 4.5 percent among females, almost everyone who wanted work seemed able to find it, albeit mostly outside the village. Just over 3 percent of the work force were employed in the community, while 29 percent traveled to Cincinnati, almost 60 percent went elsewhere in the metropolitan district, and 7.4 percent commuted outside the region.

Though scarcely self-sufficient in 1960, Forest Park seemed prosperous enough, a village of homeowners building families under comfortable if not affluent conditions. Owners occupied 86.6 percent of all dwelling units. The units' median value was $18,000, and just over two-fifths of them contained more than one bathroom. Other

2. In 1960, Forest Park lay within Census Tract C-15, which included what would become Springdale, as well as the Hollydale black subdivision. Forest Park proper contained no blacks. Charles E. Dawson to author, memorandum [winter 1978]. The absence of political boundaries separating Forest Park from other subdivisions doubtless intensified the community identity problem for Forest Park's leaders. Even after incorporation they complained that many Forest Park residents failed to register their legal residence for automobile licenses as Forest Park.

3. This is the SMSA figure. I have used the shorter term for readability.

statistics indicate, however, that Forest Park in 1960 teetered on the brink of becoming just another lower-middle-class suburb, occupied by blue-collar workers as well as white.

In most respects, Forest Park showed "better," from a middle-class standpoint, than either Cincinnati or its suburbs as a whole. But the most meaningful comparison was with rival Greenhills, whose status most Forest Park leaders hoped to top, and here Forest Park ran even or trailed behind. In median family income, Forest Park fell behind Greenhills by $8,460 to $8,887. Both placed about 83 percent in the two middle-income brackets ($5,000-$9,999 and $10,000-$14,999). But Greenhills placed a share larger by six points in the higher of those two categories, and in addition, a larger share (7.5 to 4.5 percent) in the $15,000-$24,999 column. Such figures suggested that Greenhills had an edge in the status sweepstakes. In addition, occupational statistics showed that Forest Park barely qualified as a white-collar community. Of its work force, 54 percent were white-collar, while Greenhills had 67.9 percent. In 1960, Forest Park's civic leadership came predominantly from the white-collar middle classes. But Forest Park also contained a non-white-collar group of considerable magnitude, almost large enough to divide the village's character between a blue- and a white-collar ambience. Odious as many Forest Parkers would doubtless have found the reality, Greenhills, in 1960, ranked as the more solidly middle-class and affluent of the two communities.

Within a decade, the split in Forest Park's character had disappeared. In the 1970 U.S. Census figures, Forest Park not only continued to make a "better" statistical showing than either Cincinnati or the average of its suburbs, but that year the new city also stood as one of the area's premier white-collar suburbs and topped Greenhills on virtually every index of white-collar respectability. In 1970, Forest Park's white-collar quotient for males soared to 71.2 percent, while Greenhills' dropped off to 67.1 percent. The Cincinnati suburbs as a whole stood at 49 percent and Cincinnati proper at 44 percent. Among 83 suburban census tracts, Forest Park stood eighth from the top in median school years completed and sixth in persons 25 or older holding a high school diploma, while Greenhills finished tenth and eighth respectively. Forest Park's median income per family placed it sixteenth on the list, two notches above Greenhills; Forest Park stood sixteenth to Greenhills' eighteenth in the median value of owner-occupied homes. And in the important category of median value of rent paid, Forest Park turned up second, well above Greenhills' forty-first position.

Other measures clearly indicate the widening distinction between Forest Park and Greenhills. Forest Park's median family income in 1970 came to $13,309, almost $200 higher than that for Greenhills. Forest Park put three-fourths of its families, as opposed to two-thirds for Greenhills, in the two brackets which made up the $10,000-$25,000 range; Forest Park scored lower than Greenhills (22 percent to 31) in the four income niches at the bottom of the hierarchy. The median value of Forest Park's owner-occupied structures topped that for Greenhills by $22,700 to $21,300; Forest Park's list included 55 structures valued at $50,000 or more and 268 at $35,000-$50,000, categories in which Greenhills had only 3 and 98 respectively. Between 1960 and 1970, however, the percentage of owner-occupied dwelling units in Forest Park jumped eight points, to 94.5, while in Greenhills the percentage fell one notch to 68.8. The proportion of rental units in Forest Park fell from 6.9 to 5 percent in the ten-year period. Meanwhile, the Forest Park vacancy rate plummeted from 6.4 percent in 1960 to .6 in 1970, a more significant dip even than the drop from 3.1 to 1.1 percent in Greenhills.

Although by 1970 Forest Park had outstripped Greenhills in these statistical indicators, in others the community remained essentially the same as in 1960. Its median age was 22.3 for females and 20 for males; 35 percent of females and 36.4 percent of males fell between the ages of 5 and 19, with roughly three-fourths of the total between the ages of 5 and 45. The percentage of married males over 16 years of age held steady at 75 percent, although the figure for females dropped from 81.2 to 75.9 percent. The median years of schooling rose from 12.4 to 12.8. Unemployment for males stood at 1.2 percent, down from 2.6 in 1960, while that for women dropped from 4.5 to 3.4. Now the percentage of married women searching for or holding jobs outside the home rose significantly, from 26.1 to 35.6 percent. The place-of-work statistics in 1970 matched almost perfectly those of a decade before, when just over 3 percent of the work force had held jobs in Forest Park.

Yet Forest Park had changed. While the percentage of Forest Park dwellers who had occupied the same house since 1965 edged up from 24.7 to 56, the origins of those residents had shifted substantially. In 1970, only 27 percent came from within the Cincinnati metropolitan area, a drop of 19 points from 1960. The percentage coming from outside the district stood at 20, as "organization men" from large corporations continued to find Forest Park a suitable haven. In this sense, then, Forest Park's population, though still overwhelmingly born in the United States, became more cosmopolitan, made up more than ever before of employees of national or international firms.

The most dramatic change in Forest Park's demographic profile, however, took place in its racial composition. By 1970, the village had more blacks. Not that racial change in the village during the 1960s even nearly resembled an "invasion," to use the invidious sociological term for drastic changes in a neighborhood's composition. Yet between 1960 and 1970 the number of black residents rose tenfold, from 45 to 424, pushing the black percentage from an insignificant .5 to a barely perceptible 2.8. In Greenhills, the percentage of blacks edged up from 0 to .2, with 10 blacks added to its total population of 6,066. The differences between the two contiguous places suggest that blacks with the means to move to areas like Forest Park or Greenhills found it easier to break into a new housing market than a fully-occupied selling and renting arena. In addition, the civil rights successes of the 1950s and early mid-1960s may have exerted more anti-discriminatory pressure on developers and real estate firms handling new property in rapidly growing areas. In any case, though Forest Park's black population in 1970 outnumbered Greenhills', it still fell below the figure for Cincinnati's suburbs generally (4.5 percent), for nearby Woodlawn (over half black), for Lincoln Heights (entirely black), or for Cincinnati itself (27.6 percent).

Nor did Forest Park's black population approximate the popular urban white stereotype of blacks as ignorant, impoverished, chronically unemployed refugees from the ghetto. A variety of minor differences other than skin color, however, did distinguish the village's white and black populations. Blacks, like whites, were transient, in that only 22.6 percent of those living in Forest Park five years or more had lived in the same dwelling since 1965. But the blacks with five years or more of residence had moved from closer places, 47.9 percent of them listing their previous place of residence within the metropolitan district and just 7.4 percent from beyond.[4] Educational levels were similar. In median years of schooling, both whites and blacks had 12.8. The percentage carrying a high school diploma stood at 80.4 and 81.4 respectively. Blacks showed 32 percent with some college experience, while whites showed just over 42 percent. Only

4. The census bureau failed to secure figures on 75 (22.1 percent) black persons.

27 percent of black males worked in white-collar jobs, well below the white male mark of 71.2 percent. But 61 percent of black females and 60 percent of white famales were white-collar employees. The gaps in education and male employment help explain some other differences between blacks and whites in Forest Park. Median family income for blacks stood at $9,906, well shy of the white figure of $14,409. And the median value of units occupied by black owners came to $19,100, short of the whites' $22,700. Black renters, however, paid a median monthly bill of $171, compared with a median monthly rent for whites of $142.

Still, racial change was not the most significant change in the white-collar village society of the 1960s. Not only had the village's socioeconomic and demographic structure altered perceptibly by 1970, but so, too, had the tone, structure, and concerns of voluntary organizations. In a curious fashion, incorporation itself had subtly affected the organization milieu and, some observers thought, the nature of voluntarism and the mood of organized community life. From the beginning, Forest Park had been lively and young—so young that the local press carried no obituaries and little news of "senior citizens." After incorporation, however, fear about the death of civic spirit haunted village activists,[5] as if self-government, while increasing residents' control over their lives and helping to protect the community from outside influence, somehow undermined community cohesiveness.

The demise of the Civic Association constituted one of the first events in the emergence of this uneasy state of mind. In January 1962, less than six months after incorporation, the association's *Newsletter* issued a plea for volunteers to help produce its future issues. Scolding readers for letting a handful do all the work, the *Newsletter* said that it would be "ironic to us that our village emerges as a dynamic being while our only form of communication to all the residents of Forest Park dies for lack of volunteers."[6] The harangue accomplished little, however. At the end of the fiscal year, though scheduling a budget of the $4,097.79 for the next year, the association reported a "drastic decline of interest and activity" and made yet another plea for participation.[7] The *Newsletter,* in an uncharacteristic appeal to selfish interest as the bedrock of community spirit, announced:

5. *The Village Voice,* May 1967.
6. *Forest Park Newsletter,* Jan. 1962.
7. Forest Park Civic Association, "Fifth Annual Report," May 21, 1962, n.p.; *Forest Park Newsletter,* May 1962.

There are openings on the NEWSLETTER Staff, Council Liaison Committee, Garden Committee, and many others. If you want to increase the value of your property, or better the community in general, here is your chance. . . . We need YOU. We are anxious to have YOU work with us, and us with YOU.[8]

Clearly, the organization was in trouble, and in 1963 the trouble got deeper. That spring, no one could be found to run for association president, and the May meeting failed to bring out the 10 percent of membership necessary for an election. In June, a quorum failed to appear for a special meeting. And two months later, on November 10, the association finally voted to disband. The group's remaining $900 went to the Women's Club for the volunteer fire department's life squad, with a stipulation that if the cash went unspent for three years, it should automatically revert to the village's general funds.[9]

Yet the association did not vanish without a trace. The board sold the name and assets of the *Newsletter* to Forest Park Publishing Associates, Inc., whose members came not only from the Civic Association, but also from the Swim Club, Little League, and "many other organizations." Forest Park, a village of about 10,000 people, was now assured of news coverage by three local papers, in addition to the suburban sections of the metropolitan dailies. The local papers were the *Forest Park News*, published by Kanter's Forest Park, Inc.; the *Greenhills* (sometimes called *Greenhills-Forest Park*) *Journal*; and the *Newsletter* which, in its own words, "like the Phoenix . . . has arisen from its ashes under new ownership with a rebirth of vigor and enthusiasm." The *Newsletter* claimed that it alone had an "unbiased, nonpartisan" approach.[10] As its editor explained in an article asserting the paper's absolute editorial autonomy, the *Newsletter* aimed to offer:

A free and independent choice in Forest Park—we have used these words before and repeat them now for emphasis. We believe that an unpledged voice is required in order that both sides of any question can be presented and examined. That voice must be free of any vested interests, not because vested interest is improper, but to avoid any implication that it might be. Our interest is the betterment of Forest Park, in the belief that the good of the residents and the good of the community are inseparable and identical. . . .[11]

8. *Forest Park Newsletter,* June 1962.
9. *Forest Park Newsletter,* June, July, Aug. and Nov. 1963.
10. *Forest Park Newsletter,* July and Nov. 1963; Dec. 1964.
11. *Forest Park Newsletter,* Dec. 1964.

The *Newsletter*, in short, stood for something like a higher law. It claimed a unique vision of the village, undistorted by the vested interests of developer, homeowners, renters, and public officials. The paper stood as the Civic Association's successor, in placing itself between voters and public officials as the "voice of the community." It viewed that community as a distinct, endangered entity, equal if not superior to the individuals who happened to live within given territorial boundaries at a given time. But the *Newsletter* was far weaker than the Civic Association as an embodiment of that civic spirit. And such strength was especially important in a transient community of limited liability.

To fill the void left after the Association's demise, the *Newsletter* and its successor, the Women's Club's *The Village Voice*, encouraged people to join other groups. The groups included a civil defense organization which, since there were no public fall-out shelters, trained its members for in-home self-protection in case of disaster or attack.[12] The paper berated villagers whose participation in one civic project amounted to a "deafening roar of apathy."[13] *The Village Voice* recognized how difficult it was to put down "roots" in a society where "families are relocating as frequently as . . . today," but insisted on the "personal responsibility of every citizen to contribute toward a desirable community." To clinch the point, the paper pointed to outside forces which threatened to undermine American strength if local community spirit expired.

> Our coming generation, your children, needs to acquire the sense of a localized community and to feel personal responsibility for ruling that community. This used to be characteristic of nearly all Americans. To enlarge this viewpoint, . . . we can say world leadership is rooted in local community. A 'one world' attitude is more easily instilled in young minds that have a sense of belonging locally; and a lacking in this sense leads to social irresponsibility in today's contracted and disordered world.[14]

Occasionally the aspect of the community participation campaign relating to outside threats turned into sterner stuff, making civic apathy tantamount to treason. In 1962, for example, the *Newsletter* ran a virulently anti-Communist piece in which the Reverend Jenkin Lloyd Jones blamed Johnny's inability to read on "beatniks," "educationists, and pseudo-social scientists." Shortly thereafter, the

12. *Forest Park Newsletter,* Jan. and Feb. 1963.
13. *The Village Voice,* May 1966.
14. *The Village Voice,* July 1966.

paper expressed concern about the paucity of public patriotic gestures, the general lack of "exuberance," and the "passivism" which "makes Our Nation highly vulnerable to communist [sic] domination."[15] And in 1966, inspired by Dr. Fred Schwartz and Herbert Philbrick's lecture on the Communist threat, the editor of *The Village Voice* ran an article on the subject which elicited a "tremendous response." One woman wrote, recognizing:

> that the residents of the village are interested in dogs on the loose, and planting trees . . ., and watching little league baseball—I am too!! But, I would appreciate . . . views . . . about what we 'little people' can do to keep this country (and village) free so that we may continue to enjoy all these other activities.

The editor suggested that community participation was the answer, arguing that:

> advocates of 'let the government do it' are a very serious threat to our inherited way of life. No matter how good their motives seem to be, they are building up Big Government; and Big Government—whether communist, fascist, socialist, or seemingly democratic—becomes oppressive government that threatens both freedom and prosperity. This business of letting the government run things will not work in a free society.[16]

The editor failed to note the irony of her remarks, in a city which had just begun to build up its own government and which boasted of its image as a comprehensively planned community.

For the most part, the pressure for community participation merely elicited a bland, non-ideological commitment to help make the community a nice, closely-knit place to live. One letter to the editor in *The Village Voice*, for example, admitted that "we are not all 'doers'," but contended that "you can't live in a community such as ours and not get involved."

> Call me corny but I'm glad we live here. I'm proud of my friends, neighbors and Forest Park. . . . I just thought it was time to publicly say THANK YOU to all the people who have made Forest Park the wonderful community it is. I sincerely hope we will always have interested 'oldtimers' and energetic 'newcomers' who will continue to work for it.[17]

Everybody, however, did not join in, and after incorporation there was a decline in both the proportion of active participants[18] and the

15. *Forest Park Newsletter*, Aug. and Sept. 1962.
16. *The Village Voice*, May and June 1966.
17. *The Village Voice*, Sept. 1965.
18. *The Village Voice*, Dec. 1967.

number of groups involved in community-wide efforts of the sort undertaken by the old Civic Association. To be sure, the Women's Club did fill the gap left when the *Newsletter* folded and for a time concerned itself with public policy questions such as the annexation fight with Springdale and the effort to secure a branch library. But in 1967, the Women's Club discontinued *The Village Voice* and thereafter lapsed into a familiar pattern of humanitarian and youth-oriented volunteer work.[19] Similarly, a Businessmen's Association was formed in 1965, to promote the shopping center and the Forest Park area, and to serve "the community." But the group quickly languished,[20] not to revive until the 1970s. A short-lived Citizens' Committee took as its first major task the creation of a community center for club meetings, indoor recreation, and public functions. But at its last meeting, someone suggested asking Kanter for help in raising money for the center. "Sure," someone responded, "and name it [for] Kanter?".[21] On that cynical note, the committee faded from public view.

Coincidental with the disappearance of a community-wide civic organization came efforts to stimulate community-wide civic spirit through celebrations of one sort or another—a strategy reminiscent of Kanter's early "country fair." One of the first such events was a "community recognition day," put on in 1962 by the Northwest Junior Chamber of Commerce. This event "recognized" Springdale and Greenhills as well as Forest Park, although Forest Park celebrants ignored the two neighboring suburbs in awards for "Most Outstanding Citizen," "Family with Most Children," and "Oldest Resident" (the latter competition referring to the individual who had lived longest in Forest Park).[22] Two years later, Forest Park, in the words of the *News*, "reached a new plateau of its civic growth," when the local American Legion, the Forest Park Police Department, the volunteer fire department, and others endorsed the idea of having a parade in official observance of Memorial Day. Almost simultaneously, the Forest Park Police Association announced that it would sponsor the first "community celebration" of the Fourth of July.[23]

---

19. White, "History of the Forest Park Women's Club," 2–3; *Forest Park Newsletter*, Dec. 1964; *The Village Voice*, Oct. 1965, Dec. 1967.

20. *Forest Park News*, Dec. 10, 1965.

21. *The Village Voice*, Feb. 1966.

22. *Cincinnati Post and Times-Star*, Aug. 31, 1962; *Forest Park Newsletter*, Sept. 1962.

23. *Forest Park News*, June 26, 1964.

Finally, in 1967, the year *The Village Voice* went under, the village council designated Labor Day as Forest Park Community Recognition Day, suggesting that the spirit of civic community, if no longer embodied in an active organization, at least survived in Forest Park. The *News,* commenting on the designation, predicted that "fun, excitement, entertainment, enthusiasm and esprit de corps will be filling the community's atmosphere" on that day.[24]

The switch in emphasis from organizing for the general community welfare to civic celebrations left activists to channel their energies into a proliferating number of volunteer special-interest groups. Some of these, such as the PTAs, Scouts, and garden and bridge clubs, antedated incorporation and grew almost inevitably as the village grew. Other groups, however, stemmed from the establishment of familiar institutions such as chuches or from the appearance of new interests. In either case, the multiplication of these groups eroded the general sense of civic community and fragmented village society into units competing for prestige, members, and resources. These organizations fell loosely into two groups—one closely related to governmental units, agencies, or departments; and the other involved with more "private" institutions.

The first of the government-related voluntary associations was the volunteer fire department. As we have seen, organization efforts began in 1959. In 1960, the Springfield Township Trustees established a Forest Park Fire District, authorized a tax levy and bond issue within the district, and officially recognized the existence of the volunteers. The village subsequently bought a pumper, and the volunteers were trained at Sharonville by a former Cincinnati fireman. A trucking firm loaned them a used fire truck. Finally, in December 1961, the volunteers took over responsibility for fire protection in Forest Park. Thereafter, individuals, businesses, the Women's Club, and Union Central donated money and equipment, including a resuscitator, accoutrements for the pumper, an ambulance, and a training tower.[25]

The second government-related voluntary organization in Forest Park was the volunteer fire department's Ladies Auxiliary. In October

24. Forest Park Council, "Minutes," Vol. III, June 26, 1967, 140; *Forest Park News,* Aug. 19, 1968.
25. Joe L. Valent, "Forest Park Volunteer Fire Department," pp. 1–3; Gruenschlager, "Forest Park Fire Department," research report, n.d., LAC Files.

1961, just before the volunteers took over fire protection duties in the village, the wives of four men in the group called an organizational meeting of fire spouses. The auxiliary raised $433 with its first Christmas decoration and bake sale; a series of fundraisers followed, including fish fries, rummage sales, and various events at local celebrations. Between 1961 and 1976, these activities yielded about $21,000. The proceeds financed the purchase of equipment ranging from tools and nails for the first firehouse to a "back-up" ambulance. The auxiliary also set up a Fire and Rescue Committee, which attended fires to serve food and beverages to the firefighters.[26]

Despite its chronically tight budget, the Forest Park Police Department, as a formal agency of village government, did not initially[27] attract volunteer assistance. The mid-1960s "law and order" enthusiasm, however, made the police a favorite beneficiary of the volunteer spirit. In September 1963, for example, the Forest Park Democratic Club contributed the first $50 toward $950 needed to supplement the village's police appropriation.[28] That same fall, a group was formed, calling itself the Forest Park Emergency Communications Team. After consulting the department, its leaders decided that some form of emergency communication might be necessary "during certain times in the law enforcement of the local area." Armed with citizen's-band radios and walkie-talkies and wearing headgear resembling hardhats, its members patrolled streets on Halloween, searched for lost children and animals, controlled traffic at accident scenes before the police arrived, assisted troubled motorists on area expressways, and provided communications for parades. Though the organization included residents of nearby communities, Forest Park members concentrated on village problems and took instructions from the Forest Park police chief.[29]

The Emergency Communications Team, however, soon gave way to the larger Forest Park Police Association, a group organized and dominated by local Democrats. Formed late in 1963, it sponsored the first community Fourth of July celebration.[30] The Police Association was more a special-interest group than a civic association, however.

26. Clare Cohn, "Ladies Auxiliary Forest Park Volunteer Fire Department," typescript, n.d. [ca. 1976]; LAC Files.
27. The village police officially came into existence on Oct. 3, 1961. See *Cincinnati Post and Times-Star,* Oct. 4, 1961.
28. Forest Park Council, "Minutes," Vol. I, Sept. 17, 1963, 164.
29. *Forest Park News,* July 24 and Nov. 13, 1964.
30. *Forest Park Newsletter,* Jan., 1964; *Forest Park News,* June 26, 1964.

It assisted the police in varied ways, an objective which proved powerfully attractive to local residents. In 1966, an estimated three-fourths of all Forest Park's adult residents had paid dues, either for individual or family memberships. The funds so generated allowed the association to purchase police manuals, new shoulder patches, and collar emblems needed by the force. And after the Forest Park police contributed three officers to control a black uprising in Cincinnati in June 1967, the Police Association donated a riot gun to Forest Park's police arsenal, an outside light for the police cruiser, and a trophy case for the departmental headquarters. At the same time, the association announced that one of its chief goals would be "the guidance of local teenagers and . . . the fulfillment of their social and recreational needs."[31]

A third, though much less popular, special-interest group with close government ties focused on the physical environment of Forest Park, functioning as a subcommittee of the village council's Recreation Committee. Established in spring 1965, the Beautification Committee conducted "clean-up, paint-up, fix-up" campaigns, crusaded against littering, advised homeowners on how to "fight the war against the tent caterpillar," suggested how and when to prune trees, and pushed villagers incessantly to "Help Put the Forest into the Park." Though its fifteen hard-core leaders were as enthusiastic as any other group's, the organization never attracted broad support. Consequently, it was "with a great deal of pride and a greater amount of gratification," that the committee announced Joseph Kanter's offer to help raise money for the H.O. Kanter Memorial Tree Fund. Kanter would match, on a dollar-for-dollar basis, funds donated by residents in 1966, and he would make annual contributions thereafter, in amounts to be negotiated.[32]

The few "private" voluntary groups established in the 1960s, like those with close ties to city government, both stemmed from and helped shape the character of village society. As in the older "private" and new government-connected groups, women played important roles in the new "private" organizations. And like all the volun-

31. *Forest Park News*, Oct. 1, 1965; *The Village Voice*, Feb. 1966; July 1967. It was not unusual for concern to be juxtaposed with riotous disorders and efforts to discipline teenagers, for many people in the 1960s believed that "outside agitators," usually young males, stirred up discontent, and that this discontent sometimes erupted in riots, whose participants were also largely young males.

32. *Forest Park News*, Apr. 16, 1965; *The Village Voice*, May 1965, May 1966, May 1967.

tary associations formed after incorporation, each of these groups tended to promote a special interest. The assumption was that what benefited a particular groups's cause somehow also benefited the civic welfare. This premise, however, was adopted without any systematic examination of the relationship between particular group goals and the welfare of the community as a whole. That is, the groups did not acknowledge, let alone examine, the difference between launching uncoordinated attacks on particular problems, and first defining the civic welfare and then invoking civic spirit cooperatively to assign top priority to certain problems and defer action on others.

One set of "private" voluntary organizations formed in the 1960s was associated with various religious denominations. Religion was important both to Forest Park's developers, who reserved land for churches and a synagogue, and to civic leaders such as Mayor Philip White, who once designated the week of February 5 as American Legion Religious Emphasis Week and called on his fellow citizens to engage "in regular public worship at the church or synagogue of their faith. . . ."[33] Kanter had expected ultimately to have seven churches serving Protestants, Catholics, and Jews. But the presence of seventeen Protestant churches, four Catholic churches, and a Jewish synagogue in the "greater neighborhood of Forest Park" slowed the development of religious facilities in the village.[34] With the aid of the Council of Churches of Greater Cincinnati, which refereed the timing and location of Protestant churches entering Forest Park, and of the Catholic Archdiocese, which made and kept an early commitment to purchase ten acres of Kanter Corporation land for church and school purposes, Forest Park slowly added religious structures to its organizational amenities.[35]

Methodists arrived first, opening the Forest Park Methodist Chapel late in 1959.[36] Shortly thereafter, in June 1961, the Episcopal Congregation of the Holy Spirit, a missionary enterprise organized through Grace Episcopal Church in College Hill, began building a church on

33. *The Village Voice*, Feb. 1967; Kanter to author, interview, July 5, 1975; *News-Reporter*, n.p., May 23, 1963, newsclip in Kanter Corporation scrapbook, office of Forest Park, Inc.

34. *Forest Park News*, Sept. 6, 1963.

35. Kanter to Bryant, Aug. 27, 1962, files of Forest Park Planning and Zoning Commission; *Forest Park Newsletter*, June 1962; *Cincinnati Post and Times-Star*, Jan. 26, 1963.

36. *Forest Park Newsletter*, Dec. 17, 1959; *Cincinnati Post and Times-Star*, Jan. 31, 1959.

three and a half acres at the corner of Waycross and Hanover.[37] Next came the Forest Park Christian Church, which broke ground on four and a half acres at the corner of Hanover and Kemper in fall 1962. Both it and the Episcopal group opened their buildings in September 1963.[38] After a pause, in 1967 the Covenant United Church of Christ purchased five acres at the corner of Hall-Winton Extension and Waycross Road. In the same year, Catholics organized the parish of St. Matthias the Apostle and sought ways to raise $200,000 for a building. These two churches were not built however, and Catholics were left to worship in Cameron Park School, while the Covenant congregation used "The Hayloft," a square dance party barn in Springdale.[39]

The experience of the Covenant United Church, which set out to erect a regular church edifice but ended up joining forces with Holy Spirit Episcopal in 1969 to build a shared "church center," helps explain the closure. Money comprised part of the problem. National figures at the time indicated that a standard suburban church cost an average of $400,000 in site and construction costs over a ten-year period. As Covenant United contemplated its original project, the building plans began to look too expensive "for their size and purpose." The Covenant minister and the priest at Holy Spirit finally decided that through merging they could retain the intimacy of the small parish (a characteristic they deemed especially important in a transient community of "strangers" where individuals needed the comfort and support of becoming closely acquainted quickly with members of their own sect), and at the same time afford facilities for youth and adult education programs too expensive for either group alone. By pooling their resources to support the resulting Winton Forest Church Center, the two groups could worship separately in small, tightly-knit, if unstable, congregations reminiscent of the kind they thought common in the past, and still carry out a "modern" program of social and educational activities for their members.[40]

Forest Park Catholics resolved the same dilemma in a similar way. Though lacking the option of a merger, they were able to tap arch-

37. *Forest Park Newsletter*, Apr. 1960; *Community News*, n.p., Sept. 15, 1960, newsclip in Kanter Corporation scrapbook; *Greenhills Journal*, June 16, 1961.
38. *Forest Park Newsletter*, Nov. 1962; *Forest Park News*, Sept. 6, 1963.
39. *The Village Voice*, March, July 1967; *Forest Park News*, June 26, 1967, and Mar. 4, 1968. In 1969, Baptists purchased land for a church but failed to start construction in the 1960s. See *Forest Park News*, Dec. 23, 1969.
40. *Forest Park News*, Sept. 30, 1969.

diocesan resources for land acquisition. Instead of erecting a conventional church building, however, they built a "Confraternity Center." The new center was designed especially to handle the educational programs, parish meetings, and social events which, along with religious services, seemed particularly important in this setting.[41]

A particular special interest, the civil and social discipline of teenagers, provided much of the impetus for the religious center movement in Forest Park. Holy Spirit Church in 1966 brought in a new clergyman, the Reverend John Lovatt, in part because of his demonstrated expertise and "enthusiasm" for youth work.[42] But awareness that the teenage "problem" deserved special organizational attention dated almost to the initial settlement of Forest Park. In the early years, however, younger children had commanded so much more attention than teenagers that the secular Teen Club of the late 1950s stumbled into the 1960s unable even to establish a permanent meeting place.[43]

During the mid-1960s, however, anxiety over the teenage issue mounted. In 1965, for example, Cletus McDaniel of McDaniel Realty sought to inspire "better" adolescent behavior by sponsoring a contest to choose "the best Teenage Citizens of Forest Park." He enlisted the Women's Club to select the winning male and female, "strictly on their contribution to the community as good citizens."[44] In 1966, the village council enacted legislation "to combat the rash of glue sniffing." In spring and summer 1967, Charles Dawson, the former *Newsletter* columnist who now wrote regular articles for *The Village Voice,* counted 1,500 teens in the village. He also described teenage vandalism in Forest Park as a "real problem," noting that by law parents must pay for damages inflicted on property by their offspring. And he listed the question of "what to do with teenagers' time" as the most serious problem in the village. In fall 1967, partly in response to the idea that teenage vandalism was a result of inadequate teen recreational opportunities, the police organized a Teenage Civic Communications Team to assist the force with "surveillance" during the Halloween weekend.[45] This step relieved some teenagers of the tedium of free time in order to frustrate the vandalism of others.

41. *Forest Park News,* Apr. 8, 1969.
42. *The Village Voice,* Dec. 1966.
43. *Greenhills Journal,* Nov. 17, 1961.
44. *The Village Voice,* Sept. 1965.
45. Forest Park Council, "Minutes," Vol. III, Jan. 4, 1966, 2; *The Village Voice,* May and June 1967; Forest Park Council, "Minutes," Vol. III, Nov. 7, 1967, 160.

Meanwhile, Father Lovatt had begun to mobilize volunteers to guide village teenagers into constructive leisure pursuits. In 1966, after persuading the Women's Club and the Northwest Junior Chamber of Commerce to help found a youth center, he broached the idea to Mayor White, who appointed a Youth Commission to investigate the proposal. The commission reported positively, noting that the "community and area direly" needed

> a functioning youth center where teen-agers could focus their social activities on a year-round basis—a place of their own, operated and governed by themselves, with room for ping-pong and pool, arts and crafts, dancing to live bands, a place to study or simply meet their friends, and perhaps most importantly, a place where a full-time director could provide imaginative programming to develop each youth's potential.[46]

Thereafter, planning, organizing, and seeking support and space for the youth center began in earnest. In spring 1967, the scheme's backers created an adult board of directors, with Father Lovatt as president. Officially called the Forest Park Youth Center, Inc., the center catered to all teenagers in the Greenhills-Forest Park School District. Because its 7,500 square feet were located in the basement of the Punshon Engineering Building, the youths nicknamed the center "the Cellar." Describing it as "just like a bunny club" (Hugh Hefner's popular Playboy Club for adults), the teenagers announced in May that, for $5 and $3 respectively, senior and junior high school students could purchase "keys" giving them access to the Cellar's three dance areas, game room for pool and ping-pong, snack bar, tables and booths, meeting rooms, and director's office.

Such facilities, appropriately decorated, were costly. Rent was $400 per month, and the cost of renovations, operating expenses, and salaries for a manager and youth director brought the initial annual budget to $18,000. Though the center was touted as a self-supporting venture, Central Trust Bank floated a $10,000 interest-free "start up" loan underwritten by several businesses, including the Home Builders Association of Greater Cincinnati which reasoned that the Cellar would help attact home buyers to the area. The club opened in May 1967, although the "grand opening" took place in September. Except for one councilmember's vague reported comments about unspecified "problems" and the additional workload placed on police, news

46. *The Village Voice*, Dec. 1966, Sept. 1967.

coverage of the Cellar's activities, throughout its early history, was consistently favorable.[47]

The organization, however, did not survive long. Membership fees, donations, and fundraising events failed to defray expenses; in spring 1969, the growing debt, combined with increasing parental suspicion about rowdiness, placed the Cellar in jeopardy. Its board asked the council to appropriate a $3,000 subsidy for the club. The council complied, but parents, at a "tense and explosive" public meeting in April, objected sharply to that use of tax money. To counteract adult disillusionment with the club, individual board members sponsored a "Support the Cellar" drive in May. And in June, a group of "Cellar dwellers," as the teenage patrons styled themselves, presented the Forest Park Police Department a certificate of appreciation for its interest and cooperation.[48]

The fundraising and image-polishing campaigns came to naught. In September 1969, the Cellar folded for lack of operating money. Behind the financial problem, however, lay a drop in membership—from 1,100 in September 1967, to about one hundred in September 1969. And the failure of a fall membership drive to attract more than about twenty new keyholders, a figure Mayor White, attributing the disinterest to "the affluency of kids today," called "a ridiculous number." One "Cellar dweller," however, maintained that teens had abandoned the club because of police harrassment at dances and because the adult board had refused to let members carry out their own ideas. One parent concurred. "Kids in a bedroom community like Forest Park need somewhere to go," she observed, "but parents thought the Cellar should not be just a place for kids to hang around in. . . . They want super-planned activities. . . ."[49]

The disgruntled Cellar mourner may have exaggerated in describing Forest Parkers as compulsive super-planners, or in calling this the prime cause of the Cellar's demise. There can be little question, however, that organizational enthusiasm ran strong in the village, as the proliferation of special-interest groups, both government-related and "private," demonstrated. Though concerned with special interests, the groups recruited participants and developed programs from

47. *The Village Voice*, Feb., Mar., Apr., May, Sept., and Dec. 1967; *Cincinnati Enquirer*, May 15, 1967; *Greenhills-Forest Park Journal*, Nov. 16, 1967.

48. *Forest Park News*, Apr. 8 and 29, May 20, and June 10, 1969.

49. *Forest Park News*, Apr. 8, 1969; *Cincinnati Enquirer*, Sept. 10, 1969.

a village-wide base, reflecting the belief that competition among them to advance particular interests would somehow bolster the overall sense of community and quality of life.

Throughout the 1960s Forest Park had yet another set of groups, and these drew their members from neighboring places as well as the village. They advocated causes and carried out programs not limited to Forest Park in their focus and appeal. These groups defined their constituents as members of a different community, the boundaries of which failed to match either those of a political jurisdiction or of a "defended" neighborhood. Among these groups were Courtesy to Newcomers and Welcome Wagon clubs, the Winton Hills League of Women Voters, the Northern Hills B'nai B'rith, the Northwest Junior Chamber of Commerce, and the district American Legion, to cite just a few. Apart from the fact that their activities diffused the sense of territorial community in Forest Park, the story of these groups belongs, for the most part, to another history.

Yet not entirely. For these groups, like those based in Forest Park itself, comprised special interest groups, "communities" of individuals with varied interests, connections, and organizational memberships. That such groups flourished implied that the ideal of the community of limited liability was disappearing. That ideal, while recognizing that individuals harbored plural concerns and commitments, also assumed that any place would have large numbers of responsible citizens whose voluntary activities would help sustain the locality as a civic community and not merely as place in which to live. By the end of the 1960s, little except rhetoric or an occasional "community celebration" sustained the sense that Forest Park was this type of community of limited liability. An abundance of special-interest groups served a variety of personal interests, but no organization advocated, helped define, and promoted the welfare of the local community as a whole.

It was in this context that the spirit of volunteerism generated another kind of special and essentially personal interest organization, this one rooted in economic and spatial distinctions. On September 30, 1969, the *News* announced that residents of "K" section had organized to protect that neighborhood and had designated a representative to attend city council meetings and gather information.[50] In retrospect, it seems surprising that the neighborhood had not appeared earlier as a major unit of identification and action. Though

50. *Forest Park News*, Sept. 30, 1969.

Forest Park had been planned comprehensively, Warner-Kanter and Kanter had built Forest Park a subdivision at a time, and the houses in each subdivision fell within a given price range specified for that tract.[51] So from the beginning Forest Park was a segregated community divided by the age of its housing stock, utilities, and streets, and by the income of its residents, based on the purchase or rental prices they could pay for housing. It may have been these *de facto* distinctions that led the first village council, in the interest of community cohesion, to substitute letters of the alphabet for the names Warner-Kanter had bestowed upon subdivisions. The reasoning apparently was that simple letters, unlike names, evoked little sense of a place's status.[52]

In any case, neighborhoods were not a focus of organizational activity until 1969. In the late 1960s, Forest Park residents began to have the kind of jitters which, in the big-city milieu, sparked a neighborhood organization revolution. Blacks began to move into Forest Park during 1967,[53] and in the village racial, ethnic, and economic class sensitivities mounted slowly thereafter. In spring 1968, amidst civil rights demonstrations and racial disorders in Cincinnati and parts of Hamilton County, Mayor White complained about a "potential panic" in Forest Park created by "unfounded, ridiculous, and too often repeated rumors," and the council worried about large numbers of villagers reported to be arming themselves.[54] That summer, a member of the planning commission urged the council to adopt a resolution "welcoming as citizens and neighbors all people, irrespective of race, creed, religion, color, or national origin."[55] And in 1967 and 1968, the federal government adopted new anti-discriminatory housing regulations which supplemented Ohio's recently revised fair housing law, which had taken effect in fall 1965.[56]

Alone these events might have suggested civic rather than neighborhood organization to Forest Parkers, but combined with the nature and timing of subdivision development they produced an outburst of territorial parochialism. In the mid-1960s, work began on

51. *Cincinnati Post and Times-Star,* Oct. 23, 1976.
52. *Forest Park Newsletter,* May 1962.
53. Forest Park Council, "Minutes," Vol. VII, Apr. 7, 1975, 209.
54. *Greenhills-Forest Park Journal,* Apr. 11 and 25, 1968.
55. Forest Park Council, "Minutes," Vol. IV, July 15, 1968, 40.
56. *Greenhills-Forest Park Journal,* Oct. 21, 1965; Sam Bass Warner, Jr., *The Urban Wilderness* (New York: Harper and Row, 1972), 230–246. *The Village Voice*'s "Communist Threat" column (July 1966) denounced federal open-occupancy legislation as a dangerous erosion of "freedom of choice."

the Forest Ridge subdivision in Forest Park's northwest corner, west of the proposed Circle Freeway route and hence cut off from the village's principal area. The highway "wall" failed to reduce citizens' anxiety, however, as they watched wooden houses architecturally repugnant to many Forest Parkers go up along Elkwood and Cedarcreek Drives. In winter 1968–1969, irate homeowners made Kanter and the Forest Ridge builder, Imperial Homes, targets of a "general protest" about the types of houses in the subdivision. Whether because of their alleged aesthetic shortcomings or the furor over their construction, the objectionable houses sat vacant, and the builder eventually went bankrupt.[57] It was in this context that the activists of "K" section, which lay just across Circle Freeway from Forest Ridge, created the first neighborhood organization in Forest Park.[58]

It was ironic that this variety of special-interest organization threatened to divide the village into a collection of "defended communities." For the civic community spirit so ardently nurtured by the Civic Association and advocates of community welfare in the 1950s and early 1960s itself had stemmed from perceived threats of "outside" groups to community integrity. Now the neighborhood organization revolution, familiar in big cities across the nation in the 1960s, had reached the "model" community among Cincinnati's suburbs. And in Forest Park, as in the cities, the movement started with anxieties about class and race, as well as with territorial defensiveness. The "defended community" of 1960 seemed about to become in 1970 a congeries of "defended neighborhoods."

Forest Park residents, in the 1960s, then, like other white-collar urbanites, had myriad opportunities for volunteer activity. In addition to the Baseball Association, which in 1969 was still the city's largest group,[59] other groups established in the 1950s continued to be active in the 1960s: the Swim Club, the PTAs, Boy and Girl Scouts, garden clubs, and high-culture groups. Still other "community" groups took shape after the 1961 incorporation. Some briefly sought to keep alive the spirit and program of civic community represented by the Civic

57. Forest Park Council, "Minutes," Vol. III, Apr. 5, 1966, 31; *Greenhills-Forest Park Journal,* June 2, 1966; Forest Park Council, "Minutes," Vol. IV, Jan. 6 and 20, 1969; *Greenhills-Forest Park Journal,* Jan. 23, 1969; Michael Kadlecik to author, July 30, 1976, letter in LAC Files. Kanter was surprised by the bias in the Cincinnati area in favor of brick or stone materials. Kanter to author, interview, July 5, 1975.

58. *Forest Park Newsletter,* Jan. and Aug. 1963; *Forest Park News,* Sept. 6, 1963; *The Village Voice,* Dec. 1966.

59. *Forest Park News,* Apr. 18, 1969.

Association and the editorial policy of the *Newsletter* and *The Village Voice*. After the Civic Association's death, however, that spirit was most often expressed rhetorically or in "community celebrations." For in the 1960s most organizations, whether "private" or attached to government, selected a special interest—a part of the community—on which to focus their efforts.

Except in the Baseball Association, women dominated voluntary organizations after the demise of the Civic Association. The Women's Club was the most active and versatile group, implementing within its varied program many projects suggested by sponsors throughout the community. The "organization men" of Forest Park, apparently, had married organization women, who found their outlets in the volunteer field. Except for a lonely voice now and then accusing the Baseball Association or Recreation Commission of ignoring the needs of girls, not a single exponent of women's liberation protested the dominance of children, family, home, and volunteerism over Forest Park's women, including those employed outside their homes. Indeed, with the deference males and females alike paid to the ideal of volunteerism, and the enthusiastic way potentially activist newcomers were recruited into the lush round of activities spawned by "community" organizations, few people had the time, confidence, or perspective to follow another drummer.

*. . . unless Forest Park gets additional funds
from some [local] source and assumes
responsibility for more of the services . . .
which people now pay for themselves, we will
never . . . get a more equitable distribution of
. . . state and Federal funds, and we stand to
drop back in [the] quality of personal and
property protection, and further back in the
condition of our streets and other facilities.*

COUNCIL MEMBER
LORAINE BLACKBURN, 1971

THE POLITICS OF NOSTALGIA AND THE DEATH OF THE COMMUNITY OF LIMITED LIABILITY, 1970–1974

Throughout the 1960s and into the 1970s, both community-wide and narrower special-interest groups struggled to keep alive the notion that Forest Park could be a community of limited liability—a place where responsible citizens, through widespread participation in volunteer associations, would reinforce their local orientation, promote the welfare of the whole community, and assure Forest Park's future as a model planned community. But after 1970, advocates of the community of limited liability dwindled in number. The pleas of those remaining now sounded nostalgic and attracted few listeners. Discourse about the nature and agencies of civic life still made use of the words *community* and *neighborhood*. But a new set of assumptions about the nature of urban society held sway, not only in Forest Park but in America generally. These new assumptions drained not only *community* and *neighborhood* of their civic connotations, but also the word *metropolitan*. While this discourse still took the individual as the basic social unit, the definition of that individual no longer recommended a concern to help resolve essentially civic questions through voluntary participation in genuinely civic organizations. The new individual seemed legitimately turning inward, toward an intensely personalized individualism more concerned with self-fulfillment, career, and/or property values than with civic participation to advance the general welfare.

The new way of dividing up and ordering society received a most dramatic expression in Forest Park beteen 1970 and 1974, in an acrid conflict over the role of city government. As we have seen, the village's incorporation had weakened the old faith in Forest Park as a community of limited liability, by establishing a government to do some things for its residents that they could not do for themselves. And the adoption of the city charter in 1969 gave that government the potential of taking over an even larger share of civic responsibility. In 1974 therefore, when those nostalgic for a community of limited liability clashed with advocates of a more positive city government, they suffered a crushing defeat. The defeat climaxed a complicated fight over a proposed city income tax.

Nostalgia for the community of limited liability fed on Forest Park's apparent success and sense of security as it entered the 1970s. Now the third largest city in Hamilton County, trailing only Cincinnati and Norwood, an industrial "satellite" with roots in the nineteenth century, Forest Park possessed the basic infrastructure of municipal services. The community seemed safe, too, from big-city annexation. In 1954, Cincinnati had assigned an assistant city manager to annex outlying areas, but in thirteen frustrating years, just twenty-one minor slices of territory had been added to the tax list.[1] Finally, in 1967, Cincinnati had dropped its annexation effort. Even the urbanization process seemed pro-suburban. The socioeconomic system of the late 1960s and early 1970s made suburbs competitive with their core cities, not only for residents but also as commercial, office, and industrial sites.[2] The administration of Richard M. Nixon, with its attitude of "benign neglect" toward inner-city problems, seemed favorably disposed toward suburbs generally and toward planning-oriented places such as Forest Park specifically.[3] Here, if anywhere, it seemed to many, the ideal of a community of limited liability ought to flourish.

1. *Cincinnati Post and Times-Star,* Jan. 7, 1977.
2. Paul R. Porter, *The Recovery of American Cities* (New York: Sun River Press, Two Continents, 1976), 47–68, sums up in a witty, commonsensical way the many angles from which urbanologists in this period arrived at this conclusion.
3. On Nixon's metropolitan policy, from the perspective of the early 1970s, see, e.g., Miller, *The Urbanization of Modern America* (New York: Harcourt Brace Jovanovich, 1973), 225–28.

In view of all this, it is scarcely surprising that the mood in Forest Park as it began its history as a city, was optimistic. To coincide with the tenth anniversary of Forest Park's incorporation, the Home Builders Association of Greater Cincinnati chose Forest Park as the site of its own tenth home show spectacular (see Figure 8). As if in preparation for this summer 1971 "Homerama," Kanter, through Forest Park, Inc., donated city signs at town entrances reading, "Welcome to Forest Park, Ohio, the Planned Community." On Homerama's opening day, the *Forest Park News* featured the celebration in the paper's tenth anniversary issue. Editor Eileen Kieffer, the self-styled civic community "visionary," embellished the edition with growth-focused historical accounts tracing important events and institutions and celebrating the "decade of progress" in Forest Park.[4]

Yet Forest Park's new "establishment" city council, elected in fall 1969 to inaugurate the home-rule, manager-council government, soon faced the sobering potential for serious fiscal difficulty. In June 1970, the Committee on Streets and Highways reported a shortage of funds for "desperately needed" road repairs and estimated that the current taxation rate would not be sufficient to meet future street repair needs. That same month, Alvin M. Tomb, whom the council had named "permanent" city manager in April, pointed out that several homes in Forest Park remained unoccupied and that building permits in early 1970 had declined from 1969 levels. Tomb also commented on the adverse influence of the tight-money situation on home building.[5]

To city officials concerned about the long-term community interest, conditions seemed to call for more activisim in public policy. The council decided to assess a tax on the earnings of people who worked in Forest Park and of businesses located in Forest Park, regardless of where the wage earners or business owners lived.[6] Under the terms of the new city charter, however, adoption of the earnings tax required charter amendment and voter approval. On August 17, after hearing three businessmen vigorously object to a tax on business profits, the incumbent majority approved the earnings tax ordinance for consideration by the electorate in November 1970.[7] The council majority deemed the city's financial status gloomy enough to put two levies for

4. *Forest Park News,* Oct. 23, 1970; Jan. 23, 1971.
5. Forest Park Council, "Minutes," Vol. IV, June 1, 1970, 191; *Forest Park News,* Apr. 24, 1970; *Cincinnati Enquirer,* Apr. 10 and June 18, 1970.
6. Forest Park Council, "Minutes," Vol. IV, Aug. 17, 1970, 14.
7. *Ibid.*

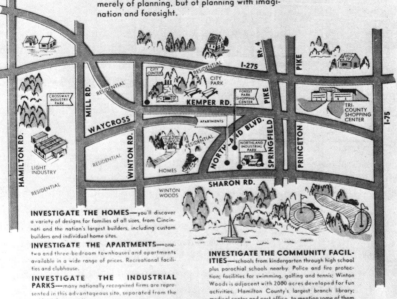

Welcome to Forest Park
THE PLANNED COMMUNITY

Everything's here for living, working and playing. Unique in its development, Forest Park was planned for progress. A drive through its 3700-acre expanse shows immediately the results not merely of planning, but of planning with imagination and foresight.

INVESTIGATE THE HOMES—you'll discover a variety of designs for families of all sizes, from Cincinnati and the nation's largest builders, including custom builders and individual home sites.

INVESTIGATE THE APARTMENTS—one-two and three-bedroom townhouses and apartments available in a wide range of prices. Recreational facilities and clubhouse.

INVESTIGATE THE INDUSTRIAL PARKS—many nationally recognized firms are represented in this advantageous site, separated from the residential community.

INVESTIGATE THE COMMUNITY FACILITIES—schools from kindergarten through high school plus parochial schools nearby. Police and fire protection; facilities for swimming, golfing and tennis; Winton Woods is adjacent with 2000 acres developed for fun activities. Hamilton County's largest branch library; medical center and post office, to mention some of them.

A Community Development of

THE KANTER CORP. **AND** *Forest Park* INC.

For Information Call 851-6000

A Good Place to Live, Work and Play

FIGURE 8. Advertisement in the *Cincinnati Enquirer's* 1971 special section on Homerama. The map features Winton Woods Lake, Park, and Golf Course, as well as the Tri-County Shopping Center. None of these amenities lay within Forest Park or resulted from the efforts of the planners whose work is cited in the ad as the source of Forest Park's distinctive attractiveness. Source: *Cincinnati Enquirer*, July 11, 1971.

fire protection on the same ballot: a one-mill renewal operating levy and a one-mill renewal equipment levy.[8]

The council's decision to ask for an earnings tax created a furor. At an August 28 hearing Union Central, the Forest Park Businessmen's Association, and Forest Park, Inc., declared their vehement opposition to the tax. The measure's administrative costs to the city and businesses and its potential for inhibiting commercial and industrial development were cited, and it was charged that the council had acted without studying the question thoroughly. Then someone discovered that, because one member of the incumbent majority had been absent, the ordinance had not received the two-thirds vote of the council required for all charter amendments. That oversight forced postponement of the referendum until a special election in December. In the interim, the fire levies on the November ballot passed,[9] and both sides in the earnings tax controversy publicly argued the merits of the proposal.

Those in favor of the earnings tax concentrated on explaining how the tax would work and what it would buy. The legislation authorized a tax of up to 1 percent on earnings. Under the proposal, any Forest Park resident who worked and paid a lesser earnings tax elsewhere owed Forest Park only the difference between the level of that tax and 1 percent; those who paid 1 percent elsewhere would pay nothing to Forest Park. Similarly, individuals living elsewhere but working in Forest Park had to pay up to 1 percent, either to Forest Park or to the government of their place of residence (if it had such a tax). Under state law, financial institutions, as companies, would pay nothing, but their employees would be liable to the tax.

Benefits to be derived from the tax sounded formidable. Its defenders claimed that, over the five-year budget planning period, revenue from the tax would permit the city to double the police force; add seven paid firemen; construct new or expanded police headquarters, two Fire Department substations, and a separate Maintenance Department building; resurface and repair streets; and perhaps begin municipal garbage collection service and reduce real estate taxes.[10]

The basis for business opposition to the tax had been clearly enunciated in August. Eileen Kieffer voiced another viewpoint in the *Forest Park News*. Passage of the tax, in broadening the scope and

8. *Forest Park News,* Aug. 28 and Sept. 11, 1970.
9. *Forest Park News,* Aug. 28, Oct. 9, and Nov. 6, 1970.
10. *Forest Park News,* Dec. 4, 1970.

improving the quality of city services, would cause Forest Park to "lose . . . the feeling of community," she wrote. If the city performed so many functions so well, it would leave "our civic-minded people and organizations little to do. . . . " Kieffer also doubted that the tax would raise as much money as projected. Another opponent distrusted the five-year budget projected without an earnings tax, because, he asserted, it showed expenses and population increasing but income decreasing.[11]

The combination of economic self-interest and community idealism proved devastating. Voters rejected the proposition in every precinct, and the total margin was 1,762 to 446, although only 30 percent of the eligible voters went to the polls. Charles Dawson attributed the defeat to the antagonism of non-residents; to the proposal's complicated language; to the council's failure to fight for ratification; to the measure's being submitted to voters at a special election; and to a "well-heeled" opposition, including the *Forest Park News* and ex-Mayor Philip White, who had headed a joint anti-tax campaign by the Forest Park Citizens Committee Against Unfair Taxation and the Forest Park Businessmen's Association's Committee on Taxation.[12]

Curiously, neither the pre-election disputes nor the post-election analyses mentioned the novelty of such a tax as a reason for its failure. To be sure, this type of tax was already in use in the metropolitan area. Cincinnati, where many Forest Park residents worked, had imposed it in the mid-1950s, on the grounds that the big city served all metropolitan communities. And many smaller municipalities, including Springdale, had subsequently found its charm irresistible. But the Forest Park tax, unlike the Cincinnati or Springdale earnings tax, forced Forest Park residents and city officials to consider the relationship between the nature of community they hoped to build and its fiscal foundation.

Kieffer had raised this issue during the campaign when she speculated that the tax would somehow undermine Forest Park's community spirit. Clearly, she still thought of community in Forest Park in the old way. A flagging of civic participation, she suggested, signaled alienation and the demise of community in Forest Park and, by extrapolation, in America generally. For Kieffer, local institutions

11. *Forest Park News*, Dec. 4, 1970; *Greenhills-Forest Park Journal*, Dec. 3, 1970.
12. *Forest Park News*, Dec. 4 and 18, 1970; *Greenhills-Forest Park Journal*, Sept. 3 and Dec. 17, 1970.

which encouraged this kind of civic community formed the very bedrock of the American system. From this perspective, the earnings tax seemed alien, almost subversive, for it suggested that government could do things as well as, or better than, public-spirited volunteers.

Indeed, the logic of the tax took Forest Park to be an economic rather than a socio-civic community. The proposal might more accurately have been called a "users" tax, for one's liability to the tax depended not on where one lived, but on which set of facilities—which "infrastructure"—one used to make one's living. Where and, within limits, how or whether one chose to exercise one's social and civic responsibilities was a matter of supreme indifference. The earnings tax, by its very nature, swept aside the notion of the metropolis as a set of small "defended" communities, whether the defenses stood to protect vested economic interests or particular socio-civic or "cultural" predispositions.

The logic of the tax also implied that communities were interchangeable. Ignoring the hoary cry against "taxation without representation," the tax assumed that each municipality provided, or ought to provide, the same services at roughly identical levels of quality, and that those services had nothing to do with the nature and character of local society. Hence voters in one place within the metropolis should feel no compunction about exercising "virtual" representation and taxing "outsiders" for what the "outsiders" themselves would support if they but lived within the municipality in which they happened to work. The tax said, in effect, that all residents of the metropolis were welcome in Forest Park, as long as they paid for the use of its municipal facilities.

During the early 1970s, that kind of open invitation evoked at the very least, ambivalence and anxiety in Forest Park. The city council majority fed the uneasiness by continuing to press for an earnings tax. The second round in the fight began in February 1971, with an open meeting to discuss the city's finances. The anti-tax forces spoke first, questioning the efficiency of the city's current form of government. Philip White, who had argued in Charter Commission hearings for the strong-mayor form of government, complained that administrative costs had increased since 1969 and suggested that the standing Charter Revision Commission investigate structural rather than fiscal changes to improve the situation. J. Stuart Mill of Union Central, who had also opposed the switch to manager-council government, said that Forest Park's government over "the last one or two years" lacked "citizen interest and participation," implying that he, too, preferred organizational to financial reform.

The pro-tax people responded by reminding the audience of the unhappy legacy of "personal" village government by amateurs. A member of the council pointed out that no major street repairs or preventive maintenance programs had been carried out in the past ten years. He cited the need for two new fire substations, a building for the Police Department, and more fire and police personnel to bring the force up to "national standards." Mayor Sullivan capped the session by describing the "news media" as so biased that the city, in order to spread the truth, was considering spending $2,000 to $4,000 in the next fiscal year to send "newsletters" to residents.[13]

The council carried the fight into August 1971 by demonstrating the futility of looking elsewhere for funds. In April, Councilmember Loraine Blackburn reported on a letter from Senator Robert A. Taft, Jr., responding to her complaint about the inadequacy of federal revenue sharing. The senator lamented the fact that the "tax productivity" distribution formula discriminated against places with a disproportionately large poor population or with little industry, but supported the formula in principle as a means "to restore the vitality of our state and local governments." Blackburn acknowledged Taft's concern, concluding that "unless Forest Park gets additional funds from some source and assumes responsibility for more of the services (such as refuse collection) which people now pay for themselves, we will never . . . get a more equitable distribution of . . . state and Federal funds, and we stand to drop back in quality of personal and property protection, and further back in the condition of our streets and other facilities."[14] Simultaneously, the council pushed the state legislature for action on two bills increasing the portion of state taxes returned to municipalities, but without result.[15]

Finally, the council decided to ask voters to face the earnings tax question once more. In mid-August, by a unanimous vote, the council placed both a .5 percent earnings tax and a 5-mill real estate tax levy on the November 1971 ballot, stipulating that if both measures passed, the one projected to return the most revenue would go into effect.[16] The tax vote coincided with the election of three council

13. *Forest Park News,* Feb. 26, 1971.
14. Forest Park Council, "Minutes," Vol. V, Apr. 19, 1971, 66.
15. *Ibid.,* Aug. 16, 1971, 106.
16. Forest Park Council, "Minutes," Vol. V, Aug. 16, 1971, 106; *Forest Park News,* Aug. 27, 1971.

members. Since the unanimous council vote on the dual tax proposition had masked real dissent among council members over the earnings tax, it now seemed quite possible that the new council could contain a majority which was against any tax and against the manager-council form of government as well.

The council race matched the English era in village politics for enthusiasm and tension. A total of eight candidates vied for three seats, only one of which, that of Mayor Sullivan, belonged to an incumbent. The list of contestants included ex-Mayor Philip White; Frederick Lamb, the former head of the Charter Commission; and Kristen Heiberg, the chief and former president of the volunteer fire department and president of Heiberg Construction. All of these men possessed considerable visibility going into the race.[17]

Those who favored increasing the city's tax revenues fired the first shot in the campaign. On August 16, the day that the council put the two tax issues on the ballot, council member Lesick gave a pro-tax speech sketching three "familiar" approaches to community development. One, which he called "the fragmented view," "proceeds on the theory that strengthening one part of the anatomy of the body politic," such as the police, "while ignoring others, can be done without adversely affecting the other parts." This philosophy, he argued, "merely maintains a crisis climate in municipal affairs." A second approach, which he labeled the "developer or large corporation approach," "assumes that what is good for the developer is good for the city." Though often "well-considered and well-intentioned," this attitude fails in the long run because it advances "on a crash basis, from program to program." The third approach he identified as "nostalgic," a yearning to have "everybody lend a hand to get and keep things moving," while ignoring the fact that "most people will not, or cannot, lend a hand." By adhering to these various approaches, he asserted, "cities are drifting into the future in a courtship of chaos bordering on the brink of disaster."

Lesick conceded that Forest Park had "moved along some of these avenues," but he maintained that "our drift can be arrested" by embarking on "a program of prevention" to "anticipate problems and avoid the consequences of present problems." What Forest Park needed, he asserted, switching into space-age terminology, was a "guidance system for the thrust into the future," a system capable of

17. *Forest Park News,* Aug. 13 and 27, 1971.

delivering "twenty-four hour complete fire protection," "comprehensive crime control," an "upgraded restorative road program," recreation "suitable for all ages," improved sanitation methods, anti-pollution measures, "and the proper staffing of all departments and facilities with capable, competent personnel."

The "one propellant . . . most important . . . to embark in a dynamic way in order to fulfill the promise of this community" was, of course, additional tax money. The citizens had a choice; either adopt a real estate levy "and pay for this program all by themselves, or . . . adopt an income tax" requiring that "non-residents also participate and pay for the use of municipal facilities and services. . . ."[18]

Lesick's speech represented the positive, futuristic side of the pro-tax campaign. But that effort possessed another face, one which insisted, in Dawson's words, "that the City is going downhill."[19] One spokesman for this line of attack pointed out that, among the eighteen "suburban cities" in Hamilton County, Forest Park stood last in per-capita expenditures for law enforcement, legal services, street lighting, and traffic safety; next to last in expenditures for legislative functions; third to last in appropriations for financial administration and engineering; and below the suburban median in outlays for street maintenance, public health, parks and recreation, and administrative costs. And it placed barely above the median, though not among the top six, in spending for fire protection and buildings and grounds.[20]

The anti-tax opposition put up a formidable front. The *News,* though it stayed out of the council campaign *per se,* took a stance on taxes. The paper regarded the council's real estate tax proposal as extravagant and unwarranted. Despite arguments that 63 percent of all Hamilton County wage earners lived in municipalities with an earnings tax, that 75-80 percent of all such wage earners paid such a tax somewhere, and that 85 percent of all Forest Parkers in the work force already paid an earnings tax somewhere, the *News* remained intransigently opposed to the income tax. Beyond that, pro-tax elected officials were charged with using a city newsletter to promote pro-tax views, a practice the *News* regarded as of dubious legality. And the paper deplored the mayor's negativism, especially his references to the "bad" developer, local press, and businessmen.[21]

18. Forest Park Council, "Minutes," Vol. V, Aug. 16, 1971, 106–7.
19. *Greenhills-Forest Park Journal,* Oct. 29, 1971.
20. *Forest Park News,* Oct. 22, 1971.
21. *Forest Park News,* Oct. 8 and 22, 1971.

Several candidates centered their campaigns on the tax question. The Forest Park Citizens Committee Against Unfair Taxation, for example, ran a full-page ad in the *News* against both taxes and another full-page ad endorsing White, Heiberg, and Brian Strachan for the council. The text of the latter ad pledged that those three, if elected, would avoid unnecessary taxes while providing economic, efficient, and "adequate" government. A fourth candidate, Fred Lamb, also focused on taxes, declaring his opposition to both proposals and suggesting instead an aggressive campaign of industrial development to broaden the tax base.[22]

As in 1970, however, another sensitive issue lay beneath the question of taxes as a simple economic matter of who would pay most for what. That issue surfaced most clearly in the candidacy of Kristen Heiberg, a veritable symbol of the socio-civic spirit. Heiberg had been president and in 1971 served as chief of the Forest Park Fire Department, which still included volunteers contracted by the city to operate municipal firefighting equipment. The volunteer organization was the very antithesis of the professional, bureaucratic, heavily planned approach to city government outlined in Councilmember Lesick's pro-tax speech. Any threat to the volunteer fire department—and the pro-tax rhetoric certainly sounded like one—threatened the ideals of those who shared Kieffer's vision of the socio-civic community.[23]

The electorate refused to make the hard choice between the property and income tax, voting solidly against both issues, and the returns in the council race strengthened the no-tax mandate. Incumbent Mayor Sullivan, who during the campaign had favored passage of either of the two tax issues, failed to finish among the winners. With 3,000 votes cast, White, Heiberg, and Lamb, in that order, swept the top three slots, while Strachan, in his first council race, finished fourth, just 39 votes behind Lamb.[24]

The new council majority was now confronted with the problem of financing a positive government and a broad range of services, without new taxes of any kind. It could, through efficiency measures, try to squeeze more out of a static budget; or it could expand the city's tax base through rapid commercial and industrial expansion, a policy

22. *Forest Park News,* Oct. 8 and 22, 1971.
23. For Heiberg's credentials as presented in the campaign, see *Forest Park News,* Oct. 8 and 22, 1971.
24. *Forest Park News,* Nov. 19 and Dec. 3, 1971; *Greenhills-Forest Park Journal,* Nov. 12 and Dec. 3, 1971.

FIGURE 9. This view (ca. 1973), northwest along Northland Road, shows part of the Northland Industrial Park (right center foreground), the office park, and Northland Tower (the dark building, taller than its neighbors, in the center of the picture). Reproduced by permission of The Kanter Corporation.

requiring the full and enthusiastic support of The Kanter Corporation. Or it could try both.

Kanter, on the face of it, possessed good reasons for cooperating. His corporation now had a program for Forest Park's development, based on recent assessments of the urbanization process and the nature of the metropolis. The Kanter program was designed to overcome past obstacles to the city's industrial and commercial growth, including the 1950s loss of the Tri-County Shopping Center. A major shopping center still seemed indispensable in making Forest Park a profitable development. Kanter's overall concept had been taking shape for some time, but he described his Grand Design and its rationale in detail shortly after the election.

In January 1972, Kanter released plans for Northland Tower, a $15-million, 52,000-square-foot, six-story office building and office park near the corner of Northland and Waycross (see Figure 9). Expressways, Kanter explained, had popularized suburban office locations. By dispersing the functions of metropolitan central business districts, the trend promised to eliminate big-city rush-hour snarls, relieve the downtown air of pollution, and liberate commuters from parking problems and long walks to their offices. Outlying office parks would be convenient to nearby banks, post offices, restaurants, shopping, and residences. Kanter saw Northland Tower as the anchor for Forest Park's business section and as an integral part of his broader development program. The elements most recently added to that program were the Promenade Shopping Center, then in the advanced planning stage (see Figure 10); and "planned unit development" (PUD), a condominium arrangement which clustered single-family homes and townhouses with apartments surrounded by green space. The city council had recently passed enabling legislation for the PUD idea. Completion of Northland Tower, Promenade Shopping Center, and the PUDs, Kanter noted, would give Forest Park a full range of business, residential, industrial, and commercial development, "creating a total human environment" and permitting people to work and shop in their own general neighborhoods.[25] Kanter's overall concept treated the metropolis, including its biggest city, Cincinnati, as a congeries of economic communities which existed solely to serve the personal (as opposed to the civic) interests of their residents. Therefore the Kanter plan stood as a plausible, pragmatic alternative to the earnings tax.

25. *Cincinnati Enquirer*, Jan. 11, 1972; *Forest Park News*, Jan. 28, 1972.

FIGURE 10. 1972 picture of Promenade Shopping Center at the corner of Winton and Kemper Roads. At the top is I-275, and in the lower right corner is part of the "I" residential section. Reproduced by permission of The Kanter Corporation.

Though Kanter's presentation stressed the virtues of suburban office sites, PUD constituted the critical element in his solution to the local tax dilemma. The PUD concept assumed that office, commercial, and industrial workers would live close to their place of employment, and each unit included parks and greenbelts. The higher population densities generated by PUD would increase real property tax revenues, while reducing the per-capita cost of local government. According to a 1971 estimate, for example, an 80-acre development of single-family homes in Forest Park provided accommodations for 200 families with 350 school-age children and one mile of streets. Such a subdivision cost $198,700 per year in school and city service expenses, but generated only $149,666 in taxes, leaving a deficit of $49,040. An 80-acre PUD, on the other hand, housed 1,000 families with 350 school-age children and one-third mile of streets. The cost for schools and city services came to $206,000, but the development produced $427,600 in taxes, leaving a surplus of $221,000 to reduce the need for other city revenue sources. The PUD's lower proportion of families with children in school comprised the primary difference in the two schemes, although the fewer miles of streets and smaller amount of land required for each family unit were also important.[26]

Kanter's solution to the tax problem in Forest Park required that the city government be willing to go along with the PUD concept and able to keep afloat fiscally until the PUD program could begin to pay off. City officials seemed amenable to the scheme and in 1971 approved one PUD site across from city hall. By 1972, however, their constituents viewed the matter differently.

In winter and spring 1972, Forest Park, Inc., asked the city, under the city's enabling legislation, to rezone an area from single-family to PUD. The request set off an uproar expressing residents' fears about the PUD's effect on property values. The *News* described the planning commission's public hearing on the matter as long, "the best attended meeting in the history of Forest Park," and "emotion packed." In the course of the session, the commission decided to reject the PUD request, and the president of Forest Park, Inc., read a letter withdrawing the proposal. This letter indicated that in the future the company would work with the planning commission and an architect in selecting a PUD site and secure general agreement among the three parties on plans for that site before making a rezoning

26. *Greenhills-Forest Park Journal,* Oct. 1, 1971.

request.[27] Nevertheless, the intensity of feeling at the hearing suggested that it would, at a minimum, take time to persuade the electorate that PUD was a wise solution to the city's fiscal difficulties.

Meanwhile, the new council, with an anti-tax majority, at its first meeting elected Phil White mayor by a 5-2 vote.[28] Succeeding decisions at that meeting, however, came on a 4-3 count, with White, Lamb, Heiberg, and Taylor (called by Dawson the "businessmen's dynasty"), voting against Blackburn, Conklin, and Lesick.

The new majority first packed the Finance Committee with its own people, than tried to cut city costs while encouraging the developer to promote commercial and industrial growth. In March 1972, for example, the council passed an appropriations ordinance which contained no wage increases except a 2 percent hike for two police sergeants; merged the jobs of clerk and finance director; cut funds for a licensed architect to review building plans; and eliminated expenses for the city manager to attend a professional convention. At the same time, Lamb attacked City Manager Alvin Tomb for failing to attract more business and industry to the city. In response, the minority charged that the council's meddling in such administrative matters as enforcement of the building code stemmed from a dangerous "Foolosophy of Government."[29]

As the majority-minority conflict deepened, centering on the city manager, White called a special council meeting to define the problems with the city manager and to discuss legislative and administrative procedures. The city manager himself had felt the need for some specific direction, and for a time after the session manager-council relations improved. In August, however, the majority attempted to change the city charter to permit the council to hire and fire a manager by a simple majority rather than a two-thirds vote. The attempt failed, but White sharply criticized the manager for refusing a Kanter Corporation request to close Mill Road temporarily for sewer construction purposes. Finally, in October 1972, the city manager resigned, effective December 2. He gave no reasons, but Dawson, now writing for the *Greenhills-Forest Park Journal*, suggested that he left "to preserve his sanity" in the face of "pressure . . ., heckling" and "need-

27. *Forest Park News*, Mar. 10, 1972.
28. *Forest Park News*, Dec. 17, 1971.
29. Forest Park Council, "Minutes," Vol. V, Feb. 21, 1972, 165–69; *Forest Park News*, Feb. 25 and March 10 and 24, 1972; *Greenhills-Forest Park Journal*, Jan. 7 and 21, and Feb. 4, 10, and 24, 1972.

ling." Dawson claimed in his column that it seemed "more and more obvious" in 1972 that Forest Park was "being run for the benefit of Kanter and the businessmen."[30]

With his new Grand Design, including PUD, hanging in the balance, Kanter did not need that kind of publicity. In fact, throughout 1972 and into 1973, both Kanter and the city moved slowly and carefully on PUD. Finally, however, in an announcement emphasizing the attractiveness of PUD housing clusters for "families" without children, the planning commission approved another PUD site. The location, a small triangular area east of I-275, toward the northwest boundary of Forest Park, was allowed a maximum density of only seven units per acre.[31]

The planning commission's approval of this second small-scale PUD did little to dispel the sense of crisis surrounding the city's financial condition. The council majority contributed to the anxiety by denying wage increases to city employees and refusing to extend and improve services. The council also refused to engage in long-term fiscal planning, preferring instead to respond to spending pressure with special tax levies. On October 6, 1972, for example, Mayor White reiterated his opposition to new taxes in general but declared his support for a recreation levy scheduled for a vote in November.[32] Two months later the council approved a $250,000 bond issue to build a fire substation in the eastern portion of the city.[33] Although both recreation and fire levies passed easily,[34] neither addressed the question of how to keep the city solvent and functioning satisfactorily until the office park-PUD Grand Design could establish a firm revenue foundation for the city.

At about the same time, Forest Park received distressing news from the county and federal governments. In October 1972, the same month in which White came out for the recreation levy, the Hamilton County Budget Commission announced that in 1973 it would reduce Forest Park's portion of the State Local Government Fund from the

30. *Greenhills-Forest Park Journal,* Apr. 21, Aug. 11 and 25, and Oct. 6, 1972; *Forest Park News,* Apr. 7 and Oct. 6 and 20, 1972.
31. Forest Park Council, "Minutes," Vol. VI, July 3, 1972, 58; *Forest Park News,* Oct. 6, 1972; Jan. 26, Mar. 9, and May 18, 1973.
32. *Forest Park News,* Oct. 20, 1972.
33. *Greenhills-Forest Park Journal,* Jan. 12, 1973. Both issues passed easily. See *Forest Park News,* Nov. 17, 1972; May 18, 1973.
34. *Forest Park News,* Nov. 17, 1972; May 18, 1973.

1972 level of $78,000 to $39,000. Simultaneously, federal officials revealed that in 1973 the city would receive $39,000 in federal revenue sharing money, enough to offset the loss in state money, but not enough to increase the budget. Dawson pointed out that the federal help remained small because of the city's relatively low municipal tax effort; Dawson noted that Greenhills, Woodlawn, and Springdale, all of which assessed an earnings tax, received from Washington $18.60, $18.50, and $10.40 per person respectively, while Forest Park, without an income tax, received a meager $2.60 per capita.[35]

During the last few months of 1972, the state of public affairs in Forest Park looked precarious. Almost everyone [36] recognized the need for more city revenue. The council majority seemed committed to piecemeal financing while, according to the *Greenhills-Forest Park Journal*, a voluble and articulate minority agitated for an earnings tax, condemned the "haphazard approach" of special tax levies for capital improvements, and asked whether a "community which promotes the image of a 'Planned Community' should "actually plan ahead or rely on last minute emergency reactions. . . . "[37] Voter suspicion of PUD, moreover, seemed to have stalled progress on The Kanter Corporation's Grand Design. And the council remained deeply divided while finding itself, after City Manager Tomb's resignation, running a city-manager government without a city manager.

It was in this context that Mayor White made a dramatic announcement. In January 1973, he revealed his decision to become director of industrial and commercial sales and leasing for The Kanter Corporation.[38] On February 5, White resigned as mayor,[39] receiving generous press commendations for his years of public service. The council, in what the *Greenhills-Forest Park Journal* called a "surprising" display of "esprit d'corps" [sic], promptly reorganized. On the night of White's resignation, Conklin, of the pro-tax group, nominated former Council Member Robert Behrendt to fill White's place. Unopposed, Behrendt's candidacy went through unanimously. Then Kris Heiberg, of the no-tax faction, nominated Fred Lamb as mayor, a motion seconded by Loraine Blackburn, a member of the pro-tax

35. *Greenhills-Forest Park Journal*, Oct. 6, 1972; *Forest Park News*, Oct. 20, 1972.
36. *Forest Park News*, Oct. 20, 1972.
37. *Greenhills-Forest Park Journal*, Nov. 10, 1972.
38. *Forest Park News*, Jan. 12, 1973.
39. *Forest Park News*, Jan. 26 and Feb. 9, 1973.

camp. Lamb, too, was elected unanimously. In his acceptance speech, Lamb set as his goals securing a "qualified" city manager and healing the divisions on the council.[40]

White's decision to join Kanter drastically changed the city's political alignment. White, as the chief spokesman and main political organizer of the no-tax forces, could scarcely have reversed his stance in mid-term; he had publicly reaffirmed his position just two months earlier when he supported the recreation levy. But by joining Kanter and resigning as mayor, he opened the way for the dominant remaining political figures to agree on some sort of tax increase. The consensus was advanced when White's council seat was filled with Behrendt rather than Strachan, who as a member of the White-Heiberg no-tax slate had barely missed winning a council seat in 1971. The movement was carried still further when both factions agreed on Lamb. As former chairman of the Charter Commission, the new mayor had established himself beyond doubt as an opponent of "imperial" mayoralty and a proponent of manager-council government. And Lamb's immediate commitment to hire a "qualified" city manager amounted to a virtual endorsement of the sort of professional management likely to produce long-term fiscal planning. Such planning was of necessity predicated upon the ability to estimate with at least a modicum of accuracy the city's long-term income, a task impossible in the absence of a resilient, established tax base.

The February 1973 compromises, in short, implied a clear rejection of *ad hoc* personal government, financed by special tax levies and staffed by "amateurs." All factions now seemed to agree that Forest Park should have an "activist" city government, more concerned with sound management practices and fiscal integrity than with fostering civic spirit in a community of limited liability. If the consensus could be sustained through the November 1973 elections, Forest Park would have turned an important corner in its history and would be ready to decide whether the new style of government should be financed with an earnings tax or a property tax.

The council cleared the first hurdle in May, when it unanimously appointed Michael D. Kadlecik as city manager. Unlike his predecessor, who had been a local resident with an engineering background, Kadlecik bore all the earmarks of a professional public management specialist, including a peripatetic career pattern. A native of Johnson City, New York, he had earned an undergraduate degree in political

40. *Forest Park News*, Feb. 9, 1973; *Greenhills-Forest Park Journal*, Feb. 9, 1973.

science from the University of Maryland and an M.A. in city management from Syracuse University. His previous experience included part-time and summer work in Bowie and Cheverly, Maryland, and posts with local governments in Baltimore County, Maryland, and Council Bluffs, Iowa. Just prior to coming to Forest Park, Kadlecik had been city administrator in La Vista, Nebraska, just south of Omaha, a city with a population of 7,000 and a budget of $1,200,000.[41]

Beginning with Kadlecik's appointment, and continuing through spring and early summer 1973, circumstances conspired to favor the consensus coalition. On May 8, voters approved the $250,000 fifteen-year bond issue for construction of a new Fire Department substation.[42] In June, the council approved a proposal to annex a 103-acre parcel of land known as Wright Farm. The area, northwest of I-275, was owned by The Kanter Corporation and ticketed by Kanter, the planning commission, and the city council for PUD zoning.[43] In July, too, the Cincinnati Reds' premier catcher, Johnny Bench, whom Kanter had hired as consultant to the Forest Park Little League, presided over the opening of the Northland Tower office building. The tower was an important element in what increasingly appeared, despite disagreements over public financing, to be not only The Kanter Corporation's but also the council's Grand Design for Forest Park's future.[44]

By that time, moreover, a crisis involving race buttressed the spreading conviction that a strong, steady tax base and forceful city action were needed in shaping Forest Park's future. In May 1973, a resident of "H" section complained to the council of "apparent" efforts by certain realtors to turn "H" section into an all-black district. Shortly thereafter, an integrated group of concerned citizens circulated a flyer protesting the methods of "unscrupulous" realtors. The group accused these realtors of "steering" blacks to particular districts and using "scare tactics" to frighten whites away from "salt and pepper" neighborhoods. The flyer asked for city assistance in stopping these practices, and 97 percent of those responding to the flyer agreed that the situation demanded council action.[45]

41. *Forest Park News,* May 4, 1973; "Resume," Michael D. Kadlecik, typescript, [1978], LAC Files.

42. *Forest Park News,* May 4 and 18, 1973.

43. *Forest Park News,* June 15, 1973; *Greenhills-Forest Park Journal,* June 15, 1973.

44. *Forest Park News,* June 15 and July 13, 1973.

45. Forest Park Council, "Minutes," Vol. VI, May 7 and June 4, 1973; *Greenhills-Forest Park Journal,* June 15, 1973.

Mayor Lamb responded by appointing a three-person committee, consisting of himself, Conklin, and Lesick, to study the possible goals and duties of a human relations or human resources committee. The mayor expected to appoint either a standing council committee or an officially constituted lay commission to deal with "problem areas," particularly "at this time" the unethical practices of real estate sales personnel.[46]

Then, in mid-July, the council turned its attention to a comprehensive sign ordinance which would ban real estate signs carrying "for sale," "sold," "open house," "new house," "by owner," or other similar notices, except on vacant land or model home sites.[47] A public hearing on the measure "packed" the council chambers,[48] so the Council held a second hearing on September 5, which also drew a large turnout.[49] Both sessions heard a variety of charges, including the assertion that corporations which had once recommended Forest Park as a nice place for new employees to live, now described the city as "not the most desirable community any more." Real estate interests advocated voluntary self-regulation among real estate firms, rather than direct city intervention, as the appropriate solution to sign saturation in some areas of the city.

The council moved cautiously on what was clearly a controversial subject. On September 15, 1973, with an election less than two months away, the council decided unanimously to give the realtors, under council supervision, a chance to try out voluntary regulations. But the council went beyond the sign issue, declaring its belief "in fair housing practices, regardless of race, creed or national origin," and noting that even if voluntary sign control were successful, it alone would not solve "the legal problem of assuring fair housing practices in Forest Park."

With that preamble, Mayor Lamb outlined an ordinance establishing an Advisory Committee on Housing, consisting of seven non-officeholding citizens to investigate a range of "problems," including illegal housing practices and the availability of varied types of housing. The ordinance also prohibited steering and other forms of housing and real estate discrimination. Though the ordinance duplicated

46. Forest Park Council, "Minutes," Vol. VI, June 18, 1973; *Greenhills-Forest Park Journal*, June 29, 1973; *Forest Park News*, July 13, 1973.
47. *Forest Park News*, July 27, 1973.
48. *Forest Park News*, Aug. 10, 1973.
49. Forest Park Council, "Minutes," Vol. VI, Sept. 5, 1973, 227–29; *Greenhills-Forest Park Journal*, Sept. 14, 1973; *Forest Park News*, Sept. 21, 1973.

some state and federal laws, Lamb contended that it would facilitate action on violations by bringing offenders to a local instead of a "downtown" court.[50] The mayor presented the creation of the housing committee as a will-of-council consensus in favor of it, making the ordinance's passage a foregone conclusion, and on November 5, 1973, the day before the council election, it became law.[51]

Two other "crises" erupted before the election, both of which helped turn public opinion in favor of strong local government. In September, the police chief and one patrolman, the second in two months, resigned from the force. In his parting statement, the chief lashed out at the council for its failure to respond to his year-old complaints about heavy turnover in the department, lack of trained officers, improperly maintained equipment, inadequate manpower and equipment, and lagging salaries. Following that blast, a group of residents from "H" section "arrived en masse" in the council chambers "to protest the situation in their neighborhood." They complained about a burned-out house which remained standing and vacant after nine months, and about uncut weeds on empty lots, accumulated trash, rats, empty houses with broken windows, and the absence of street lights.[52] By their account, Forest Park seemed on the verge of acquiring a slum, a frightening prospect for middle-class, white-collar individuals already alarmed over the threatened erection of a black ghetto and the demoralization of the city's police.

As the sense of crisis intensified, the election campaign moved into high gear. Seven candidates ran for five council seats, and all of them came out for positive city government and additional taxes of some kind.[53] Samuel Lasley, an independent making his first race, advocated beefing up the police force, repairing and replacing worn-out police cruisers, adding more street lights and stop signs, curbing speeders, and restricting PUD to one area until its effect on home values, school crowding, and traffic could be evaluated.[54] Brian Strachan, in his second race, flayed the old council for responding too slowly to obvious needs and for encroaching on the city manager's administrative turf. And while continuing to oppose the earnings tax, Strachan admitted that the city required more money, as all depart-

50. *Forest Park News,* Sept. 21 and Oct. 19, 1973.
51. *Forest Park News,* Nov. 16, 1973.
52. *Forest Park News,* Aug. 24, Sept. 21, and Oct. 19, 1973; *Cincinnati Enquirer,* Sept. 18, 1973.
53. *Forest Park News,* June 15, Oct. 19, and Nov. 2, 1973.
54. *Forest Park News,* Oct. 19 and Nov. 2, 1973.

ments faced difficulties similar to those plaguing the police. Richard Metcalfe, another non-incumbent, stressed police needs but also deplored the city's generally low salaries and poor equipment maintenance record.[55]

A slate composed of two incumbents, Blackburn and Conklin, and one newcomer, Alfred A. Mangels, pulled even fewer punches. Blackburn charged that ex-Mayor White and his allies had used misleading tactics to defeat the earnings tax and "take over" the city, which they subsequently drove into financial "crisis." They also, she asserted, had excluded the pro-tax minority from major council committees, harrassed the city manager into resignation, permitted city employee salaries to drop from among the top 25 percent in Hamilton County to the bottom 50 percent, and allowed the Police Department to deteriorate. For all this, she added, the "former mayor" received his "reward" in the form of a job with The Kanter Corporation. As a result, the city, for "a several month period," had "the developer's employee in our Mayor's chair."[56]

The rest of Blackburn's slate embellished her description of the former council majority. Mangels charged that the earnings tax issue never had received a "fair test" before the voters, and claimed that higher taxes were now required merely to maintain current levels of service, not to mention improving or expanding them. Conklin, too, concentrated on the financial "crisis," alleging that the old majority had failed to engage in long-range planning and had ignored the corrosive effect of inflation on a budget financed from a static tax base. Finally, the slate's campaign chairman lauded PUD's high tax yield, adding it would help alleviate the city's woes if that sort of development were supplemented with an earnings tax.[57]

The election produced few surprises. Conklin ran first in the contested races, followed closely by Blackburn and Metcalfe, while Mangels, whose only previous campaign had placed him on the Charter Commission, joined the other three in the winner's circle. Strachan garnered more votes than any other candidate, an impressive showing even though he ran unopposed. The most unexpected result was the defeat of incumbent Herbert Taylor, which violated conventional wisdom about the advantages of incumbency. Dawson

55. *Forest Park News,* Nov. 2, 1973.
56. *Ibid.*
57. *Ibid.*

explained the anomaly as a consequence of Taylor's failure to erase his no-tax image in a period of financial crisis.[58]

The new council expeditiously and unanimously elected Lamb as mayor and Metcalfe as vice-mayor. City Manager Kadlecik, who, except for a September 1973 attempt to patch up the police budget, had remained conspicuously silent on taxes and municipal finances throughout the campaign, now moved into the discussion of the city's fiscal affairs. On November 16, 1973, just ten days after the election and before the new council was officially seated on December 1, Kadlecik unveiled a thirty-page fiscal report projecting insufficient revenue from the current tax base to fund even current personnel and programs through 1979. To restore the city to solvency, he preferred the adoption of an earnings tax because of its "growth potential." But if the council chose a property tax increase, he suggested staged increases of 1.5 mills each in 1974, 1976, and 1978.[59]

Kadlecik's fiscal report scarcely had sunk in when he released his 1974 budget, calling for a 6-percent cost-of-living increase for all employees. He also budgeted for two more police employees and added a full-time mechanic to the city's maintenance crew. Kadlecik suggested abrogating the city's contract with Hamilton County for public health services and hiring a Forest Park health officer with a "construction" and environmental health background.[60] For two months, the council subjected Kadlecik's analysis to intensive study. After "refining the City Manager's suggestions," Mayor Lamb issued a public report in February 1974, explaining the council's view of the city's needs and why those needs should be met.[61] As with the Housing Commission ordinance, Lamb presented the report as a sense-of-council document. Clearly, the council members had achieved important compromises in order to present a united front and persuade the city's varied interest groups to support some kind of tax hike.

The council's report was in two parts. The first laid out needs of "immediate urgency," requiring $177,000 in additional revenue. The police were to receive the lion's share. An initial $55,000 would

58. *Forest Park News*, Nov. 16 and Dec. 14, 1973; *Greenhills-Forest Park Journal*, Oct. 26 and Nov. 9, 1973.

59. *Forest Park News*, Sept. 21 and Nov. 16, 1973.

60. *Forest Park News*, Dec. 1 and 14, 1973.

61. *Forest Park News*, Feb. 8 and March 22, 1974.

increase the force's numbers from fifteen to nineteen, create a "detective and juvenile division to meet the rising trend in burglaries and juvenile related crime," and add a night patrol officer whose canine work in commercial and industrial areas would free other officers for service in residential districts. In addition, the report allotted $19,000 to bring police salaries to the middle of the upper 25 percent of municipal police salaries in Hamilton County; $6,000 to bolster the cruiser fleet; and $23,000 to meet inflationary costs, especially for gasoline and salaries, in the police budget. Police needs alone, therefore, came to $105,000, well over half the cost of the entire minimum needs package.[62]

Three other categories remained. The report allocated $45,000 to cover an impending 1973 deficit; $6,500 to raise the salaries of the building commissioner, public works director, and fire inspectors; and $20,000 to pay for a "modest" street resurfacing program.

That level of expenditure, as Lamb noted, shortchanged the street resurfacing program and ignored both the volunteer firemen's demands for more fire stations and equipment and the complaints of those who deplored the city recreation program's emphasis on organized sports such as league baseball. To meet those shortcomings, the second half of the report set out the price and rationale for "future needs" to cost an additional $70,000. Among these needs were $20,000 for street resurfacing; $30,000 for fire protection; and $20,000 for recreation. The recreation program would provide for that segment of the city's 9,000 young people uninvolved in recreational activities; pay for work on eight undeveloped park areas; start a tot lot program; serve more effectively the "thousands of women . . . isolated in their homes day after day"; and, in general, help make the " 'Park' in Forest Park a reality."[63] Together, the "minimum" and "future" needs added up to $247,000.

The report, so precise to this point, ended on an ambiguous note. Describing as "apparent" the fact that the council must seek additional revenue "to meet even this minimum program of services costing $177,000," the report left open the option of going for the whole package. It also asked citizens to help decide how to raise the necessary money, whether by a "3-mill property tax or an earnings tax." The magnitude of the earnings tax was not specified. Though the

62. *Forest Park News,* Mar. 22, 1974.
63. *Ibid.*

report set a hard "by March" deadline for the council's decision on the 1974 budget, it by no means wedded the council to any particular income or expenditure figure. In the final analysis, it specified neither who would get what, nor at whose expense.[64]

On February 14, 1974, Kadlecik filed two more reports bearing on the city's financial prospects. The first estimated the income from a .5-percent earnings tax at between $193,000 and $213,000, more than enough to cover the $177,000 in "immediate needs." Of the total, moreover, $109,000 would come from "outsiders" working in Forest Park, $79,000 from "natives" working elsewhere, $15,000 from business profits, and $5,000 from "growth."

The second report announced the results of a poll, taken in the single-family residential areas, including duplexes, which surveyed citizen preferences between a 3-mill property tax and an earnings tax. The table showed that 78 percent favored the earnings tax and 13.8 the property tax; 1.1 opposed any tax; and 7.1 displayed no preference. Kadlecik closed by reminding the council that the poll figures merely represented "general trends" and preferences and did not prove that citizens would or would not vote for a tax increase.[65]

Despite Kadlecik's disclaimer, the data encouraged the council. If the projections were even nearly accurate, an earnings tax would both pass and generate enough money to cover the city's "immediate" needs and start on the second priority projects. It would not, of course, yield enough to cover entirely all three items on the "future needs" list. In March the council voted to put a .5-percent earnings tax on the ballot in a special May 1974 election. The council vote, however, was 4 to 3, revealing a split in what to that point had seemed a united front. Three council members had tried unsuccessfully to make the tax expire automatically whenever city income from real estate taxes reached a prescribed dollar level. Dawson identified these three council members as anti-tax advocates who had been supported in 1971 by businessmen, "certain officials" of Union Central, and Kanter employees.[66]

The council split, however, was only one factor casting a pall over the 1974 earnings tax campaign. The terms of the tax proposal, for

64. *Ibid.*
65. Forest Park Council, "Minutes," Vol. VII, Feb. 19, 1974, 8–9; *Greenhills-Forest Park Journal,* Feb. 22, 1974.
66. *Forest Park News,* Mar. 8, 1974; *Greenhills-Forest Park Journal,* Mar. 8, 1974.

example, restricted its use to police and fire protection, street maintenance, deficit elimination, and inflationary expenses.[67] Parks had lost out, eliminating the chance of using "let's make the 'Park' in Forest Park a reality" as a slogan. Street repairs had slipped to second priority level, giving little solace to drivers weary of dodging pot-holes. And the *News*, which had shown signs of "softening" on the tax issue, remained neutral, carrying information on the earnings tax but withholding editorial endorsement.

During the final stages of the campaign, however, three developments strengthened the earnings tax case. First, Brian Strachan, who had run unsuccessfully for council in 1971 on the no-tax slate and successfully in 1973 on a platform opposed to the earnings tax, now emerged as one of the earnings tax's staunchest promoters.[68] Second, the council amended the earnings tax ordinance to terminate on October 1, 1979, and the business community in return agreed not to oppose the measure.[69] Finally, four days before the vote, the *News* came out for the amended tax. Pointing out that all seven council members supported the tax, the paper noted that the Police Department needed bolstering to cope with "juvenile problems," because Forest Park's school enrollment had risen 17.2 percent in three years while its juvenile crime rate had skyrocketed by 61 percent.[70]

On election day, voters approved the earnings tax by the largest majority ever garnered in Forest Park history, 2,379 to 810.[71] This 60 percent margin of victory matched the percentage by which voters had defeated Forest Park's first earnings tax proposal in 1970.

From the outset, supporters of the earnings tax had held a special conception of the kind of positive, professional government Forest Park should have, as well as, by implication, the kind of community Forest Park would inevitably become and the kind of metropolis within which it would exist. The metropolis would be an amalgam of communities, each with a basic infrastructure of municipal services equivalent in kind and quality to those in other communities. Such a metropolis would fit newly-defined individual needs and circumstances, and residential communities would function as interchangeable parts within it. The passage of the income tax in 1974 marked the

67. *Forest Park News*, Mar. 8 and 22, 1974; *Greenhills-Forest Park Journal*, Apr. 5, 1974.
68. *Forest Park News*, Mar. 22 and Apr. 19, 1974.
69. *Greenhills-Forest Park Journal*, Apr. 5, 1974.
70. *Forest Park News*, May 3, 1974.
71. *Forest Park News*, May 17, 1974.

triumph of that conception. Forest Park's new, soundly-financed, professional government saw local community in economic and service, rather than socio-civic, terms. The individual person was to be taken as the basic community unit. And the government's primary goal was not to foster civic, ethnic, religious, neighborhood, or some other form of social cohesion, but rather to provide a convenient, comfortable place for those liberated individuals to move through, or linger within, as their self-defined commitments and life-style choices might determine.

The new conception of Forest Park ran counter to the old notion of the community of limited liability—cohesive, civic-centered, participatory, and essentially voluntaristic—with which Warner-Kanter, the Civic Association, and the Women's Club began Forest Park, and which Kieffer, of all the civic leaders, championed the longest. But in the 1974 earnings tax campaign, they all abandoned the older vision, in their rhetoric as on their ballots. With it, they abandoned the sense of Forest Park either as a unique and "defended" community or as a model for the emulation of others. What emerged was a new consensus about the proper allocation of community responsibilities. The city government would provide a varied array of services. The developer would provide housing and encourage economic growth. Local voluntary organizations would tend to personal and essentially private needs. The growing sense of fiscal emergency seemed, in short, to have healed the divisiveness which had been building around the racial issue and other conflicts. However, differences between the concept of a professional police and the idea of a volunteer fire department, between business and residential interests, and between the developer and the municipal corporation, like the question of race, were real and persisted. In the last quarter of the twentieth century, it remained to be seen if the new Forest Park stood on sufficiently sturdy and durable foundations to contain those deep divisions.

. . . because of the diverse background of its residents [and because] a certain segment of the population enjoy [sic] the benefit of the community but do not contribute their time, energy or revenues in turn, [Forest Park] needs a method of involving its people and organizations in the affairs of the community.
Forest Park Advisory Committee on Housing, 1975

[The K and C's] efforts . . . often turned inward toward its members [sic] psychological and spiritual well being.
JOHN G. FELDMAN,
"Glenmary Council Knights of Columbus, #5675—History," 1975

RACE, CLASS, AND THE COMMUNITY OF ADVOCACY: TURNING INWARD

Forest Park's adoption of the earnings tax was a victory for those who believed that city government should be the exclusive keeper of the civic welfare. That victory stemmed from the recognition of a serious fiscal problem, one which both reflected and veiled deeper disturbances in the city. With the adoption of the earnings tax, city officials could turn their attention to other matters. When they did, however, they found that Forest Parkers in the early 1970s defined their problems in such a way that appropriate responses to those problems transformed the mechanisms by which the city dealt with its internal contradictions and disagreements.

These shifts marked the metamorphosis of Forest Park into a *community of advocacy,* a community of competition for power and scarce resources, a community of distrust and disbelief in established ways and institutions as channels for realizing aspirations or satisfying grievances. It was a fragmented community, turning inward to psychological concerns and to economically motivated anxieties about Forest Park's "deterioration."

In the early 1970s, then, Forest Park's civic morale sagged. It was supported neither by a civic association nor by a steadfast, confident government. And it was undermined by the pressure of voluntary organizations which were parochial, inward-turning, and backward-looking, and whose "civic" activities masked an intensely narrow individualism which placed concern for each person's psychological or material well-being above the welfare of either the city government or the community as a whole. A period of political crisis ensued, as the expectations which instituted a new city charter and earnings tax persisted. But now people sought to use the city government and Forest Park's voluntary associations to protect individual interests. The urge to participate was as strong as ever, but in the early 1970s it took new forms, raised new questions, and viewed familiar issues from new perspectives.

None of this grew out of gross, fundamenal, or sudden changes in the city. To be sure, the population continued to grow rapidly, by 1,000 persons per year between 1970 and 1974. But the city's socioeconomic profile remained unaltered. Data collected in 1972[1] by a team of social scientists from the University of North Carolina at Chapel Hill indicated that Forest Park was still essentially white, middle-class, and white-collar, though its population proved younger, less educated, lower in occupational status and family income, and slightly blacker than other new towns the team surveyed (*see Table I*).[2] But locally no one made that sort of comparison.

Analysis of Forest Park's residential structure, however, reveals the roots of the new mood. By 1974, Forest Park's socioeconomic geography displayed a distinctly split pattern. By that date, the city's built-up portion formed a giant crescent defined by Greenhills on the south, the arcing line of Southland Road around the top, the west corporate limit of Springdale, and I-275 on the north and west (see Figures 11 and 12). Generally speaking (*see Table II*), the cheapest housing lay along the northern perimeter of the crescent in the Birch

1. *Forest Park News,* Nov. 17, 1972.
2. The other ten new towns were Columbia, Maryland; Elk Grove Village, Illinois; Foster City, California; Laguna Niguel, California; Lake Havasu City, Arizona; North Palm Beach, Florida; Reston, Virginia; Sharpstown, Texas; Valencia, California; and Westlake Village, California. Two new towns studied by the team failed to reach the minimum population required for inclusion in the social-structure portion of the research. See *Community Profile–Spring, 1973, Forest Park Ohio,* New Community Development Project, CP Report #3, July 1974, Center for Urban and Regional Studies, Univ. of North Carolina, Chapel Hill, N.C., 2, 13–14.

Table 1. WHO LIVES IN THE COMMUNITY	Forest Park	13 New Communities
Race		
White	91.4	95.7
Black	8.6	3.1
Other	0.0	1.1
Age of Household Head		
Under 40	61.6	49.4
40–54	30.8	32.8
55 or older	7.5	17.7
Household Composition		
Unmarried adult(s), no children	5.2	12.4
Married couple, no children	18.4	26.9
Unmarried adult(s) with child(ren)	3.0	4.3
Married couple with child(ren)	73.4	56.4
Households with child(ren) under 6	39.9	28.1
Households with child(ren) 6–13	49.1	36.5
Households with child(ren) 14–30	28.7	23.5
Education of Household Head		
High school graduate or less	39.6	27.8
Some college or college graduate	39.2	48.1
Graduate or professional training	21.1	24.1
Employment Status of Head and Spouse		
Only household head employed	57.8	56.6
Both head and spouse employed	38.4	32.1
Neither employed	3.8	10.1
Occupation of Household Head		
Professsional or managerial	48.7	59.2
Other white collar	19.1	18.9
Blue collar	32.1	21.9
Family Income in 1972		
Under $10,000	12.8	11.7
$10,000–$14,999	34.6	22.0
$15,000–$24,999	45.0	46.9
$25,000 or more	7.6	19.4

Source: New Community Development Project, "Community Profile—Spring 1973: Forest Park, Ohio" (Chapel Hill: Center for Urban and Regional Studies, Univ. of North Carolina, 1974), 2.

Hill, Forest Ridge, and "F," "G," and "H" sections; each of these had an average housing value between $20,000 and $30,000, while all of the interior subdivisions fell above the $30,000 mark. "B" section, which formed the southeastern foot of the crescent, was an exception

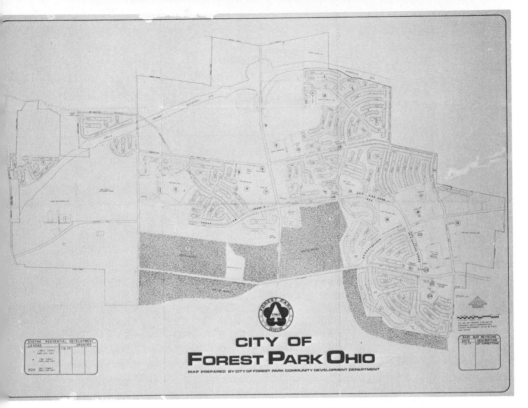

FIGURE 11. Street Map and Informational Guide to the City of Forest Park, Ohio, 1977.

FIGURE 12. Detail from Figure 11. Shows Forest Park's various residential sections, 1977.

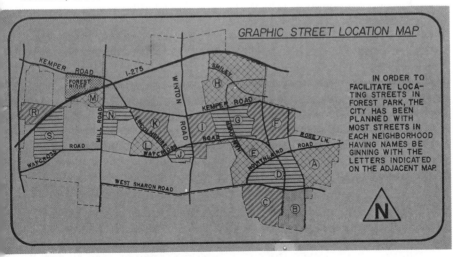

Table II. CHARACTERISTICS OF FOREST PARK NEIGHBORHOODS [1974]

Section	No. of D.U.s	% Black	% Owner occupied	Turn-over*	Value of Housing 1970	1974
B	235	10.1	97.9	6.8	29,350	44,200
West C		0.0	96.4	7.0		
	495[a]				24,070[a]	26,800[a]
C		1.9	95.0	7.4		
D	227	1.8	89.2	9.8	26,050	33,400
E	213	3.6	93.2	5.0	40,810	50,000
East F		10.9	95.1	9.0		
	586[a]				18,770[a]	23,200[a]
West F		18.6	94.7	8.2		
G	389	9.0	95.6	9.1	22,280	24,300
H	924	21.9	98.7	7.7	23,880	27,900
I	204	9.0	97.8	8.9	29.350	35,700
J,K,&L**	590	7.7	98.9	15.1	32,640	35,100
M**	81	8.3	100.0	20.0	25,800	45,000
R	181	10.9	97.4	11.1	21,500	23,500
Forestridge	221	9.5	99.3	2.2	——	24,300
F.P. Apts.	412	9.1	——	30.1	——	——
Vers. Apts.	180	14.3	——	28.1	——	——
Rev. Apts.	95	2.9	——	43.5	——	——
Total City	5023	10.7	82.4	11.5	24,700	30,700

*Turnover=percentage of residents living in the school district less than one year.
**The apparently high turnover in these sections was due to their newness—both were being occupied at the time this table was compiled.
[a]This figure represents the total for both parts of the pertinent section.

Source: David M. Ascher, "Characteristics of Racial Change in Suburban Communities: A Case Study," (Master of Community Planning thesis, Univ. of Cincinnati, 1975), 56.

with its average housing value of $44,200. But 'B' section also contained a population 10.1 percent black, just .6 percent below the city average of 10.7. All the other peripheral subdivisions, moreover, combined their low average housing values with black percentages at or well above the citywide percentage, and "F" and "H" sections, the two outer districts with the highest percentages of black population, also constituted the most densely-built single-family portions of town.

Indeed, in 1974 even the city's three multi-family complexes fell into the general core-periphery pattern. The two with the highest percentage of blacks, the Forest Park (9.1 percent) and Versailles Apartments (14.3 percent), lay on the outer edge of the crescent (see Figures 13 and 14), while the third, Revere Village Apartment (2.9 percent black), was situated toward the interior (Figure 15) across from the "D" section (average housing value, $33,400).[3] The socioeconomic geography of Forest Park, then, fell into a center-periphery pattern suggesting a real territorial division within the city. In contrast with metropolitan cores, the center of Forest Park seemed to be encircled by a poorer and blacker rim. Fear began to spread that "blight" on the periphery might spill over into the interior, inspiring concern about class and race distinctions, and provoking a discussion about steps to thwart the expected spread of this blight.

Among other things, these anxieties helped revive the notion that Forest Park needed some sort of civic association, despite Council Member Blackburn's contention that Forest Parkers had "passed the point where they want 'do it yourself' government," and her "vibrations" to the effect that it "is difficult to get enough . . . volunteers . . . for Scouts, Baseball, Church Groups, P.T.A.s" and other similar organizations, "without getting help to do the everyday city type duties which really can't wait till Saturday or until someone maybe has the time."[4] Predictably, the principal spokesperson for a new civic volunteerism was the venerable *News* editor, Eileen Kieffer. Though she wrote nostalgically about the old Civic Association, with its emphasis on general welfare and public policy, she now called for the establishment of a different kind of group.

Kieffer finally put her ideas into proposal form, and in spring 1971, she called a meeting to assess public interest in her scheme. She began by elaborating her plan. The new organization would center on the question of deterioration. The group's officers should not include elected city officials, but teenagers as well as adults and even non-residents who worked in Forest Park should be eligible for membership. The board of directors should contain a resident of each of the city's neighborhoods. Thus Kieffer introduced the idea of territoriality, which the old Civic Association and village and city governments

3. See *Street Map and Informational Guide to the City of Forest Park, Ohio: A Friendly, Forward Looking City that Cares* (Forest Park, Ohio: City of Forest Park, Community Development Department, 1977); David M. Ascher, "Characteristics of Racial Change in Suburban Communities: A Case Study" (Master of Community Planning thesis, Univ. of Cincinnati, 1975), 56.
4. *Forest Park News*, Dec. 18, 1970.

FIGURE 13. This picture (1973) looks northeast across the Forest Park Apartments (center) toward the Northland Industrial Park (top right). The Forest Park Swim Club is in the center foreground, and the Versailles Apartments stand to its right. Reproduced by permission of The Kanter Corporation.

FIGURE 14. 1972 view south along Southland Road. Shows the Forest Park Apartments (bottom), Sharon Road, the Versailles Apartments (center), and part of the "B" residential section. Reproduced by permission of The Kanter Corporation.

FIGURE 15. In this shot (1974), the Revere Village Apartments line the right side of Northland Road. At the top is part of the "E" section; in the lower right is part of the "D" section. Reproduced by permission of The Kanter Corporation.

184

of the 1960s had tried to suppress as inimical to true community spirit, and which the new city charter itself had skirted by prescribing at-large rather than district election of city council members. Kieffer closed by noting that the nearby communities of Glendale and North College Hill each had a volunteer association which conducted periodic "Ecology Drives" to collect recyclable materials as a means of conserving resources, fighting pollution, and cleaning up the neighborhood.[5]

The initial meeting attracted fifty people, who decided to organize the Forest Park Citizens Forum. In May, the forum's members held an unstructured discussion of master planning, suggesting their uneasiness with the direction of community development. But in June, they decided to leave planning to the city and organized, instead, a Forest Park "Ecology Drive." In July, at its third meeting, the group heard an address by E.E. Johnson, president of Forest Park, Inc., and decided to incorporate to facilitate the handling of funds. By fall 1972, both the ecology drives, one of which netted twelve tons of refuse, and the forum itself, which discussed subjects of personal interest to its members, such as drug abuse among youngsters, seemed well-established institutions. And in October the organization laid plans to start a municipal swimming pool fund from the recycling project profits.[6] The proposal acknowledged both the city's tight budget and the presence in Forest Park of people either unable to afford a private swim club or unwelcome there.

The only other effort to create a civic organization in the 1970s produced an even more narrowly-oriented group. In spring 1970, a steering committee chaired by Philip White set up the Businessmen's Association, ostensibly to advance cooperation, coordination, and communication among the city's business and professional people. City Manager Tomb suggested that a more perfect instrument of civic self-improvement, particularly for fostering business and industrial development, could be established if the association merged with the Citizens Forum. The new group not only rejected that idea but also narrowed its scope from the original intentions. Instead of uniting the city's businessmen and professionals to provide a cohesive business perspective on general civic questions and projects, the group made

5. *Forest Park News*, Mar. 12, 1971.
6. *Forest Park News*, Apr. 9, May 7, May 21, June 18, July 9 and 16, Aug. 13 and 27, and Oct. 8, 1971; Sept. 8 and 22, 1972.

opposition to the earnings tax proposal its most visible activity throughout this period.[7]

Indeed, the most distinctive expression of citywide civic spirit in the early 1970s occurred not in the form of organizations and projects, but in symbolic ceremonial events attempting to create a sense of tradition and of continuity with the past. In 1975, for example, looking forward to the national Bicentennial in 1976, the council appointed a committee to honor citizens for making outstanding contributions to the city. The committee instead developed a plan for producing a community history.[8] The city and The Kanter Corporation, moreover, joined forces to refurbish "Founder's Park," the site of the flagpole monument bearing the dedicatory inscription commemorating the birth of the planned community and honoring the American homeowner. On July 4, 1976, there was a "rededication" ceremony, in which a Forest Park flag was hoisted alongside those of the United States and the Ohio American Revolution Bicentennial Commission.[9] In the same spirit, The Kanter Corporation gave the city a lot containing a giant oak tree thought to be 300 years of age and the most ancient in Hamilton County. Though the tree succumbed to disease shortly thereafter, and vandals tore down all three flags from the Founder's Park pole, the two projects served to remind citizens of their common heritage as Forest Parkers and of the new town's primordial connections to the natural order of things.[10]

Yet neither flag-raisings nor commissioning a community history could conceal the fact that the city's liveliest and most innovative organizational action lay not with civic or special-interest groups, but with a new type of voluntary organization. These new associations ignored social, economic, and civic questions and directed their attention to the psychological problems of their chosen clientele. In fall 1970, for instance, an ecumenical group of religious volunteers called FISH opened a round-the-clock "hotline" telephone number which distraught persons could call for assistance.[11] Shortly thereafter, a newly formed Forest Park Mental Health Advisory Group set up a Mental Health Walk-In Center to deal with alcoholism, behavior

7. *Forest Park News,* July 31, 1970; Forest Park Council, "Minutes," Vol. V, Jan. 17, 1972, 159–60.

8. *Forest Park News,* July 12, 1974; Forest Park Council, "Minutes," Vol. VII, Jan. 6, 1975, 160–61, Apr. 21, 1975, 215.

9. *Forest Park News,* July 23, 1976.

10. *Forest Park News,* Mar. 8, 1974; July 23, 1976.

11. *Forest Park News,* Nov. 6, 1970.

problems, divorce, suicide, and parent-child tensions.[12] And from the late 1960s into the 1970s, a local La Leche League flourished. It promoted the breast feeding of babies, on the grounds that the practice built "a bridge of tolerance, understanding, patience and love" between mother and child which carried over into all other personal relationships.[13]

The perennial concern with teenagers also tended to be defined and treated in psychological terms in the early 1970s. At a Citizen's Forum discussion of drug use among the young, one adult described Forest Park as a "boring community" for adolescents, claiming that local parents destroyed their children's "identities" by treating them like babies and drove them to drugs by denying them the psychological support of holding a job.[14] Some teenagers agreed, arguing that Forest Park had no constructive distractions at all for unemployed young people, since the city had no movie theaters, bowling alleys, youth center, or municipal swimming pool. When one teenager suggested establishing a youth center, the *Forest Park News* curtly dismissed the proposal, recalling the disastrous Cellar experience. Instead, the *News* advocated constructing a city swimming pool.[15] But neither pool nor center materialized. And an entrepreneur who sought to open a pool hall for persons twelve years of age and older ran into stiff resistance from the city council.[16]

The one successful institutional response to the teenage problem in the 1970s stressed a psychological approach. Alateen, an organization for young people whose parents suffered from a drinking problem, was formed in 1973. Recognizing the need for broader teen services, in 1975 a group of adults from the Mental Health Advisory Group organized a Citizens Youth Committee of adults from Forest Park, Greenhills, and Pleasant Run, an unicorporated subdivision immediately northwest of the two municipalities. The Citizens Youth Committee worked to drum up support for a local Youth Services Bureau, citing soaring school suspensions and juvenile delinquency in Greenhills and Forest Park, and the high divorce rate in Pleasant Run. The group proposed an agency to assist "troubled young people" by providing, among other things, "counseling services for

12. *Greenhills-Forest Park Journal*, Dec. 20, 1974.
13. *Forest Park News*, Aug. 28, 1970; July 26, 1974.
14. *Greenhills-Forest Park Journal*, Sept. 8, 1972.
15. *Forest Park News*, July 12 and 24, 1974.
16. Forest Park Council, "Minutes," Vol. VII, May 5, 1975, 226; *Greenhills-Forest Park Journal*, Dec. 19, 1975; *Forest Park News*, Oct. 17, 1975; Jan. 23, 1976.

individuals, groups and families; . . . supportive services to schools, police and community in a mutually positive outreach to youth, without breach of confidentiality . . ."; and "youth advocacy by establishing a mutually positive relationship between the young person and the Youth Services Bureau youth advocate."[17]

Churches also tended now to focus not on general civic issues, but on the special personal needs of individuals and groups, in terms of their stage in human development. The Forest Park Methodist Chapel, whose minister described his edifice as "a tent in the desert," provided accommodations for Alateen.[18] The Winton Forest Church Center, housing both Covenant United Church of Christ and the Episcopal Church of the Holy Spirit, in the early 1970s established a "congregate" home for the elderly on a site originally purchased by Covenant for a church building.[19] But a new Protestant religious group carried farthest the tendency to turn inward. In 1969, eighteen people from the Missionary Bible School in another suburb came to Forest Park to organize the Forest Park Community Church. The name carried a special irony, however, for the group described the institution as "a place . . . to meet with neighbors and friends to worship God, a church dedicated to helping you *individually* [italics added] to know Jesus Christ." Its special emphasis on "Bible study and knowledge in all of its services" apparently struck a responsive chord, for the group more than doubled its membership in two years.[20]

Emphasis on the personal and psychological also characterized the city's Catholic organizations. The parish of St. Matthias the Apostle ran a Parish Center, but the center's programs largely revolved around religion classes rather than civic concerns.[21] In addition, the Glenmary Council Knights of Columbus, chartered in 1965 and housed until 1972 in Springdale and Sharonville, conducted a set of inner-directed activities. Upon moving to Forest Park in 1972, the organization received a special zoning exception to hold senior citizen meetings and classes, dog obedience instruction, and family

17. *Greenhills-Forest Park Journal*, Mar. 9, 1973; *Forest Park News*, Apr. 18, 1975.
18. *Cincinnati Enquirer*, Sept. 27, 1970; *Forest Park News*, Mar. 9, 1973.
19. *Forest Park News*, July 27, 1973; *Greenhills-Forest Park Journal*, Dec. 21, 1973; June 6, 1975. The elderly also attracted the concern of school officials, who gave them free admission to extracurricular events. *The Village Voice*, Oct. 1967; *Forest Park News*, Sept. 24, 1971.
20. *Forest Park News*, July 9, 1971.
21. *Forest Park News*, July 9, 1971.

receptions in its headquarters on Southland Road. In 1973, the city council approved the organization's request to conduct bingo games and secure a liquor license.[22] Two years later, the Knights of Columbus' official historian proudly noted that its "efforts . . . often turned inward toward its members," in an attempt to promote their "psychological and spiritual well being. . . ."[23]

The resort to a psychological, personal, and highly individualistic approach to community problems also influenced the handling of a variety of perennial annoyances. The question of peripatetic dogs, for example, which in the early 1960s seemed a nuisance to be eliminated once and for all by the enactment of a leash law, now seemed a "problem" created by ignorance of the facts of dog life and capable of being solved privately by individuals. The author of a 1970 letter-to-the-editor was amazed, given "all the controversial subjects in the news today—the pill and planned parenthood programs; air pollution and water pollution, dope, protesters, riots, etc., . . . why someone hasn't looked into the problem of the increasing animal population and the causes." Noting that male dogs will always seek out females for breeding purposes, the writer proposed an educational campaign to encourage spaying, kennel breeding, and the use of dog birth control pills to lower the number of wandering canines, reduce the dog population, and relieve the city of what he regarded as unsightly mixed breeds of the "Heinz variety."[24] Another reader, who preferred neutering to spaying, pointed out that dogs roamed for purposes other than breeding, and that dog owners still had children who left fence gates open. This respondent concluded cynically that the "animal problem along with all the other problems of the world are not going to be settled in one day, week, or year, but if everyone . . . would do a little it would help a lot. In other words, everyone should try a little harder to keep their own dogs home,"[25] but also everyone should accept the inevitability of the dog nuisance.

Similarly, in June 1970, Dawson abandoned his decade-long campaign to get public officials and The Kanter Corporation to alleviate the nuisance of drainage ditches in Forest Park. Now he called the

22. *Greenhills-Forest Park Journal,* Feb. 23 and Mar. 9, 1973; *Forest Park News,* Feb. 23, Mar. 9, and Apr. 6, 1973; Forest Park Council, "Minutes," Vol. VI, Feb. 19, 1973, 135; Mar. 5, 1973, 142; May 21, 1973, 179.
23. John G. Feldman, "Glenmary Council Knights of Columbus, #5674—History," typescript, June 1975, LAC Files.
24. *Forest Park News,* Mar. 13, 1970.
25. *Forest Park News,* Mar. 27, 1970.

existence of the ditches, with their threat to person and property, "a permanent fact of life." Instead of treating the problem as a civic issue, Dawson now advised individuals to cement or pipe their ditches to prevent the banks' progressive crumbling.[26]

Another manifestation of inward turning, the rising interest in neighborhood, fed on a new sense of creeping deterioration in the quality of life and the threat of sinking property values. Such matters had, of course, always concerned Forest Park's civic activists. In the past, however, they had treated them as problems slated for ultimate resolution through the planning process and under the benign influence of economic growth and development. Indeed, during the 1950s and 1960s, the dual faith in growth and comprehensive planning had nourished the belief that Forest Park would become a sort of white-collar utopia.

Now, however, Forest Parkers treated the specters of vacant low-cost housing in the Forest Ridge section northwest of I-275, the appearance of blacks, and a drop in residential building activity as problems requiring different solutions. In 1969, those events provided the occasion for the city's first formal expression of local territoriality, the formation of a neighborhood organization in the "K" section. The founding of the Citizens Forum, with its neighborhood and ecological orientations, followed quickly.

The number of neighborhood organizations multiplied steadily until the *Greenhills-Forest Park Journal* in 1975 pronounced it a "movement."[27] That year, too, the city council's Advisory Committee on Housing made a set of recommendations reflecting the new concern with psychological and economic values. In discussing deterioration in the quality of life, local commentators, neighborhood leaders, and city officials seldom if ever referred directly to class and race. Instead, they focused on how individuals created and could remedy Forest Park's environmental disarray.

From 1969 onward, Forest Parkers besieged city officials with complaints about individual behavior deemed likely to undermine property values. The mayor, in 1970, promised one group of offended citizens that he would watch closely the residence of a man who allegedly was operating a private detective agency in his home, in

26. *Greenhills-Forest Park Journal*, June 11, 1970; *Forest Park News*, Apr. 20, 1973.

27. *Greenhills-Forest Park Journal*, June 27, 1975. Apparently, all Forest Park's neighborhood organizations were integrated. Robert Wildermuth and Robert Rhein to author, interview, Mar. 26, 1980; Charles Dawson to author, interview, Apr. 1, 1980.

violation of an ordinance which prohibited persons from conducting businesses in their houses.[28] The Zoning Board of Appeals reluctantly granted blanket approval to all homeowners who had converted their carports or garages into extra rooms, but simultaneously announced an absolute ban on the practice in the future.[29] The council banned boats, trailers, and campers from driveways and front yards because, as the *Forest Park News* put it, "No one wants our city to look like a trailer court."[30]

Gradually, the agenda of anxieties about the deteriorating quality of life lengthened, and concern about individual behavior mounted. Police investigating a 1970 report about three families living in one house in the F section found, instead, one family with three grown children. A short time later, when a citizen complained that "general housekeeping" needed to be done in the "F" section, police also checked on violations of the junk ordinance and health regulations, in an effort to get offenders to take "pride in their property" and prevent the development of "slums and downgrading of investments."[31] In summer 1971, Kemper Road residents complained of speeders, trash-littered yards, empty houses, rats, and poor drainage in a new subdivision in the western part of the city. Shortly thereafter, a rumor spread that a builder was planning to erect government-subsidized homes in the area.[32] A year later, the council fretted over charges that residents of some single-family homes were taking in boarders. The following fall, an ordinance was adopted prohibiting the storage of junk or junked cars on private premises.[33]

When Forest Park residents thus exhibited lifestyles deviating from the white-collar norm, public reports seldom identified the address or neighborhood of the offenders. Nevertheless, the "F" section and the subdivisions west of I-275 attracted the most attention. By spring 1973, the Birch Hill or "R" section, west of I-275, ranked as the most distressing neighborhood in the area, and forces outside that neighborhood soon mobilized its residents into yet another neighborhood organization.

In March 1973, The Kanter Corporation donated four Birch Hill

28. *Forest Park News*, Oct. 23, 1970.
29. *Forest Park News*, June 19, 1970.
30. *Forest Park News*, July 31, 1970.
31. Forest Park Council, "Minutes," Vol. IV, Feb. 16, 1970, 166; May 18, 1970, 189; *Forest Park News*, May 22, 1970.
32. *Greenhills-Forest Park Journal*, May 14, 1971; *Forest Park News*, Aug. 25, 1972; Forest Park Council, "Minutes," Vol. VI, Feb. 5, 1973, 131.
33. Forest Park Council, "Minutes," Vol. VII, Feb. 4, 1974, 1; Nov. 4, 1974, 134.

lots and offered to lease four additional acres there for $1 per year, for the city to groom into a park. When municipal officials moved slowly in improving the land, Birch Hill residents responded with protest demonstrations, a new mode of complaint in Forest Park. In July, they packed the council chambers, "infuriated" that a previous Recreation Commission meeting had ignored their questions about the delay, and demanded that recreational facilities be provided immediately. *The Forest Park News* explained a few days later that Birch Hill's peculiar location accounted for the city's neglect of its recreational needs, and reported that work had begun on the park.[34]

Birch Hill dropped out of the news until the following spring, when the question of race inspired its residents to move from protest to organization. In March 1974, the Advisory Committee on Housing turned up evidence that realtors operating in Birch Hill might be steering blacks to that subdivision.[35] While the committee gathered evidence on the distribution of blacks within Forest Park and related real estate practices, one of the committee's members, who also lived in Birch Hill, organized the neighborhood. In April, in a story which did not mention the racial question, the *Forest Park News* announced that the area, often referred to by its inhabitants as "a 'suburb' of Forest Park" because it had been "isolated from the mainstream of Forest Park activities by I-275," now possessed its own Civic Association. This organization, the story said, aimed to "have everyone involved, politically and socially, in their community, to provide a vehicle for communications of all sorts and to make Birch Hill (R Section) in particular and Forest Park in general a better place in which to live."[36] The implied identification of Birch Hill as Forest Park's first slum, Birch Hill's potential for becoming a black ghetto, and the organized efforts of its residents to shore up their property values, drew attention to Forest Ridge, another subdivision west of I-275.

Though Forest Ridge was a relatively new development constructed in two bursts of activity, in 1969–1970 and 1972–1973, by 1974 it had already become a veritable instant slum. The first set of houses sold slowly, and as their builder lapsed into bankruptcy, the

34. *Forest Park News*, July 13, 1973.
35. Forest Park Advisory Committee on Housing, "Minutes," Mar. 7 and 14, 1974, files of the Forest Park Advisory Committee on Housing, Office of the City Manager, Forest Park Municipal Building.
36. Forest Park Council, "Minutes," Vol. VI, March 5, 1973, 137; *Forest Park News*, July 13, 1973.

second set, constructed under the federal FHA-235 home subsidy program, went up. No one, apparently, questioned the wisdom of erecting subsidized low-cost housing in an already troubled area. So by 1974, the average value of houses in Forest Ridge stood at $24,300, just a shade above the figure for Birch Hill, $23,500.

Those figures placed Birch Hill and Forest Ridge among the six of Forest Park's fourteen subdivisions (see Figure 12) in which the average value of houses fell below $30,000. Three others (*see Table II*), the "F," "G," and "H" sections, lay just across I-275 in the northeast quadrant of the city and reported 1974 average house values of $23,500, $24,300, and $27,900 respectively. All five of these sections shared one other characteristic. Each contained a black population between 10 and 22 percent of the total. In contrast, the venerable "C" section in the city's southeast corner, with an average house value of $26,800, in 1974 reported a black population of just 2 percent.[37]

Forest Ridge's isolation, relative poverty, comparatively large black population, and proximity to Birch Hill made it a likely target of concern for the Advisory Committee on Housing, which itself was an integrated body. In March 1974, while touring Birch Hill, the committee looked Forest Ridge over, too, and turned up a long list of health and housing code violations.[38] Yet in the spring and summer, the committee concentrated on the "F," "G," and "H" sections, the first two of which, with populations nearly 20 percent black, lay closer to the heart of Forest Park and also seemed in more imminent danger of going completely black.

Forest Ridge, however, refused to be ignored. In mid-August, an angry resident presented the city Council with a list of derelict houses on streets within the subdivision. Describing the houses as "boarded up and in general disrepair," he recommended that the city tear them down, because they endangered the health and welfare of Forest Ridge residents, especially children. The mayor responded by asking the city manager to investigate the possibility of securing federal funds to "rehabilitate" that area of town.[40] This was the first proposal for urban renewal under federal auspices ever considered by the

---

37. Kadlecik to author, July 30, 1976; Ascher, "Characteristics of Racial Change," 56.
38. Forest Park Advisory Housing Committee, "Minutes," Mar. 27, 1974.
39. *Ibid.*, June 20 and 27, July 12 and 25, and Aug. 8 and 9, 1974.
40. Forest Park Council, "Minutes," Vol. VII, Aug. 19, 1974, 96–97.

council. In the next three weeks, the mayor and other council members met with Forest Ridge residents, conferred with Congressman Willis Gradison, Jr., held a public hearing on the Forest Ridge problem, and heard a frustrating report from City Manager Kadlecik on the abandoned buildings and what might be done about them. Owners of many vacant houses, Kadlecik noted, could not be found and therefore could not be served with citations for housing and health code violations. FHA repossession procedures for federally-subsidized houses could take up to a year before the FHA would begin deciding what course to pursue with a given structure.[41]

At that point, Forest Ridge joined Birch Hill and the other three sections with growing black populations as a top-priority problem in Forest Park. Throughout fall 1974, Forest Ridge residents besieged the council with complaints about vandalism, careless driving, curfew violations, lack of bus service, lack of recreation facilities, the failure of parents to discipline their children, and the dirt and debris which littered the area.[42] By October and November, Forest Ridge residents had organized a teen group with forty-one members, which wanted a swimming pool and a teen center; a Women's Club, which sponsored a clean-up day and planned a spring festival featuring bingo, a dance, and block parties with craft booths; and a Forest Ridge Civic Association.[43]

Forest Ridge's neighborhood organization elicited the admiration of the *Greenhills-Forest Park Journal,* which noted that the crisis had made Forest Ridge "the most closely-knit and cooperative" neighborhood in Forest Park. Its "community spirit," the paper said, was "the most exciting and gratifying development we have seen here in many years."[44] Forest Ridge's organization, and the set of concerns which produced it, had a ripple effect. The Valley View Civic Association was set up in 1975 to express to the city council the views of "B" section, which was one of the three wealthiest districts in Forest Park in terms of housing values, and one of the six districts with a 1974 black population of 10 percent or more. The Bellbrook Civic Association, in turn, was established in 1976 to speak for a new

41. Forest Park Council, "Minutes," Sept. 3, 1974, 102–3; *Forest Park News,* Sept. 20, 1974.

42. Forest Park Council, "Minutes," Vol. VII, Oct. 7, 1974, 119; *Forest Park News,* Nov. 1, 1974.

43. *Forest Park News,* Oct. 18, 1974; Jan. 24, 1975.

44. *Greenhills-Forest Park Journal,* Oct. 11 and 25, 1974.

subdivision directly across from I-275 from Forest Ridge.[45] With this group's founding, the outer edge of the Forest Park crescent was completely lined with neighborhood organizations. The movement also helped institutionalize city council "rap" sessions which came to be held regularly with citizens of each of the city's neighborhoods.[46]

Clearly, the 1974 excitement over Birch Hill and Forest Ridge, and the consequent interest in neighborhood organization, forced public officials and the press to think of Forest Park as a set of neighborhood fragments and to ponder the consequences of that view. That way of thinking broke sharply with the 1950s and 1960s' conception. Then most civic leaders, however they might have differed otherwise, had assumed that a general sense of community existed and had claimed the ability to forge a consensus about which particular interests must sacrifice in order to advance the public good. Now the city seemed about to break apart into a collection of neighborhoods, each represented by a "civic" association advocating local over citywide concerns and defensively resistant to compromise.

In reviewing the situation, the city's leaders decided that it was the issue of race which contributed more than any other single factor to the peculiar configuration of the 1974 crisis. Since each of Forest Park's neighborhoods and its neighborhood organizations contained at least some blacks, the problem was not residential integration, however. Rather it was the tendency toward uneven integration—the threat of creeping ghettoization, beginning in the outer and poorer subdivisions and spreading into the inner and more prosperous ones. That was "blight." And the persistence of the question of race in that form generated suspicion and fear in *all* of Forest Park's neighborhoods, and created neighborhood defensiveness and divisiveness which threatened to paralyze the political process at a critical juncture in the history of the city and the metropolis.

Throughout 1974 and 1975, the Advisory Committee on Housing searched for a strategy to stop the process of ghettoization in the city. Encouragement of neighborhood organizations, though never officially adopted as policy, constituted one part of the design. The committee continued to examine real estate practices for evidence of

45. *Forest Park News,* June 27 and July 25, 1975; *Greenhills-Forest Park Journal,* June 25, 1975; *Forest Park News,* July 23, 1976.
46. *Forest Park News,* Feb. 21, Mar. 7, and Nov. 14, 1975; Forest Park Council, "Minutes," Vol. VII, Dec. 2, 1974, 145; Mar. 3, 1975, 195; Mar. 17, 1975, 203.

block-busting, steering, and violations of the voluntary sign ban. It wrote to the Cincinnati Board of Realtors describing Forest Park's fair housing ordinance. And it also considered, but never approved, a proposal to write to major firms in the Cincinnati area, urging them not to steer new personnel away from Forest Park.

The race issue also fed the fear of metropolitanism latent in Forest Park. In 1974, for example, the housing committee recommended that the city council oppose a proposition tendered by OKI, a metropolitan regional planning authority. The OKI proposal urged that housing for the poor, aged, and handicapped be dispersed across the metropolitan area. Arguing that the policy would "overwhelm" Forest Park with low-income families, the housing committee suggested building new middle-income housing in the core city and inner suburbs of the metropolitan area and upgrading what already existed there. Then, poor families could move into the existing stock of lower-middle-income housing, as the middle-income families moved into the new structures. This proposal might have mitigated metropolitan housing problems, but it also would have preserved the racial and economic segregation traditional in the metropolis. At the same time, the committee urged OKI to find ways of locating industry in rural and semi-rural locations, thereby moving jobs even farther from the older and cheaper housing of the inner regions of the metropolitan area. The committee further recommended that any regional housing plan be implemented simultaneously in all communities.[47]

These activities and positions may seem conventional enough. But the longer the committee grappled with the issues of race, housing, and blight, the more drastic the proposed remedies became. Late in June 1974, one committee member advocated a "crackdown" on loiterers, speeders, and people who failed to mow their grass. One citizen suggested "monitoring" the behavior of all *new* residents of the city. The committee also considered barring all FHA financing as well as the construction of any house costing less than $40,000. Another proposal would have broken The Kanter Corporation's land monopoly by having the city buy all vacant land through condemnation proceedings and then sell it to other builders and developers. While collecting all these ideas, the committee decided to survey new

47. Forest Park Council, "Minutes," Vol. VII, Mar. 4, 1974, 17; *Forest Park News,* Mar. 27, 1974; Forest Park Advisory Committee on Housing, "Minutes," Feb. 21, Mar. 14 and 22, May 16, and June 2 and 6, 1974.

homeowners in Forest Park to establish a profile of incoming residents. The survey revealed that the black movement into Forest Park was not, as some suspected, an "invasion" from the nearby suburbs of Hollydale, Lincoln Heights, and Woodlawn, but that it originated instead in Cincinnati and places outside the metropolis.[48]

Finally, in spring 1975, the Advisory Committee on Housing issued its first report, with a set of recommendations for council action. The report contained several not entirely consistent parts, and it viewed the integration of Forest Park as both desirable and a problem. The aim of the report was to suggest a strategy to permit the integration of Forest Park while arresting the development and spread of black ghettos. It contained recommendations for social, physical, and economic programs. The recommendations drew on an analysis comparing Forest Park's housing and socioeconomic profile with that of other less-integrated nearby communities, correlating the race of Forest Park residents with their previous place of residence, and listing by subdivision the average price of all houses sold in Forest Park between August and October 1974.

Yet the most important part of the report was an analysis of "the process of integration."[49] The analysis rested upon two very important implicit assumptions. First, Forest Park's integration was seen as a local event, not as a consequence of a metropolitan process taking place over time, within the changing framework of the national system of cities. Second, the analysis posited as a norm a pattern of residential segregation in American metropolitan areas by race, religion, nationality, culture, and wealth—a norm compared to which an integrated Forest Park seemed an anomaly.[50] Both those assumptions suggested the appropriateness of a local rather than a metropolitan or national solution to the problem. They also considered the integration

48. *Ibid.*, Nov. 14, 1974; Ascher, "Characteristics of Racial Change," 46.

49. Forest Park Advisory Committee on Housing, "Report on Housing Conditions," typescript, 1975, 1–10, 18, files of the Forest Park Advisory Committee on Housing.

50. There is a growing body of new literature in the field of history which suggests that, except where the question of race is involved, the "process of integration" of American urban residential neighborhoods has not been characterized by the formation of stable neighborhoods segregated by religion, nationality, or wealth. See, e.g., Humbert S. Nelli, *The Italians in Chicago, 1880–1930: A Study in Ethnic Mobility* (New York: Oxford Univ. Press, 1970); Howard P. Chudacoff, *Mobile Americans: Residential and Social Mobility in Omaha, 1880–1920* (New York: Oxford Univ. Press, 1972); Kenneth L. Kusmer, *A Ghetto Takes Shape: Black Cleveland, 1870–1930* (Urbana: Univ. of Illinois Press, 1976); Thomas Kesner, *The Golden Door: Italian and Jewish Immigrant Mobility in New York City, 1880–1915* (New York: Oxford Univ. Press, 1977); James W. Sanders, *The Education of an Urban Minority: Catholics in Chicago, 1833–1965* (New

of any segment of the metropolis as a prelude to its segregation. Thus, these two assumptions help explain why the discussion of residential integration in Forest Park took on a tone of beleaguerment over inevitability postponed.

These same assumptions also dictated the procedures by which the committee selected and arranged its data, and the methodology in turn determined the character of its recommendations. The recommendations rested upon a conclusion that the behavior of individuals in "stable" white communities, when confronted with the question of race, differed from the behavior of individuals in "unstable" white communities in that circumstance.[51]

Although the report itself contained no quantitative evidence on the point, the commmittee concluded that Forest Park differed from its less-integrated neighboring suburbs chiefly in being "unstable," i.e., in containing a "relatively large percentage of transients" who moved quickly through the city because of job transfers and therefore failed to sink roots in the place.[52] This apparent instability, combined with the city's growing stock of sub-$30,000 housing and the availability of FHA financing,[53] made Forest Park exceptionally susceptible to an accelerating cycle of deterioration.

Interestingly, the report placed the blame for that cycle on the shoulders of individual homeowners. The cycle began when people unaccustomed to homeownership deferred maintenance and parked cars and campers in their yards. Then came integration; a stage of panic selling, encouraged by unscrupulous real estate operators; and the erosion of the city's attractiveness to middle- and upper-middle-class white-collar employees. Ultimately the afflicted area emerged as a low-income, black community. The committee recommended a strategy to strike at the major elements in the crisis of stability. Assuming that "communities compete for top-notch citizens,"[54] the committee suggested steps to attract "quality" residents who, by definition, would take pride in their homes and act in ways certain to

York: Oxford Univ. Press, 1977); Bruce Stave, "A Conversation with Richard C. Wade," *Journal of Urban History,* Vol. 3, No. 2 (February 1977), 229–31; Thomas Lee Philpott, *The Slum and the Ghetto: Neighborhood Deterioration and Middle Class Reform, Chicago, 1880–1930* (New York: Oxford Univ. Press, 1978).

51. Forest Park Advisory Committee on Housing, "Report on Housing Conditions," 4–5.

52. *Ibid.,* 7.

53. *Ibid.,* 9.

54. *Ibid.,* 11.

stop the cycle of deterioration. A program was also advanced to improve the behavior of those who ranked as somewhat less than "top-notch citizens."

One group of proposals affected The Kanter Corporation. The committee, for example, wanted larger lot sizes, more single-family housing $50,000 and up, an examination of the possibility of breaking up the corporation's land monopoly, and a minimum housing standards ordinance.[55] With the possible exception of the last item, all these ideas ran directly counter to the developer's plans for higher-density residential construction in the city's remaining vacant housing tracts.

Another set of proposals was addressed to city officials. The committee asked for a "balanced recreation program and community activities for all age groups," including "activities besides organized sports leagues." But this was one of the few "civic" recommendations; most of the suggestions dealt with individual behavior. For example, the anti-litter ordinance in particular and all local laws in general should be "strictly" enforced. Laws should be passed prohibiting parking vehicles anywhere but on streets or driveways, banning real estate signs, punishing realtors for "utilizing unprofessional methods," and outlawing loitering on public or commercial property. Home-improvement drives and paint-up-and-clean-up campaigns should be introduced.[56]

The third set of proposals was aimed at the city's voluntary organizations and the citizens themselves. It argued that "because of the diverse background of its residents" and because "a certain segment of population enjoy [sic] the benefit of the community but do not contribute their time, energy or resources in turn," the city "needs a method of involving its people and organizations in the affairs of the community." Designed explicitly "to instill a community spirit in Forest Park," these recommendations called for organizing not one citywide civic group, but rather "street and section groups." Local businesses were encouraged "to identify with, strengthen pride in," and promote Forest Park, in magazine articles, advertisements, letters to industries, and brochures.[57]

But that was not all. The committee wanted the council to hire public relations professionals to promote Forest Park through a

55. *Ibid.*, 19–20.
56. *Ibid.*, 19–20.
57. *Ibid.*, 19–20.

"civic communications program," complete with all the "media elements which will provide a well balanced community, social, physical, and economic growth image."[58] The committee obviously placed great stock in its image-building civic communications proposal. It placed the recommendation at the top of its list and took seven pages of a twenty-five-page report to describe it. The layout included organizational and flow charts and a thirty-item list of things that might be done to polish the city's image, including personal visits to service groups to deliver the "Forest Park Identification Pitch."[59] The primary target for this extraordinary barrage, however, was not the outside world, but residents of the city themselves. And the key to the system was establishing a city-operated Forest Park Community Information Bureau. The committee grounded this proposal in public relations theory, expressed in psychological jargon:

> To build pride and respect in a community is not an easy task. . . . The city government should provide a community information bureau that provides support and service to all good features and promotes them to the fullest through all segments of our community. . . . *Yes, we must realize the importance of Public Relations upon our community, because Forest Park is built upon the composite of each individual's feelings created from every visual and sound impression.* These . . . communicate a message . . . that stimulate and eventually motivate [sic] our citizens to some form of action. This action can be positive or negative.[60]

Clearly, the committee expected a positive reaction to both its public relations program and its other proposals. The mayor, for one, liked the report, and he challenged other suburban municipalities to set up Advisory Committees on Housing.[61] The report's adoption in Forest Park, however, depended on the response of other city officials, politicians, the developer, voluntary organizations, homeowners, and voters. And that response in turn hinged on whether these groups—or some combination of them—thought there was a crisis sufficiently grave to warrant the kind of action the committee suggested.

The Advisory Committee on Housing report may have established some facts, but by itself it could not break the city's paralysis. The words *neighborhood, community,* and *civic,* which had seemed synonymous and compatible before, now struck a dissonant chord. It

58. *Ibid.,* 19.
59. *Ibid.,* 14.
60. *Ibid.,* 11.

was difficult in the 1970s to conceive of Forest Park as a single neighborhood pervaded with a community spirit compelling enough to sustain civic ideals and action in the public interest. Instead, the city now seemed to, and indeed did, function as a collection of individuals, neighborhoods, quasi-public voluntary organizations, and private interest groups, whose interaction failed to generate a strong feeling for the civic welfare. These associations seldom took the civic ideal as their point of departure in defining and attacking problems. Rather they stressed individuals' economic and psychological motives for, and their benefits from, participation. Even the Advisory Committee on Housing, one of the city's most self-consciously civic groups, made a series of extremely divisive recommendations—recommendations which antagonized the developer, encouraged the formation of neighborhood organizations, and advocated the manipulation of individual psyches through the magic of imagery—as a means of handling "blight" and "integration." To be sure, a form of community existed in Forest Park in 1974, but it was a community of advocacy, a collection of inward-turning individuals and groups unable or unwilling to cooperate to promote the civic welfare.

Yet the crisis, which the housing committee defined as the overly rapid "integration" of Forest Park, persisted. In spring 1975, the mayor announced that the city's blacks now comprised over 12 percent of the total population, up from 2.9 percent in 1970. In reaction, the council banned the display of real estate signs, the first such ordinance enacted in Hamilton County, and a step which precipitated a hot exchange of letters in local papers.[62] Nonetheless, a housing committee survey indicated that 30 percent of all houses sold in the city the following year had gone to minority buyers. And throughout 1975 and 1976, the committee heard reports about, and sought to curb, unethical practices by realtors.[63]

At the opening of the last quarter of the twentieth century, then, it remained to be seen whether "blight" and "integration" would unite Forest Park and spark a revival of civic spirit, or continue to fragment the city into defensive advocacy groups. The "problem" had been

61. Forest Park Council, "Minutes," Vol. VII, Apr. 7, 1975, 210.
62. *Greenhills-Forest Park Journal,* Apr. 18, 1975; May 2, 1975; *Forest Park News,* Apr. 19 and May 2 and 16, 1975.
63. Forest Park Advisory Housing Committee, "Minutes," July 31 and Sept. 18, 1975; Mar. 4, May 20, and June 17, 1976; *Forest Park News,* July 23, 1976.

defined as early as 1969, but, as of spring 1975, the city government's only major policy response had been the adoption of an ordinance banning real estate signs. The Advisory Committee on Housing, to be sure, had filed its report, but those recommendations were at odds with the master plan, the character and practice of city government, and the developer's design for the city's future. And the city's voluntary organizations seemed unwilling even to discuss the issues of race and class in the framework of a genuinely public policy.

I don't intend to build an Indian Hill.
JOSEPH KANTER, August 1976

*The intent behind the establishment of the
position of Director of Community
Development is to provide professional
planning advice from a person who knows what
the citizens . . . want and who is accountable to
their elected officials.*
FOREST PARK CITY MANAGER
MICHAEL KADLECIK, August 1974

POLITICS AND PLANNING
IN THE COMMUNITY OF ADVOCACY:
STARTING OVER, 1974–1976

The simultaneous "integration" and discovery of blight in Forest
Park reduced the willingness of some of its civic and political leaders
to carry on the city's tradition of planning systematically and comprehensively for a balanced model community of work, residence,
and leisure. They seemed tempted now by the vision of Forest Park as
a conventional bedroom suburb, a static vision which saw Forest
Park as a place with housing sufficiently high-priced to insure a
homogeneous upper-middle-class population, and a vision which
eliminated any commercial or industrial development which might
jeopardize that dream. For different reasons, both Kanter and City
Manager Michael Kadlecik resisted that vision. But both also wanted
to give the city, as it entered the last quarter of the twentieth century, a
new vision of its future.

As we have seen, Kanter took the first step in 1972 when he
proposed his corporation's Grand Design. That design promised residents a "total human environment," the city fiscal solvency, and the
developer a profit, in a mixed development strategy calling for industrial and office parks, additional commercial facilities, and extensive
use of the PUD residential concept. Kanter's scheme seemed both

flexible and pragmatic. Given soaring costs for construction, financing, energy, and municipal services and utilities, the plan provided a neat way to keep Forest Park viable economically. If the rate of economic growth and metropolitan sprawl should decline in the face of inflation and energy shortages, moreover, the Grand Design could accommodate a less mobile and more diverse population than the transient professionals who, oriented toward single-family homes, had formed Forest Park's foundation. Kanter's proposal made sense demographically, too. As population growth approached the zero mark and the baby-boom generation moved toward middle age, the demand for single-family homes in which young adults could rear children seemed likely to diminish.

Such thinking, coupled with the dictum that the cost of government should be minimized, appealed to a broad range of urbanologists in the early and middle 1970s. Mayor Pete Wilson of San Diego used it to justify his program to "densify" the city and discourage "leapfrog" development scattering residential projects beyond the range of existing municipal services.[1] Philip Klutznick used the rationale in the 1970s to sell Chicago 21 Corporation's grandiose South Loop New Town in the abandoned railroad yards just south of Chicago's central business district.[2] Such thinking so appealed to the University of North Carolina research team studying new towns that it recommended increased use of PUD in new communities.[3] And Cincinnati area builders and planners, including Orville Brown, executive secretary of the Home Builders Association of Greater Cincinnati, also found it compelling; but "the public," Brown felt, associated PUD's clustered housing with "cheap housing," assumed that the PUDs attracted "cheap people," and regarded apartment dwellers as "second class citizens, or something."[4]

Though Brown viewed the general resistance to PUD as irrational, suspicion of high-density housing had deep roots in American urban life. The apotheosis of the homeowner as the archetypical American began in the late nineteenth century, when the advent of rapid mass transit set off the country's first wave of urban sprawl. It became possible for even the working class to escape the incredibly congested

1. George F. Will, "New Voice for the GOP," *Cincinnati Post and Times-Star*, Mar. 1, 1977.
2. Jerry C. Davis, "Wrong Side of the Tracks," *Chicago Sun-Times*, Jan. 16, 1977.
3. *Forest Park News*, June 14, 1974.
4. Glenn Williams, "Land Use Plans: Whose Interest is Best Interest," *Cincinnati Enquirer*, Aug. 22, 1976.

"walking city" residential districts built in the nineteenth century and move to a modest home on the city's cool green rim.[5] In the 1920s, the automobile's growing popularity fortified the view that the single-family home was a sign of success. And after the Depression and World War II, the baby boom and vast metropolitan explosion made the acquisition of a house, a yard, and a few trees a "given" article of the national faith. By that time, in fact, the single-family home had been defined as the norm, while high-density apartment living was seen as characteristic of "abnormal" groups, such as young singles, married couples without children, older people whose children had left home to take up a single-family home of their own, the poor, and colored minorities.

Once established, moreover, the characterization of single-family and multi-family houses as "normal" and "abnormal" helped to segregate low-density single-family areas from high-density apartment areas. By the 1950s, high-density housing came to be identified with "the city" and "urban," and low-density housing with "suburbia" and "metropolitan." This identification was engraved in the federal Housing Act of 1949, which set as a national goal "a decent home and a suitable living environment for every American family."[6] In this socio-geographical and ideological context, PUD seemed odd because it "mixed" groups which were perceived as separate in lifestyle and culture and which therefore should be segregated spatially.

Despite the public uneasiness about PUD, however, The Kanter Corporation pushed ahead with its Grand Design. City officials, lured by the prospect of municipal solvency, for the most part went along. Indeed, by spring 1974, when Kanter asked for a shopping center and PUD north of I-275 at Kemper and Mill Roads, the Forest Park zoning code accommodated all elements of Kanter's Grand Design. One PUD, across from the municipal building, had already received the council's blessing. But this new one ran into stiff opposition.

During the public hearing on the Kemper-Mill PUD, the president of Forest Park, Inc., speaking for Kanter, devoted most of his time to the planned shopping center. It would, he said, provide area residents, including the subdivisions of Forest Ridge and Bellbrook, a

5. Sam Bass Warner, Jr., *Streetcar Suburbs: The Process of Growth in Boston, 1870–1900* (New York: Atheneum, 1976); Miller, *Boss Cox's Cincinnati: Urban Politics in the Progressive Era* (New York: Oxford Univ. Press, 1968), 34–35.

6. Quoted in Porter, *The Recovery of American Cities*, 128.

highly convenient place to shop, would contribute to the tax duplicate, and would not create a traffic problem. The city manager
presented a consultant's report supporting these contentions. And a
planning commission spokesman announced that his group had voted
five to one in favor of the package, describing the PUD as the best the
commission had yet seen.[7]

The "public" was not impressed. The first speaker said he would
gladly pay higher taxes to retain Forest Park as a "bedroom community." The second declared flatly that all shopping centers created
more traffic, encouraged shoplifting, and inflicted assorted other
burdens on the Police Department. One woman from a neighboring
town warned that the proposal might damage "intercommunity relations," and someone else suggested either making the area into a park
or developing it as a "controlled PUD" or single-family subdivision
in the R-2 zoning category.[8]

After the session, a local paper noted that the tract's lack of sewers
made PUD residential construction a distant prospect. Both the
Greenhills-Forest Park Journal and the *Forest Park News* reported
that objections to the shopping center at the hearing had been almost
"unanimous."[9] The council thought it over for a month, during which
time Union Central also registered its opposition. Then, by a four-to-
three and a six-to-one count respectively, both the Kemper-Mill PUD
and the shopping center were voted down.[10]

The rejection of the Kemper-Mill proposal did not dampen Kanter's enthusiasm for PUD. The narrow council vote against PUD and
the planning commission's continued enthusiasm for the PUD concept suggested that the idea still might be salvaged during the terms of
the officials who occupied city hall between 1973 and 1975. To be
sure, the 1974 passage of the earnings tax had relieved some of the
pressure to improve the city's financial picture by endorsing high-
density development. And public concern over race and blight made
officials edgy about housing innovations.[11] The nervousness ran

7. Forest Park Council, "Minutes," Vol. VII, May 6, 1974, 43–45; *Forest Park News*,
May 17, 1974.

8. Forest Park Council, "Minutes," Vol. VII, May 6, 1974, 44–45.

9. *Greenhills-Forest Park Journal*, May 24, 1974; *Forest Park News*, May 17, 1974.

10. Forest Park Council, "Minutes," Vol. VII, June 3, 1974, 59–60; *Greenhills-Forest
Park Journal*, June 7, 1974; *Forest Park News*, May 17, 1974.

11. Forest Park Council, "Minutes," Vol. VII, June 3, 1974, 61; July 1, 1974, 72; July
15, 1974, 81; Aug. 5, 1974, 84; Dec. 16, 1974, 148; *Greenhills-Forest Park Journal*, Mar.
22 and Aug. 9 and 30, 1974.

strongest among homeowners, and it intensified and spread in spring 1975, when the Advisory Committee on Housing released its report and the news came that Forest Park's black population had increased from 2 percent in 1970 to 12 percent in 1975. Kanter, instead of giving up on his Grand Design and PUD, or postponing action until after the fall 1975 election when voters might select a violently anti-PUD council, decided to push cautiously ahead.

Kanter devoted summer and fall 1974 to other zoning matters, then revived the PUD question. In December 1974, Robert Rhein, then president of Forest Park, Inc., invited the council, at Kanter Corporation expense, to visit a recently-opened PUD development in another place. Nothing came of that, but a week later Rhein approached the planning commission with a proposal to rezone the recently-annexed 103-acre Wright Farm tract west of I-275 from single-family R-1 to R-2.[12] The planning commission, however, first suggested rezoning just 73 acres, rather than the entire plot, then recommended that "the best use of the area would be PUD."[13]

As a consequence of the planning commission recommendation, Rhein laid two different Wright Farm proposals before a public hearing on March 3, 1975. The first, a single-family plan, showed 275 residences built at a density of 2.4 houses per acre, with 25 acres reserved for parks. The second, a PUD, displayed 217 single-family homes with lot sizes larger than in nearby Bellbrook, Birch Hill, or Forest Ridge; 45 townhouses; and 210 apartments; yielding a density of 4.7 dwelling units per acre, with 15 acres for parks. Rhein estimated that city revenue from the PUD would be $22,000 a year in real estate taxes; $8,000 in earnings taxes; and $5,000 in miscellaneous income. Thus, the city would derive $35,000, to cover $24,500 in service and other city expenses.[14]

Except for the Birch Hill Civic Association representative, who said his constituents disliked the PUD's high density, the citizen interrogators seemed friendly or, at worst, indifferent to the PUD concept. In response to questions, Rhein indicated that he preferred 103 acres of PUD to 73 acres of R-2 single-family houses. He agreed to work with the city council in reformulating the details of the plans for Kemper-Mill. Rhein admitted that square-footage requirements could determine housing price ranges. He had revealed his general

12. Forest Park Council, "Minutes," Vol. VII, Dec. 2, 1974, 145; Dec. 16, 1974, 152.
13. Forest Park Council, "Minutes," Vol. VII, Mar. 3, 1974, 197.
14. *Ibid.*

expectations in this regard by figuring the tax estimates for the PUD on values of $38,000 for single-family houses and $32,000 and $20,000 for townhouse and apartment units respectively.

No one seemed particularly distressed by these remarks. Council Member Conklin went on record as favoring PUD, provided that the developer made firm commitments to the city on planning and design details before rezoning took effect. Council Member Blackburn pointed out that the council, in annexing Wright Farm, had passed a resolution of intent to develop it as a PUD. Thus, a consensus between the council and the planning commission existed on the appropriateness of PUD in that district. Blackburn also observed that the area lay outside the Greenhills-Forest Park School District and consequently carried a school tax 1.4 mills below that of the rest of Forest Park.[15] For that reason, the developer might be able to market more expensive housing than Rhein anticipated. Clearly, Rhein and the PUD concept could have received much harsher treatment from the public. And city officials apparently remained impressed with PUD's feasibility from the standpoint of municipal fiscal policy.

Still, residents' concern about blight kept the situation volatile. In March alone, on two different proposals, the developer incurred the wrath of the Birch Hill and "H" sections where concern over deterioration centered. The first plan, a request to rezone two plots of land in Birch Hill from residential to office use, elicited complaints from the Birch Hill Civic Association about potential traffic hazards, violation of the area's residential character, and Birch Hill's lack of park and recreational space.[16] The major eruption, however, occurred when irate "H" section residents learned that a builder planned to erect $30,000 homes on Hitchcock Drive. The protesters crowded the council chambers to denounce the "low cost" housing, by which, as Dawson of the *Greenhills-Forest Park Journal* wryly observed, they meant anything costing less than their own homes. Some of these protesters also wanted the city to set a minimum price on housing in Forest Park, a proposal which, Dawson explained, federal courts had held unconstitutional as discriminating against the poor.[17] Despite the public protests, during the summer the developer not only pushed ahead with the Wright Farm PUD, but also reapplied for the Kemper-Mill PUD and shopping center rezoning.

15. *Ibid.*, 198.
16. Forest Park Council, "Minutes," Vol. VII, Mar. 17, 1975, 199.
17. *Ibid.*, 202–3; *Greenhills-Forest Park Journal*, Mar. 21, 1975, 199.

Now, with the fall 1975 council elections just three months away, officials of the city and The Kanter Corporation toured PUD sites in the area of Washington, D.C. They went, Mayor Lamb explained, because the council had already slated one-third of Forest Park's undeveloped land for PUD, while Kanter was pressing for two more PUDs, and the council wanted to "do a credible job" of evaluating the new proposals. Accompanied by Rhein, the group visited PUDs in three new towns—Columbia and Montgomery Village, Maryland; and Reston, Virginia. What they saw, they agreed, ranged from excellent to mediocre to "just plain horrible." By all accounts, however, the entire group returned open-minded and receptive to the PUD concept, though cautious about its application in Forest Park.[18]

Shortly after the July trip, the willingness of the council and other public officeholders to countenance more PUDs received a stringent test. The city council had on its agenda August 18 and September 15 public hearings on the Kemper-Mill and Wright Farm projects. By that time the contours of the 1975 council campaign had taken shape. Council Member Heiberg chose not to stand for reelection, as did Mayor Lamb, who felt that he had for too long neglected his duties as vice-president and general counsel of Merrell-National Laboratories. Council Member Strachan, an aerospace engineer for General Electric, filed for another term, teaming up with Charles Imhoff, a newcomer to local politics who was a General Electric organization and manpower manager. Two other non-incumbents, Cletus McDaniel and Michael Menrath, were realtors; Menrath, in addition, had served on the Forest Park police force.[19] Not surprisingly, given the general anxiety over race and blight, the PUD controversy was to play a major role in the contest.

Early in August, the campaign began on a sour note, when a citizen who had run well but failed to win in the 1973 council race, responded to the mayor's appeal for dedicated citizens to run for public office. He did not, however, announce his candidacy. Instead, he claimed that the council had lost touch with voters on PUD and that disillusionment with the traditional political process was spreading. The ". . . ugly specter of PUD and all that it represents," he noted

18. *Cincinnati Enquirer*, July 29, 1975; *Cincinnati Post and Times-Star*, July 29, 1975; *Forest Park News*, Aug. 8, 1975; *Greenhills-Forest Park Journal*, Aug. 8, 1975. The local press ignored the question of who picked up the tab for the trip, and metropolitan dailies differed. The *Enquirer* credited the city and the *Post and Times-Star* The Kanter Corporation.
19. *Cincinnati Post and Times-Star*, Aug. 5, 1975; *Forest Park News*, Aug. 8, 1975.

ominously, "still hangs heavily over all our property values . . . ," and "many of us who have offered our services are beginning to feel disenchantment and discouragement. Perhaps some good men and women will come forward . . . , but I for one am beginning to doubt it."[20]

Within a week, a leader in the Birch Hill Civic Association took up the same theme. Repeating his opposition to PUD, he claimed that "screaming, argumentative, uninformed mobs" seemed to have more influence with the council "than a group of calm, polite, informed people under one banner and statement." His organization, he added, would reconsider its tactics, as it continued to try to impress upon the public its view "that PUD stands for Maximum People Packing" and that "the primary concern of the City in condoning PUD is the biggest tax bite available."[21]

Those outbursts of anger and political alienation alone might not have focused the campaign on PUD. But in mid-September, the council held a public hearing on the Wright Farm PUD, followed immediately by a regular session at which it voted on the Kemper-Mill project. At that time, the council tabled the shopping center but approved the PUD, despite the strenuous objections of Strachan, the only council member facing reelection that fall. Strachan reminded the council that a large stretch of land across from the municipal building already bore the PUD designation and remained undeveloped; why not, he asked, test the idea in one place before rezoning more of the city's vacant acreage?[22]

At this point, frustrated parties on both sides resorted to the politics of advocacy, seeking to move the decision on Kemper-Mill outside the usual political processes. A group of anti-PUD citizens sent the council a message by assembling a referendum petition carrying over 1,000 signatures, enough if formally filed to place the Kemper-Mill PUD on the ballot for a popular vote in November 1976. At the same time, The Kanter Corporation, disgusted by the council's veto of its shopping center, for the first time began to act as if it were ready to assume the posture of an outsider. Although Kanter himself continued to reside part-time at Dixie Dale Farm, in October the corporation sold its share of the *Forest Park News* to the group with whom it had, since 1967, shared control of the paper. Simultaneously, the

20. *Forest Park News*, Aug. 8, 1975.
21. *Forest Park News*, Aug. 22, 1975.
22. *Forest Park News*, Sept. 19, 1975.

developer threatened to sue the city for breach of contract if the council did not restore the shopping center to the Kemper-Mill project.[23]

The council now faced an angry citizenry on one side and a disaffected developer on the other. In the month before the election, the council managed to appease just one of the offended parties. During October, the council and the developer reached an understanding by which the city sanctioned the Wright Farm PUD and rezoned Kemper-Mill from PUD to R-2 single-family. Kanter in turn agreed not to litigate the Kemper-Mill shopping center question.[24] The hastily contrived deal kept the city out of court, at least temporarily, but it failed to defuse PUD as a political issue.

The same issue of the *Forest Park News* which announced the Kanter-council compromise carried three significant campaign statements, each indicating PUD's salience in the contest. Strachan and Imhoff pledged to secure for the city larger and better homes, to oppose additional low-cost or subsidized housing, and to "contain" PUD until it had proved feasible on one site in Forest Park. Cletus McDaniel, in a slightly more moderate stance, talked about the need for "proper balance" in housing, and spoke of the developer in a vaguely critical tone. McDaniel implied that Kanter ran the council, which in turn ignored the wishes of homeowners. The third statement, from Menrath, criticized the council's abandonment of PUD in Kemper-Mill, and praised Council Member Conklin (who in October had resigned his seat effective January 1, 1976) for standing up for the PUD concept. Three weeks later, Imhoff, Strachan, and McDaniel, all skeptical of PUD, won seats on the council.[25] PUD seemed dead, and with it, Kanter's Grand Design. The city was left with its old 1963 master plan, which Kanter felt was inappropriate for the 1970s.

After the 1975 election, Kanter's relationship with the council deteriorated rapidly. Within a year, Kanter took the city to court twice, first over the Kemper-Mill PUD and shopping center, and, second, over the council's refusal to permit McDonald's fast food chain to establish an outlet near the Plaza Shopping Center.[26] On election day, the council received from disgruntled citizens their notice of intent to file for a referendum vote on the Wright Farm PUD,

23. *Greenhills-Forest Park Journal*, Oct. 10, 1975; *Forest Park News*, Oct. 17, 1975.
24. *Forest Park News*, Oct. 31, 1975.
25. *Forest Park News*, Oct. 17 and 31 and Nov. 14, 1975.
26. *Forest Park News*, Feb. 20, Mar. 5, and Apr. 2, 1976.

a step which reportedly led Kanter to go to court over Kemper-Mill.[27] In July 1976, the council rescinded its part of the October 1975 PUD compromise, by rezoning Wright Farm from PUD to R-1 single-family. This action stripped the city of all but one of its PUD sites and reduced the November 1976 referendum, which also went against PUD, to a symbolic gesture.[28]

Meanwhile, the council members fell to quarreling among themselves, and the council's enmity toward Kanter deepened. In one memorable flap over parking in the Plaza Shopping Center, various council members accused each other of saying that so long as Kanter was suing the city, none of his requests would receive consideration. In July 1976, an informal meeting was set up between the council and the developer's representatives, to work out "mutually agreeable goals and how they might be implemented." But the effort collapsed when only three council members attended. One of the absentees commented later that he did "not wish to listen to Kanter," because The Kanter Corporation had taken the city to court.[28]

While the feud between Kanter and the council over McDonald's and Kemper-Mill simmered, another dispute arose, this one over lot sizes. The disagreement began as the council took up a finding of the Advisory Committee on Housing, now dubbed the Housing Commission, that in recent years Forest Park had put more low-cost housing on the market than competing nearby communities.[29] In an effort to restore "balance," the council decided to revise the zoning code, by establishing larger lot sizes of 7,500 square feet for a new R-3 designation; 12,000 for R-2; and 20,000 for R-1. Kanter opposed the change, declaring that he did not "intend to build an Indian Hill," a reference to an exclusive upper-income suburb on the northeastern edge of the metropolis. Kanter did, however, indicate his willingness to accept selective, rather than blanket, lot size enlargement, including some home sites at a maximum of 18,000 square feet in the 840 vacant acres he still owned.[30]

The council nonetheless pushed ahead with its scheme. In August 1976 Kanter tried to derail the effort by offering to hire a consultant to help the city develop a "total housing strategy" and "a master plan." As part of this surprise offer, Kanter also offered to spend $6,000 to

27. *Forest Park News,* Nov. 14, 1975; Feb. 6, 1976.
28. *Forest Park News,* Apr. 30 and July 23, 1976; *Cincinnati Post and Times-Star,* Nov. 10, 1976.
29. *Forest Park News,* May 14, 1976.
30. *Forest Park News,* July 23, 1976.

landscape the two chief entrances to town, and $20,000 on a public relations effort to improve the community's image. The latter proposition apparently drew on the first report of the Advisory Committee on Housing. Kanter also proposed to create two large-lot residential areas, to reinstitute his financial support of the *Forest Park News*, and to cooperate in enforcing anti-steering laws against city realtors. "I am convinced," Kanter contended, "that the long range objectives of the planning commission, housing commission, city council, and The Kanter Corporation are the same."[31] All they lacked was a master plan embodying those objectives.

The council was tempted by Kanter's offer and voted to recess for two weeks and take another look at the city's housing studies before deciding on the lot size issue. However, on August 30, 1976, after reconsidering the housing situation, the council adopted its original lot size scheme, with only Strachan and Imhoff opposed.[32] Shortly thereafter, the council denied a Kanter request to reduce the size of lots in industrial parks from 43,800 to 22,000 square feet, but also, on a conciliatory note, eliminated the need for planning commission approval of warehouses and wholesale establishments on land zoned for manufacturing and industrial parks.[33]

As Kanter observed of the new residential zoning ordinance, the city council's 1976 actions on housing and commercial questions scarcely amounted to a new master plan for an innovative twentieth-century new town. Indeed, they more resembled the sort of *ad hoc* decisions characteristic of post-World War II developmental suburbs. But for the first time the council, rather than Kanter, was taking the initiative in designing the community. Behind that switch lay citizen anxiety over race and blight, and a declining faith in the ability of established political processes to alleviate that anxiety. Together these forces had transformed Forest Park politics into those of a community of advocacy, a community governed by referendum petitions and court cases.

The council, however, did not have the last word on housing or zoning. As the 1976 crisis reached its climax, an initiative from the new city manager suggested that Forest Park might yet renew its quest for a master plan appropriate to the latter twentieth century.

31. *Cincinnati Post and Times-Star*, Aug. 3 and 20, 1976; *Cincinnati Enquirer*, Aug. 17, 1976.
32. *Cincinnati Enquirer*, Aug. 17, 1976; *Cincinnati Post and Times-Star*, Aug. 31, 1976.
33. *Cincinnati Post and Times-Star*, Nov. 5, 1976.

Kadlecik was by training a manager of community in general rather than of particular places, and he "naturally" tended to view the city in terms of long-run civic interests. Standing above mere politics, he was loyal first of all to his perception of the larger community welfare, rather than to the developer's or the individual homeowner's economic interest. Ironically, then, this effort to resuscitate civic community in Forest Park came not from a local "civic" association but from an administrative officer technically charged with carrying out, rather than initiating, public policy. To double the irony, Kadlecik undertook the task with funds dispensed by a federal administration seeking to encourage local autonomy and self-determination among the "silent majority" by making national revenues available to local units of government for planning purposes.[34]

Kadlecik's professional civic welfare "bias" placed him in a delicate position, suspended between developer and voters, both of whom for the moment were preoccupied with the economic aspect of their commitment to the community. Kadlecik depended for his job, moreover, on a city council listening intently to homeowners' demands. And he relied heavily on Washington for money to plan for the overall long-range welfare of the community.[35] He therefore proceeded cautiously, moving first to "rationalize" the city's budget. He also used the budget to encourage the city to engage in long-range planning for the general welfare.

The new city manager's appropriation budget for 1975 was clearly a professional document, with its narrative introductory summary, detailed analysis of the sources and estimated magnitudes of municipal revenue for 1975, and a comparison, by budget account, of 1974 appropriations with those recommended for 1975. The appropriations, approved in January 1975, totaled $1,584,500, most of it for pressing problems of municipal housekeeping. Clearly responding to the council's early 1974 report (discussed in Chapter VII), the budget provided, for example, for expanding the police cruiser fleet, enlarg-

34. Otis L. Graham, Jr., *Toward a Planned Society: From Roosevelt to Nixon* (New York: Oxford Univ. Press, 1976), 188–263.

35. I am indebted to Professor Barry D. Karl, Department of History, University of Chicago, for clarifying my thinking about the mid-twentieth-century role of the "urban professional—in this case a city manager—in community planning. See Barry D. Karl, "The Urban Professional and the Promise of Life After Death," paper read before symposium, "The Future of the Metropolis," University of Cincinnati, fall 1975, Urban Studies Collection, Archival Collections of the University of Cincinnati, published in Paula Dubeck and Miller, eds., *Urban Professionals and the Future of the Metropolis* (Port Washington, N. Y.: Kennikat Press, 1980), 19-31.

ing the police force from sixteen to nineteen officers, and hiring a part-time animal control officer. In the public works area, the budget included funds to lease a new street sweeper, make a down payment on a public works garage site, add one truck to the street maintenance fleet, purchase a mower for use in parks, and reconstruct Mill Road. Funds were scheduled for purchasing a fire engine, constructing park shelters and restrooms, and adding to the recreation program bikeways, two new tot lots, and three teen dances.

Except for the format and the diversification of the recreation program to include non-athletic and non-organized sports events, nothing in the budget seemed out of the ordinary. But the document also set aside $32,340 to establish a Community Development Department "under the direction of a professional planner."[36]

The fact that Kadlecik gave that item a top priority place in his budget indicated his determination to curb blight and deterioration of housing stock in the city. To the new department's director, Kadlecik gave both a voice in building inspections and "broad responsibilities to coordinate planning, zoning administration, site plan implementation, building plan review, capital improvement staging and implementation, and basic municipal engineering." The new director, in short, would function as the city's chief of planning and housing, and Kadlecik hoped to hire either a "professional planner or planning engineer" to fill the slot.[37]

The council had authorized the post in 1974, and in August 1974, the city manager announced the appointment of Robert Eaton, who had studied architecture and then in 1971 had taken a degree in community planning at the University of Cincinnati. After graduation, Eaton had accumulated "considerable experience with planned unit developments as well as normal residential projects." In a news release announcing Eaton's appointment, Kadlecik observed that the hiring of a director of community development "represents an important forward step for Forest Park and deserves some explanation."

> There is a critical need not met in our planned community for the continuity of effective professional planning advice. This in no way demeans the efforts and skills of the Planning Commission. But the Commission is comprised of, and is intended to be, a panel of citizens reflecting the democratic input to the planning and zoning process. The City has long recognized the fact by

36. City of Forest Park, "Appropriations Budget, 1975," typescript, n.d., 1-2, Office of the City Manager, Forest Park Municipal Building.
37. *Forest Park News*, May 31, 1974.

employing planning consultants. . . . However, a consultant cannot maintain effective continuity of thought and community attitudes operating at an on call basis. . . . This lack of continuity and . . . of understanding of the wishes of the citizens . . . has put the City at a disadvantage in its dealings with its prime developer who has maintained a continuity of his goals.

The intent behind the establishment of the position of Director of Community Development is to provide professional planning advice from a person *who knows what the citizens of Forest Park want* [italics added] and who is accountable to their elected officials. . . .[38]

Thus, in a subtle way, Kadlecik expressed his view that the initiative in planning should rest with a professional planning staff and not with the developer, the elected city officials, or their citizen appointees. He proposed, in effect, to make these three together a sort of board of trustees, for whom the new director of community development would work.

In this bold, if mildly stated, stroke, Kadlecik had designed much of his housing and planning strategy to mesh with federal urban policy. This became obvious in September 1974, when he submitted to the council his recommendation for a minimum housing standards ordinance. He asked for "tools" to "strike at the broken window or door, the filth and debris inside or the burned out house," as well as at such "potentially controversial" problems as houses that needed to be painted, unpaved side or front yard parking spaces, and irretrievably dilapidated buildings that should be demolished. The code, Kadlecik noted in closing, also met federal requirements for funding under the new Community Development Act (CDA), "which will place $170 million in the Cincinnati area over the next five years." The city manager wrapped up his comments on housing by announcing that Forest Park tentatively had been offered "701" federal planning grant funds for updating the master plan and broadening it into the areas of housing and economic analysis. Washington would contribute $6,700 to match $3,300 in local money.[39]

Thereafter, Kadlecik and Eaton, the new director of community development, pushed hard for both the minimum housing standards ordinance and the "701" funds. In March 1975, Eaton sent to all builders and "interested parties" a memorandum clarifying the city administration's position on construction in Forest Park. It proclaimed a tightening of building requirements, including the elimination of "many procedures which in the past have been permitted and

38. *Forest Park News*, Aug. 23, 1974.
39. Forest Park Council, "Minutes," Vol. VII, Sept. 16, 1974, 111–12.

which depended upon the 'good faith' of builders. . . ."[40] Later that month, the council heard experts testify about the "many" substandard and inadequate houses in the city, and recommend that the building code be strengthened and enforced more strictly.[41] The next month Kadlecik put together a technical committee to review and revise the building code. Eaton chaired the committee, which included representatives from The Kanter Corporation, small contractors and builders, big builders, architects, the Planning and Zoning Commission, the Housing Commission, realtors, and the police, plus one "interested citizen."[42]

A year later, when Kadlecik faced "insinuations by the Developer and a couple of builders" that the city enforced the building code too stringently, he responded that the ordinance existed for the protection of consumers, not for the convenience of builders, and stated that more than one citizen had expressed gratitude that "someone in City Hall is looking after us." That "someone," the manager noted, was the Community Development Department, acting under policies outlined by the council.[43] And the council backed Kadlecik up. That fact, noted the *Greenhills-Forest Park Journal,* represented a complete turnabout from four years earlier, when the previous city manager had left office under fire for his "enthusiastic enforcement of the building code."[44]

Meanwhile, Kadlecik and Eaton had secured the "701" planning grant.[45] Surprisingly, no one protested the federal assistance, even though Forest Park had previously opposed such infringements upon its autonomy as Greenhills' abortive 1961 annexation attempt. To be sure, direct federal intrusion in Forest Park affairs proved rare if not non-existent during the Kennedy-Johnson era. But in the late 1960s, in the tradition of home rule and self-determination, Mayor Sullivan had expressed resentment at moves to strengthen county government. The same mayor had also joined thirty-seven other mayors in the Hamilton County Municipal League in an effort to water down Cincinnati's influence in a proposed countywide crime council. The league had also questioned the county prosecutor's effort to secure a federal grant for creation of a regional narcotics enforcement unit,

40. Forest Park Council, "Minutes," Vol. VII, Mar. 3, 1975, 189.
41. *Greenhills-Forest Park Journal*, Mar. 21, 1975.
42. Forest Park Council, "Minutes," Vol. VII, Apr. 7, 1975, 267.
43. *Forest Park News*, May 28, 1976.
44. *Greenhills-Forest Park Journal*, May 21, 1976.
45. *Forest Park News*, Jan. 24, 1975.

and had flatly rejected a *Cincinnati Enquirer* proposal for countywide standardization of Halloween observance rules and practices.[46] Both the council and the city manager of Forest Park, moreover, had resisted the OKI attempt in 1974 to distribute public housing through-out the metropolis.[47] But federal financial assistance, including a revenue-sharing program set up by the Nixon administration, met no opposition, even when the money came encumbered by red tape involving more than the provision of a new master plan.

Early in 1975, Kadlecik explained to the city council the obligations incurred by the city in accepting the "701" funds. He had, he reported, just returned from a seminar designed to explain the Equal Opportunities Act of 1972 guidelines, to which municipalities must adhere in order to qualify for federal grants, including revenue-sharing and 701 funds. The city must commit itself to "positively improving the employment opportunity for minorities and women" in city government, by bringing the proportion of minorities and women on the city's payroll to 12 percent, the standard goal developed for the Cincinnati Standard Metropolitan Statistical Area, and by spreading them through job classifications "equally and at all levels." Although Kadlecik characterized many aspects of the affirmative action program as "certainly controversial" and as an apparent "invasion of our home rule powers and intrusions on our self-determination," he urged the council members to attend another seminar designed specifically to "orient local officials on their responsibilities in EEO."[48]

The 701 planning grant called for the city to set up a three-year planning process, including citizen participation features which had the effect of further eroding the influence of the planning commission. The process was to allow the city to determine its own goals and objectives, especially in housing and economic development; at the same time, planning was to be coordinated with area policies developed by OKI.[49] For these purposes, the city manager established a Citizens Committee for Community Development. It was, however, difficult to secure resident participation, and the "J," "K," "L," and "H" sections were particularly deficient in representation. The prob-

46. Forest Pak Council, "Minutes," Vol. V, July 6, 1971, 90–91.
47. Forest Park Council, "Minutes," Vol. VII, May 20, 1974, 48–49; Aug. 5, 1975, 88; *Forest Park News*, May 31, 1974.
48. Forest Park Council, "Minutes," Vol. VII, Mar. 3, 1975, 189–90.
49. *Forest Park News*, Jan. 24, 1975.

lem was thoroughly congruent with the inward orientation of most of Forest Park's residents and neighborhood organizations at the time.[50]

The appeal for federal assistance also generated another frustration, centering on the persistence of black ghettos within the jumble of political jurisdictions within the metropolis. This factor made most federal programs simply irrelevant to Forest Park's major concern, the worry that racial animosities would confine blacks, regardless of their incomes, to isolated residential enclaves which spread contiguously instead of dispersing as the black population grew. So long, therefore, as blacks as a group lagged behind whites in income levels, integrated neighborhoods would eventually be flooded with lower-class black newcomers, forcing middle-class blacks seeking the amenities of a middle-class area either to put up with "blight" or to search for another "integrated" neighborhood, in which their arrival would again set off the process of ghettoization.

Under these circumstances, the federally-mandated 1974 effort by OKI to distribute minorities and the poor across the metropolitan landscape (like federal court decisions which prevented the use of zoning to exclude certain people, in the interest of establishing, within a given community, block-level racial integration and a balance of low-, middle-, and high-income housing), worked against everybody's interest in Forest Park. For, measured against other metropolitan neighborhoods, Forest Park in 1976 already had its share of blacks and the poor, as did several of the nearby suburbs encompassed in the Princeton, Mt. Healthy, Lockland, North College Hill, and Wyoming school districts (see Figure 16). What Forest Park and these nearby communities (and the city of Cincinnati, for that matter) needed was a national and metropolitan policy which would both redress the persisting income gap between blacks and whites, and open up the wedges of overwhelmingly white suburbs on the metropolitan area's western and eastern flanks, and the pockets, some of them quite large, of white neighborhoods within Cincinnati.[51] Until that happened, the pattern of metropolitan ghettoization within scattered political jurisdictions would persist. And it was the persis-

50. Forest Park Council, "Minutes," Vol. VII, Feb. 3, 1975, 172; *Greenhills-Forest Park Journal*, Jan. 23, 1976; Forest Park Housing Commission, "Annual Report: Summary of Activities, 1976," typescript, Dec. 1976, Office of the City Manager, Forest Park Municipal Building.

51. *Cincinnati Post and Times-Star*, Aug. 4, 1976; David R. Rosenbaum, "Civil Rights: An Active White House?", *New York Times*, Mar. 7, 1977.

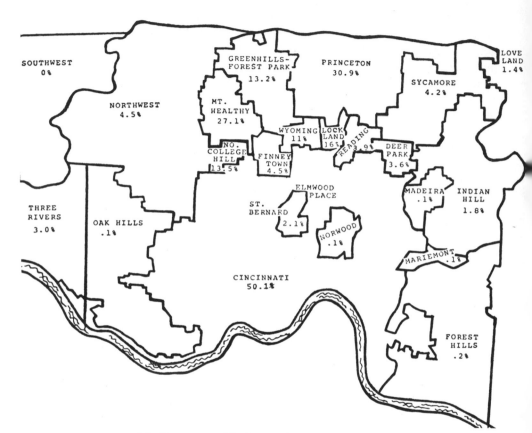

FIGURE 16. Percentage black enrollment of school districts in Hamilton County, Ohio, 1976. Reproduced by permission of the Metropolitan Area Religious Coalition of Cincinnati (MARC).

tence of that pattern which made it seem not only plausible that Cincinnati might go all black, as a lawyer in a Greenhills Presbyterian Church school desegregation forum suggested,[52] but also likely that the metropolitan area would develop a large new black ghetto on its north-central rim as the various smaller ghettos in that area expanded and merged.

Whatever the burdens and shortcomings of federal assistance, Forest Park's city administration seemed fully committed to securing outside funding. In 1976, however, under the city manager's leadership, the municipal corporation's employees wanted not only to meet the city's immediate problems of blight and residential segregation, but also to exert a strong influence on the process by which citizens, voluntary organizations, The Kanter Corporation, and elected officials charted the direction of community development during the entire last quarter of the twentieth century. What might come of that planning process remained to be seen. But Kadlecik's initiative had helped prevent Forest Park from abandoning its old commitment to long-range planning for "balanced" land use. The initiative had also kept the city, faced with a developing "balanced" socioeconomic and racial mix, from retreating into an irretrievably segregationist "bedroom" suburb mentality.

Yet the city manager's initiative also plunged the city back into the uncertainty which, before the Kanter push for PUD in 1974 and 1975, had paralyzed planning. In 1976, no one could foresee the outcome of the three-year planning process adopted upon the manager's initiative. Kadlecik himself likened the 1976 mood of civic leaders to that in 1973, in the midst of the great earnings-tax dispute, "when we sat back and evaluated our finances and everything else."[53] A similar attitude prevailed in the 1976 city budget discussions.

The 1976 budget's theme was "hold the line."[54] Projected expenditures came to $1.5 million, $132,000 below 1975. The lion's share of the money—29 percent—went to the Police Department, reflecting a continuing concern for security, law, and order. The Public Works Department took the second largest portion, 18 percent, and the Fire Department, with 14 percent, the third. The state auditor's skepticism

---

52. Lyle Koehler, "Meeting on School Desegregation, Greenhills Presbyterian Church, May 12, 1976," research memorandum, [1976], Forest Park Papers, Urban Studies Collection, Archival Collections of the University of Cincinnati.
53. *Cincinnati Enquirer*, Jan. 4, 1976.
54. *Ibid.*

about the fiscal etiquette of the city's dealings with the volunteer fire company, however, prompted a budget provision for development of a full-time municipal fire department "some time in the future."[55] Recreation received $105,000, over $50,000 less than in 1975 and just half what the firefighters got. The council vetoed $22,000 for a Community Information Center.[56] This idea had been culled from the earlier Advisory Committee on Housing report and inserted in the budget by the city manager. Until July 1976, when the council announced its intention to place a municipal swimming pool bond issue on the November ballot, the 1976 budgetary deliberations yielded nothing new.

The administration's disinclination to "rock the boat" carried over into school affairs. Voters had approved education tax levies in 1970 and again in 1974, although in 1974 one issue squeaked through by only 15 votes, and another by 184.[57] By 1976, Forest Park's high school, finished in 1971 (see Figure 17), had its own athletic Booster's Association but not a full complement of athletic facilities.[58] In addition, the Greenhills-Forest Park School District's black enrollment had risen from 11 percent in 1970 to 13.2 percent in 1976, fifth highest among all Cincinnati area school systems. The Greenhills-Forest Park middle schools had adopted special ethnic heritage programs dramatizing the contributions of blacks to American history. And in 1972, the system had hired a black human relations counselor to ease the process of integration through a "preventive program," and to recruit minority faculty.[59] But in 1976, no one in Forest Park seemed inclined to move forward with new educational or racial programs in the schools.

Yet the need for action on the question of race in school affairs was apparent to many; an NAACP discrimination suit against the Cincinnati public schools seemed likely soon to spill over into the suburbs. Anticipating the possibility of court-ordered county desegregation, the Metropolitan Area Religious Council (MARC) in 1976 conducted a "forum" for the Greenhills Presbyterian Church on the implications

55. *Ibid.*; *Forest Park News*, Apr. 16, 1976.

56. *Cincinnati Enquirer*, Jan. 4, 1976; *Forest Park News*, July 23, 1976. Some public relations "gilding" of Forest Park's image occurred dispite the $22,000 cut. See the "Habitat" section of the *Cincinnati Post and Times-Star*, Oct. 23, 1976, and *Cincinnati Enquirer*, July 4, 1976.

57. *Forest Park News*, Apr. 24, 1970; May 17, 1974.

58. *Greenhills-Forest Park Journal*, Feb. 8, 1974; *Forest Park News*, Jan. 10, 1975.

59. *Greenhills-Forest Park Journal*, Apr. 23, 1976; *Cincinnati Post and Times-Star*, Aug. 4 and Oct. 23, 1976.

FIGURE 17. View of Forest Park High School (center right), Forest Park Municipal Building (lower center left), and the Greenhills-Forest Park School District headquarters (lower center), n.d. The "J" residential section is at the top of the picture. Reproduced by permission of The Kanter Corporation.

of metropolitan school desegregation for the Greenhills-Forest Park district. The four-person panel consisted of the MARC director, a Cincinnati lawyer, a University of Cincinnati education professor, and a representative from the state education agency, all of whom in one way or another supported the concept of desegregation. But the all-white audience, according to one outside observer, saw things differently. Remarks from the floor and after adjournment conveyed the group's "sense of imposition," "unwillingness to join with the Cincinnati school system," and desire to stay free of any metropolitan school district.[60]

Despite these and other manifestations of a siege mentality, Forest Park as a community had not done badly. To be sure, University of North Carolina researchers ranked Forest Park twelfth out of thirteen new towns on an index weighing fidelity to the mid-twentieth century "national" new-community concept.[61] But Forest Park's experience ought to be measured in terms of its own history and the histories of its neighbors and of "regular" as well as "new" communities elsewhere. On that scale, Forest Park was not the embodiment of an abstraction nor a single community, but many communities. In the 1940s, Forest Park had appeared in Justin Hartzog's plan as an extension and adaptation of the greenbelt ideal and as a characteristic expression of the metropolitan mode of thought. Immediately after World War II, federal officials saw the place simply as another suburban tract ripe for private development. It would have become just such a tract, had not city planners, Cincinnati officials, and metropolitan area civic leaders intervened to preserve what they could of the greenbelt idea and still relieve Cincinnati's housing shortage. From there the community had passed through several stages. Starting as an exuberant Warner-Kanter adventure in civic community without self-government, it had moved through village into city status and from being a community of limited liability to being a community of advocacy. Through it all, Forest Park had remained open to a variety of people and land uses, though not meticulously "balanced" on either score. It remained, too, an experiment in community compellingly interesting to its civic activists, and an investment profitable to its principal land owner and most of its homeowners.

60. *Greenhills-Forest Park Journal*, May 7, 1976; Koehler, "Meeting on School Desegregation." The NAACP extended the suit to Greenhills-Forest Park and other suburbs on Sept. 29, 1976. See *Cincinnati Post and Times-Star*, Oct. 23, 1976.
61. Burby and Weiss, *New Communities U.S.A.*, 97.

In 1976, however, Forest Park teetered on the edge of particularly important decisions. The roles of the city council, neighborhood groups, voluntary associations, political organizations, the developer, and the city administration in planning and the political process remained unclear. Indeed, given the general uncertainty on these issues and the fluidity of the political structure, it even seemed conceivable that PUD might be resurrected. In any event, uncertainty about the future seemed a hallmark of Forest Park as a community of advocacy.

As of 1976, one aspect of Forest Park's history even more disturbing than its monumental inconclusiveness was that virtually none of its residents measured its unresolved problems in the larger context of contemporary urban life. For example, few considered the consequences for Forest Park of such important general trends as the neighborhood organization revolution; the revival of ethnic consciousness; the possibility of severe energy and resource shortages and economic stagnation; zero population growth; the end of the great migration of blacks from south to north, and the appearance of a new inter-metropolitan pattern of black mobility; the deepening divisions between metropolitan core cities and their suburbs, and among suburban political jurisdictions; the imminence of general municipal insolvency; and the shift in national metropolitan dominance from the old urban-industrial heartland to the "sunbelt" around the southern and southwestern rim of the continent, and the conflict between the "frostbelt" and the "sunbelt." That sort of thinking preoccupied civic leaders in big cities around the country, including Cincinnati,[62] in 1976, though no one seemed sure what those trends meant. But in Forest Park, unresolved local problems and a general inability to propose well-defined solutions drew attention away from these simultaneously national and local issues and contributed to the parochialism of local politics. The larger questions were left to Kanter, the city manager, and individuals outside the community.

In sharp contrast with the situation in Forest Park before 1969, in the 1970s no one seemed willing to pose serious questions about the nature of community in the city, in the Cincinnati metropolitan area, or in urban America generally. No one, for example, asked how a community of advocacy ought to work or explored the range of institutional arrangements possible within the community of advo-

---

62. See Walter Friedenberg, "Cincinnati, Suburbs and Region All Share a Common Future," *Cincinnati Post and Times-Star*, Feb. 3, 1977.

cacy. And no one asked whether the community of advocacy was appropriate for conditions of urban life in the last quarter of the twentieth century, or if the community of advocacy should be changed. It was simply taken for granted. Unless the community of advocacy itself becomes a matter of thought and action, it seems unlikely that Forest Parkers will be able to alter the patterns of planning and politics which emerged between 1974 and 1976.

10

FOREST PARK, THE COMMUNITY OF ADVOCACY, AND METROPLEX

Forest Park's history, I have argued in this book, is not unique, not merely local. Rather, that history has derived from more general modes of arranging social reality, modes which Forest Parkers shared with other Americans. These more general modes fall into three periods. During the first period, people took metropolis and region as organic, basic units of society. During the second, people took autonomous individuals as basic units of society. The third period, in which people took inward-turning individuals as basic units of society, produced what I have called the community of advocacy. This period has not terminated and been replaced by a new social taxonomy, and therefore it cannot be treated conclusively. It is possible, however, to comment on tendencies within the community of advocacy and to clarify its nature, by contrasting it with its predecessor, the community of limited liability, and by making connections between events in Forest Park and in the larger metropolitan area. Such a commentary may also help us to think in new ways about the present state and future prospects of Forest Park, the Cincinnati metropolitan area, and important aspects of American civilization; such a function constitutes a "symptomatic" history's chief claim to "practical" utility.

As a preface to that commentary, however, it is appropriate to acknowledge that others, albeit in different ways, have also described turning inward as a principal characteristic of our times. The national print and electronic news media, for example, have reported extensively on individuals turning inward to "personal" evangelical religion or EST or transcendental meditation, and on the enormous vogue of personal physical and psycho-spiritual therapies, such as jogging, health foods, or sauna baths. Similarly, some pollsters, pundits, and politicians, including President Jimmy Carter, have stressed the sagging of confidence in the "American spirit" of optimistic self-sacrifice for the national good, suggesting that the inward-turning tendency has bred a certain meanness of spirit if not genuine selfishness. Many social critics have issued crisis warnings about the ways in which the drive for self-fulfillment, self-actualization, and other forms of what Christopher Lasch has called "the narcissism" of our times diverts its practitioners and chroniclers from considering and acting effectively on serious social and economic issues.

These descriptions and explanations of the inward-turning tendency, however, posit different sources for the phenomenon. Some attribute it to God's intervention in earthly affairs. Others see it as the end of American innocence, the product of our disillusionment in the wake of Vietnam and Watergate. Still others attribute it to our frustration at being unable to control the vast, impersonal social and economic forces involved in the energy crisis and stagflation. Yet others follow Lasch in ascribing it largely to the bureaucratization of almost every aspect of private as well as public life during the twentieth century.

These varying accounts of the sources of the inward-turning tendency, however, share a similar focus and similar concerns, and have produced similar analyses. They center their attention on individualism and individual behavior. They concentrate on the psychological and spiritual concerns of inward-turning individuals. They suggest that such individuals are diverted by these concerns from considering and acting effectively on serious social and economic issues.

In contrast, my analysis of the inward-turning tendency, as it manifested itself in Forest Park and the Cincinnati metropolitan area, concerns different issues and reaches different conclusions. Community, rather than individuals and individualism, forms the central focus of my analysis. I have concentrated on the community which was produced by inward-turning individuals and on how that community worked. And my analysis suggests that the inward-turning tendency does not divert attention from serious social and economic questions, for Forest Parkers after the mid-1960s not only were persistently preoccupied with social and economic questions but also acted on these issues in ways which some Forest Parkers, at least, thought quite effective.

In Forest Park, however, there was a tendency to define and act upon social and economic problems in new ways. And the source of these new modes of defining and acting upon social and economic issues was not, so far as I can tell, divine intervention, disillusionment with the Vietnam and Watergate experiences, frustration growing out of the energy crisis and stagflation, or massive bureaucratic dependence. Instead, the source was a new social taxonomy, one which started from the unspoken assumption that inward-turning individuals comprise the basic units of society. Unlike the previous social taxonomy, which produced what I have called the community of limited liability, this one ascribed to those individuals not even a partial obligation for civic commitment to territorial community.

These two assumptions both made the inward-turning tendency possible and made it a different tendency, with different consequences, than the various "me generation" interpretations suggest.[1] To be sure, the fundamental characteristic of the community of advocacy was the tendency of individuals to turn inward to essentially personal concerns. Yet those concerns included not only psychological or spiritual self-fulfillment, but also careerism, job security, personal safety, property values, and other personal anxieties, objectives, and causes. All of these non-psycho-spiritual concerns, by their nature, were, or were involved with, social and economic questions and therefore became subjects of public discourse and action. In addition, these social and economic questions tended to be addressed in smaller as well as larger territorial arenas, or "turfs," including neighborhoods as well as such political jurisdictions as villages, townships, and cities. It is these characteristics of the inward-turning tendency and the spatially diffuse structure of political discourse and action in the community of advocacy which make it possible to talk about community rather than anarchy, and which make community rather than individuals or individualism an appropriate subject of analysis.

1. These interpretations follow the predominant American academic and "amateur" modes of social analysis by seeking to find out why individuals behave as they do. These modes suggest that the critics of inward turning have also turned inward. Finding out why individuals behave as they do is a difficult if not impossible task, however. It is rather like asking the face in the mirror every morning why it got up: the results of this "poll," like the reasons for conducting it, tend to vary. I am therefore conceding an ignorance of why and concentrating on how people defined and acted on "public" problems.

This book, then, concludes in a period in which the inward-turning tendency created a new kind of territorial community. In the past few chapters, I have tried to lay out some of the social, political, and institutional characteristics of that community. In a more general sense, however, one of the most important characteristics of that community consisted of a paradox. Increasingly, after the mid-1960s, Forest Parkers talked about the need to guard and advance the territorial "civic" interest, by which they usually meant both the welfare of individual Forest Park residents and the welfare of the City of Forest Park as a municipal corporation. At the same time, they acted as if a civic interest did not exist. The source of this unacknowledged paradox lay in a new and unacknowledged definition of the term *civic*.

After the mid-1960s, most Forest Parkers seemed unable to conceive of social and economic problems as problems of the Forest Park residents as a whole (as a group). Nor could they conceive of a civic solution to such a problem in terms of how it would affect the general welfare, as opposed to the individual or personal interest. Indeed, it was the prevalence of that concern for the general welfare which before the mid-1960s had so persistently placed the issue of comprehensive planning high on the agenda of Forest Park's municipal politics. For that kind of planning presumed the existence of a general (civic) welfare which encompassed, yet transcended, the interest of both the individual and the municipality. It posited a kind of interdependence among the three—the general welfare, the individual interest, and the interest of the municipality—which made them inseparable in the arena of municipal action. After the mid-1960s, however, most Forest Parkers could not think and act in those terms, and that inability led to a new conception of territorial community and to a lack of interest in comprehensive planning. Forest Parkers now saw Forest Park (and the Cincinnati metropolitan area) as a congeries of territorial and associational organizations and institutions, in which individuals and particular groups bore no ascriptive obligation to the civic welfare as opposed to essentially personal concerns for self-fulfillment, careerism, or property values.

One of the most characteristic aspects of the community of advocacy in Forest Park, in short, was the tendency of individuals, for the sake of personal interests of one kind or another, to organize territorial and associational institutions of one kind or another and to turn these institutions away from a consideration of the civic interest and inward to satisfy their members' personal goals and needs. One of the most striking particular consequences of this phenomenon was the disappearance of the Civic Association and the appearance of the neighborhood organization revolution in Forest Park (and the Cincinnati metropolitan area). But there were other and more general consequences, including a paralysis (if not eclipse) of public policy. For the absence of an (even partial) obligation to the civic interest left only individual interests, and without a civic interest there could be no public policy, only particular policies.

This analysis suggests, then, that the inward-turning tendency of the mid-1960s created a distinctive style and system of politics in Forest Park. Between 1950 and the later 1960s, the business of politics in Forest Park was the business of the civic interest. That is, political disagreements during the council elections and in the process of making council decisions were disagreements over how a particular policy related to, or might influence, the civic interest and the nature of the civic community of limited liability in which all the actors in the political process assumed they lived. The Civic Association, Donald English, Phil White, or Kanter might disagree on the wisdom of a particular policy, or they might disagree over particular visions of what the civic community was or was becoming or ought to be. But they all agreed that something called the civic interest (or general welfare) existed and had to be guarded and nurtured through public policy, which by definition consisted of measures or a plan to advance the civic interest. In this system, moreover, Alvin Tomb, the first city manager, played a role peculiar to the system itself. He might participate in the formulation of public policy, and he might be reprimanded for the way he carried out that policy. But his role was managerial, in a narrow sense. Others, inside and outside government, took the initiative in defining the civic interest and in formulating and adopting the public policy required to advance that interest.

In the community of advocacy, however, people played the game of politics under different rules. These new rules permitted discussion of the "civic" interest but inhibited the emergence of a clear and generally accepted definition of that interest and of an appropriate public policy to advance it. That is, the inward-turning tendency stripped citizens of an obligation to the general welfare, without eliminating the possibility that an individual might speak as an advocate of the "civic" interest, which in the community of advocacy meant the welfare of individual residents and the welfare of the

231

municipal corporation. Indeed, some tried to speak as this sort of double advocate, but they found it a frustrating and often inconclusive task. For the mode of speaking struck others as a pose, a mask for concealed personal interest. Council members and candidates, whose political aspirations rested on their popularity with a large number of voters, found the advocacy of the "civic" interest particularly risky. Any significant venture they undertook in behalf of that interest, regardless of the venture's particular content or direction, invariably and inevitably aroused the distrust of individuals who were pursuing their own particular interests rather than the "civic" interest.

Yet some individuals, by virtue of their jobs, professional training, or some other circumstance, found it virtually impossible to avoid trying to define, formulate, and advance the "civic" interest. Given the nature of elective politics in the community of advocacy after the mid-1960s, guardianship of the "civic" interest tended to fall to the city manager. As a professional manager of the city's interest, he defined "general" problems, formulated policy, and—through budget control, community development, and planning—sought to impose policies he felt appropriate for the welfare of both the municipal corporation and its individual residents. But the manager found this assignment as difficult to carry out as it was to avoid, for in a community of advocacy the champion of the "civic" welfare necessarily threatened the particular interest of someone or some group. Thus the manager's mid-1970s drive for a new city plan faltered when neighborhood organizations showed more enthusiasm for promoting their own particular interests than for planning on a municipal basis for the "civic" welfare. In short, the city manager, like the city's politicians, by the mid-1970s had learned that any significant venture in the "civic" interest would arouse distrust. This fact was likely to make long-term tenure by a city manager extraordinary.

In the community of advocacy, then, the political process tended toward stalemate. Recurring crises failed to generate satisfactory resolutions. Dissatisfaction with the political system was persistent and general, for the system seemed unresponsive to, or disrespectful of, the desires of particular interest groups, as well as of the desires of those who occasionally advocated the "civic" interest. The community of advocacy also generated a political process which was no longer dominated by elections, bargains, and compromises. The new process resorted more frequently to demonstrations, litigation, referenda, and city charter revision or amendment; all of these instruments seemed especially useful in advancing particular interests. There was also a growing unwillingness to vote taxes to be used by city and school bureaucracies. Finally, the system, which presented problems as unrelated one to the other, made most actors in the political process see the expediency of piecemeal attacks on particular problems, as opposed to designing a general plan to solve a variety of problems.

In addition to a new political system, the inward-turning tendency also generated within Forest Park, as a territorial community of advocacy, a new and distinctive view of itself, of its functional nature, of its relationship to Cincinnati and other suburbs, and of the nature of the metropolis. This shift could be seen in several events, but it was most apparent, perhaps, in the great earnings tax debate. In the Cincinnati metropolitan area, the earnings, or "users," tax first appeared in Cincinnati, which adopted it in the 1950s. Then, the implicit rationale for the "users" tax held the big city to be a distinctive place and community. It was also seen as the historic source of suburban growth and *the* central location and vital force on which suburbia drew for its existence and welfare. But when, as we have seen, Forest Park and other suburbs adopted the tax after the mid-1960s, the action heralded the appearance of a new definition of the metropolis as a collection of essentially independent and equal places. In other words, in the new taxonomic context, the "users" tax treated Forest Park as one of the several individual service and economic areas which together constituted the larger metropolitan area. These areas competed among themselves for the resources (taxes, in this case) necessary to maintain their independence and to fulfill their functions. To view Forest Park as such a unit was to place a premium, not on creating a sense of civic community in Forest Park (or in Cincinnati or the metropolitan area), but on making it attractive and convenient for users, regardless of their residence. Such a view also blurred the old distinction between the city as one kind of place and community, and suburbia as another, which in their interdependence together constituted a functional system called the metropolis.

Kanter's Grand Design for Forest Park, which was announced in 1972, also viewed the metropolis as nothing more than a geographic assemblage of independent, equal places competing for a variety of resources. It envisaged Forest Park as a territory with a "balance" of commercial, industrial, office, residential, and recreational land uses.

This scheme reduced the metropolitan downtown from being *the* metropolitan central business district to being merely one of several potentially equal and competing localities, of which Forest Park was one. As a business location, Forest Park differed from Cincinnati in that it offered relatively large amounts of land for business development, with attractive nearby residential facilities. These advantages Cincinnati leaders sought to overcome in the late 1960s and the 1970s by offering tax abatement and other incentives for business and residential development in and near its downtown, and by encouraging preservation and rehabilitation of the old housing stock surrounding the central business district.

In Cincinnati, then, as well as in Forest Park, the distinction drawn in the 1950s and early 1960s between the city and suburbia as different places with distinctive ways of life gave way to a new view of the metropolis as a collection of competing economic and service areas. Indeed, in the late 1960s and early 1970s, Cincinnatians expressed the new view in a variety of programs besides tax abatement and historic preservation. In the late 1960s, for example, planners, city officials, and residents of a Cincinnati slum called Queensgate II drew up a plan for the neighborhood's revival. Their aim was to create a "new town in town" not unlike that proposed for Forest Park in Kanter's Grand Design. Queensgate II would have a balance of industrial, commercial, office, recreational, and residential land uses and a socioeconomic and racial balance of population.

Others in Cincinnati were thinking the same way. After the 1960s it became common for participants in the neighborhood organization revolution in Cincinnati to insist that each neighborhood should have a "viable" business district and be "viable" economically, and to resist certain kinds of business and residential development on the grounds that they might destroy the "balance" within those neighborhoods. In fact, in these years some ardent Cincinnati proponents of what came to be called "neighborhood conservation" argued that such places deserved the right of self-determination in planning and zoning. Others lobbied for distribution of a share of municipal revenues to "neighborhoods" for each to allocate as its residents saw fit. Clearly, the drives for local independence and "viability" cut across the once-familiar line between big-city and suburbia.

Forest Park's response to racial "integration" after the mid-1960s rested upon this same new way of thinking about suburbs, relationships among suburbs, and relationships between the big city and its suburbs. Since blacks did not move into Forest Park between 1950 and the mid-1960s, we do not know if whites would have seen them as a problem, or, if so, how the problem would have been handled. Such a move probably would have been considered as it was elsewhere, as a problem of the civic interest and general welfare. Forest Parkers probably would have argued for either integration or segregation in terms of how it would affect their views of the civic interest. Indeed, just such thinking appears to have dictated the fact that, at the time of Forest Park's incorporation, village boundaries were drawn so as to exclude the black subdivision of Hollydale, and, immediately after incorporation, great concern existed over the price of housing in the Forest Park subdivision closest to Hollydale. To Forest Parkers, apparently, as to Americans generally during these years, blacks were identified with the big city, as part of its inherent if segregated diversity. Within that framework, the question of race did not seem to be a suburban problem. Black suburbs then appeared as an exception to the norm, and the integration of suburbia seemed inappropriate.

After the mid-1960s, however, when "integration" came to Forest Park, the appropriateness of integration or segregation was never raised. Instead, people became concerned about individual behavior as it related to property values, the problem of "blight," and how to attract "top-notch" citizens. For in a society of inward-turning individuals, everyone seemed alike, if not equal, in that they lived in pursuit of personal goals and objectives, regardless of race (or sex, age, marital status, income, or physical or mental handicap, for that matter), which by definition had nothing to do with individual choices of goals and objectives, including the choice of where to live. Such individuals were therefore alike, but not necessarily equal, as Forest Park's concern to attract "top-notch" citizens suggests. They were only potentially equal. Blacks, therefore, like other individuals, deserved the right to select any place, whether central-city ghetto, some other segregated locale in the metropolis, or an integrated area, to exercise and develop that potential. In that place, their neighbors would judge their success in achieving equality (becoming a "top-notch" citizen).

It was this view of things which made "integration" such a dilemma for Forest Parkers. According to this view, individuals possessed the right to live wherever they chose, regardless of such criteria as race, age, income level, marital status, or physical or mental competence, for each person by definition possessed the potential for equality (each might become a "top-notch" citizen). This view meant that Forest Parkers could neither exclude nor set quotas on the basis of those criteria. Nor could they draw up *any* specific criteria for defining individuals likely to become "top-notch" citizens because anyone might, after coming to Forest Park, prove to be such a person. Forest Park, in short, must remain open and by remaining open would inevitably attract individuals who proved to be something less than "top-notch" citizens. This view therefore raised the questions of how to treat or where to put those who, after moving to Forest Park, fell short of becoming "top-notch" citizens, and how to get them there.

The rules of this game, in other words, stipulated that for Forest Park both segregation and quotas were inappropriate, but failed to prescribe ways of maintaining "integration" in either a qualitative (which individuals should be admitted) or a quantitative (how many less than "top-notch" citizens could be accommodated in one place) sense. Indeed, the rules of this game could not define integration in either of these ways, because these questions were essentially civic questions. That is, they could be answered only in the context of criteria developed to define the general interest, criteria for action which could be justified not because such action advanced the welfare of individuals (though it might), but because it put forward a particular concept of the general welfare and how to advance it. In other words, by definition, a policy of integration in a civic community meant that only so many blacks (a quota) could be tolerated in a predominantly white area, and that they should be distributed randomly within that territory.

In the new taxonomic context, however, Forest Park's response to its racial integration presented the city, and the metropolitan area in which it was located, as an assemblage of open service and economic areas for individuals (as a community of advocacy rather than a civic community). No one in Forest Park after the mid-1960s asserted publicly either that blacks should be excluded or that only a certain number of blacks should be admitted. Nor did anyone assert publicly that the city should become an entirely black municipality. The problem seemed rather that, out of residential "blight," black enclaves might form and spread until Forest Park became, against the will of its residents, a black ghetto. But since everyone had a right to reside in the community of advocacy, there could be no segregation and no precisely quantifiable definition of integration (quota); either could be construed as denying the right of individuals to exercise and develop their potential for equality. So there seemed no alternative but to leave Forest Park "open" and by a variety of public relations schemes to compete with other locales in the metropolitan area in attracting "top-notch" individuals (people unlikely to carry "blight" into the community) as residents of Forest Park.

Forest Park's responses after 1950 to the issue of integration, it should be noted, were not unique. Cincinnati also confronted the problem, and with similar results. Between 1950 and the mid-1960s, the rediscovery of local community sparked an increased concern with neighborhood identity and integrity. Out of that rediscovery came new neighborhood organizations, including the Clifton Town Meeting and the North Avondale Neighborhood Association (NANA). In defining neighborhood boundaries and the meaning of neighborhood, these groups began referring to their territories as suburban, seeking thereby to identify their neighborhoods with the traits of suburbia (serenity and homogeneity) and to dissociate them from the traits of the big city (excitement, activity, heterogeneity). The movement of blacks from a nearby ghetto into North Avondale and toward Clifton, just west of Avondale, however, was seen as a threat to the presumed suburban ambiance. Both neighborhood associations took a stance in favor of integration, as the strategy most likely to promote the neighborhoods' general welfare. This welfare they defined as achieving and maintaining a serene and socioeconomically, though not racially, homogeneous area. White neighborhoods well removed from the ghetto, moreover, remained white and felt no compulsion to advocate their own integration. To them, a strategy of segregation seemed most likely to promote the neighborhood's welfare and preserve the suburban ambiance.

After the mid-1960s, however, Cincinnati neighborhood organizations treated the question of race differently, not as a question of neighborhood but as a question of individual welfare. Whether representing integrated or segregated places, and while pursuing policies designed to attract and hold "top-notch" citizens, they invariably asserted the right of individuals, regardless of race, to live in any neighborhood. Sometimes this assertion was expressed obliquely in conflicts centered on "blight." Thus, neighborhood organizations from white, middle-class Westwood, Hyde Park, and Mt. Washington just as angrily denied charges of racism and other kinds of bias as they protested proposals to put into those neighborhoods of predominantly (but not *exclusively*) single-family homes federally subsidized apartments or deinstitutionalized communal living facilities for the mentally incompetent, all of which would have housed at least some blacks. Specific complaints about such projects varied, but never raised the question of race. Instead, they usually expressed concern about the adverse effects on individuals of increased traffic, drainage and sewerage problems, or the lowering of property values. Whatever the specific complaint, however, protestors united in asserting that the services provided by the projects would be more appropriate in some other neighborhood (usually unspecified), that they were not acting on racist motives, and that individuals had the right to live in the neighborhood of their choice, regardless of their race.

Two other manifestations of the assertion that race was irrelevant in residential decisions were the emergence of "gentrification" as an issue in Cincinnati and the rise to local prominence of Carl Westmoreland, a young, black neighborhood organizer. In the middle and late 1960s, Westmoreland led a successful effort to clean up and revive—in part through historic preservation—the sinking black neighborhood of Mt. Auburn. This effort, which included making the area attractive to "top-notch" citizens by driving its pimps, prostitutes, and drug pushers into some other neighborhood, led both blacks and whites to move to Mt. Auburn. Indeed, so many whites moved in that by the mid-1970s Westmoreland feared that the movement of too many middle-class whites into the area to rehabilitate its nineteenth-century homes might drive "top-notch" blacks out of the neighborhood. While no one denied the right of whites to move in, the cry of "gentrification" implied that they should either stay in their current neighborhood or move to some other one. They seemed to be the wrong kind of individuals for Mt. Auburn, not because of their race, but because their growing numbers threatened the right of other individuals to choose their own residence. They kept moving in, nonetheless, for they believed, and no one denied, that they had a right to.

In the 1970s, Westmoreland also became a participant in another and different conflict involving the issue of gentrification. This fight emerged when the Cincinnati Business Committee (CBC), a group of downtown business leaders organized in the mid-1970s, and the Miami Purchase Association (MPA), a historic preservation organization established by middle- and upper-income people in the 1960s, began a joint drive to restore the historic area around Music Hall in the poor but "integrated" Over-the-Rhine district in the inner-city. In part because of Westmoreland's impressive record and reputation in the field, and in part because the CBC and MPA's role in the venture had aroused acute fears of gentrification in Over-the-Rhine, the two sponsoring organizations brought Westmoreland in to organize neighborhood participation in the project. One of his first tasks was to attempt to allay fears among the neighborhood's poor, black, white, and elderly residents that historic preservation would raise housing costs generally in Over-the-Rhine and drive all of them to a neighborhood which served their needs less well. Here, too, nobody challenged the right of anyone to move into Over-the-Rhine, but the code word *gentrification* implied that potential, and presumably more prosperous, newcomers might more appropriately go to some other neighborhood. In short, here as elsewhere, the issue was not the welfare of the neighborhood, the city, or the metropolis—a question of "public" good—but the welfare of individuals and how well a particular neighborhood served their needs as they defined them. And put that way, there seemed no way of resolving the issue by developing a policy designed to serve the welfare of neighborhoods, the city, and the metropolis. Indeed, in Cincinnati and its metropolitan areas, as in Forest Park, there seemed no way of resolving the issue at all, a circumstance reminding us of both the possibility and the futility of defining problems in a way which renders them insoluble.

After the mid-1960s, then, the metropolitan area seemed to be composed of a mélange of service and economic areas, varied in size, which existed to foster pursuit by individuals of personal goals and objectives. Each of these areas competed for economic resources, power, and "top-notch" citizens, and the competition not only pitted Cincinnati against its suburbs but also big city neighborhood against big city neighborhood, suburb against suburb, and neighborhoods within a particular suburb against one another. Each of these localities, in other words, comprised a community of advocacy. And the larger units, such as Forest Park or Cincinnati, constituted a community of advocacy made up of smaller communities of advocacy.

This view of the metropolitan area also rendered ambiguous the meaning of the familiar word *metropolis,* which had suggested the existence of a metropolitan civic interest and public policy. The new ambiguity produced a search for a new and more appropriate term to describe what once had seemed a "natural" area of dependency and interdependence. None has yet appeared. But a likely candidate is the word *metroplex,* which retains a sense of the geographic scope connoted by *metropolis* but excises the half of that word (*polis*) which implies a civic interest within the area. I first heard the word *metroplex* when a television announcer in Dallas referred to the station's audience as "the Dallas-Ft. Worth metroplex." When I asked a local resident what *metroplex* meant, he replied that originally the term had been used to define the area from which the new Dallas-Fort Worth airport would attract outbound passengers. The television station had subsequently appropriated the term to designate the area it served. I next heard the word a few days later, in New Orleans, where a physician told me that *metroplex* designated an area for the delivery of health care services, explaining that such an area need not, and usually did not, coincide with political jurisdictions or with any of the socioeconomic areas defined by federal censuses.

I have since heard *metroplex* used elsewhere. A "disco" radio station in Hamilton, Ohio, just north of Forest Park and roughly halfway between Dayton and Cincinnati, describes itself as serving "the Cincinnati-Dayton metroplex." Here again the term refers to a service area, albeit one of a different kind and size. The usage is strikingly similar to the definition of a neighborhood, suburb, or city as an economic and service area for individuals in pursuit of personal goals and objectives—what I have called a community of advocacy. It suggests, in short, that the metropolis itself is now conceived of as a community of advocacy composed of overlapping communities of advocacy of a variety of kinds and sizes.

The eras of the metropolitan mode of thought and of the community of limited liability, then, are irretrievably past. We live in a different epoch, characterized by a paralysis of public policy (policy designed to serve the general welfare) and by a new view of the meaning of metropolis, big city, suburb, neighborhood, community, and civic. This is a period in which the dissipation of the older civic sense of community has left the residents of a locality in an awkward relationship to their history, as the circumstances under which this book came to be written suggest.

As we have seen, the political process in the community of advocacy shifted the initiative in defining general problems and formulating city policy into the hands of an expert in managing the "civic" welfare, the city manager. A similar shift occurred when Forest Park prepared to celebrate the bicentennial of the American Revolution.

The city council first thought to commemorate the event by appointing a committee of residents to designate a list of exemplary community leaders of Forest Park after whom to name parks. The committee, however, could not agree on a list of names, and decided instead to write a history of the city, which also proved impossible for the committee. To produce the history, the council called in a professional historian with a reputation for doing community history. In return for a modest grant to cover research costs, the council asked only for authority to review the final manuscript, unanimously agreeing that such a review would address matters of fact and not of interpretation. The entire project suggested first, that Forest Parkers were unable to imagine criteria for measuring the relative importance of community leaders (in a community of advocacy individuals are by definition equal) and events, and second, that Forest Park was a new kind of community, whose past might be worthy of recording and studying as a means of understanding and accommodating to the new reality. But that past also seemed so strange, and perhaps so irrelevant, that it seemed safe and appropriate to ask an "outside" professional to record facts and events from the past and to leave him free to define, interpret, and place in perspective those facts and events. By definition, such a history would be personal and perhaps interesting to Forest Parkers, but not for them an "authoritative" history.

Nonetheless, perhaps this history will be useful to residents of Forest Park and others concerned with the current state and future prospects of that city, of the Cincinnati metropolitan area, and of communities in America generally. By arguing that the past is past, this book suggests the inappropriateness of past modes of thought and action for the present and future. But it also suggests two questions about the more recent past in which we still live. Is the community of advocacy the only kind of community possible within the current mode of thought and action? If not, what kind of community do we want, and how, under current constraints, can we create it? Those questions, however, are the business of another and different kind of book. This volume aims at an understanding of the past and at contributing to the discourse over the current state and future prospects of community. It intends to free us of the past by suggesting that we can neither return to older modes of thought and action nor learn practical lessons from the past. This book also asserts, however, that such an understanding of the past indicates that we, as others before us have done, can think and act in new ways in the present and future.

APPENDIX

The building of the Greenbelt Towns in 1935 marked the beginning of a long needed practical experiment in the urbanization of suburban expansion around large cities in a form that would stop repetition of the mistakes that had caused and still were causing the alarming spread of blight through intown city areas. It is extremely important that this experiment continues and that its essential features be preserved in any proposal for the further development or disposition of those towns.

This country owes its greatness to its capacity for successful experimentation in vital fields of national endeavor. Its very origin was an experiment in a new form of government. The cotton gin, the steamboat, the electric light, the automobile, the airplane—all are symbols of the progress that came from the constant search for new and better methods.

Our major cities stand as a glaring exception to this tradition of progressive experimentation. By and large, their structure follows the same pattern that it did when the Dutch occupied Manhattan. They are bigger and more numerous but they are less able to serve the country's contemporary needs than were the cities of colonial days.

There are many reasons why the traditional American process of experimentation and development has not been applied to the production of better cities, but underlying them all is the great size and complexity of the subject itself. It is one thing to develop and put on the market, where the public may see and appraise its merits, a motor-driven carriage or an improved farm cultivator. It is quite another thing to develop and demonstrate a working model of a full fledged city in which science has provided facilities for the efficient conduct of modern business and a wholesome and pleasant home environment for all the citizens.

Private enterprise and government both have pioneered improvements in specific elements of city structure. Here and there throughout the country there are working demonstrations of modern city highways, modern shopping centers, modern industrial districts, modern residential neighborhoods, but nowhere is there a demonstration of a complete city structure in which all the elements have been combined to form a community that is wholly convenient and economical and pleasant for those who live and work in it.

Today's achievements in automobile design did not come from the separate and unrelated development of better carburetors, better tires, better engines, better bearings, etc. They came through the successful combination in modern automobiles of all the elements that make them so vastly different from the horse and buggy. That success was achieved only through continued experiment and improvement with complete working models.

The same process must be employed if this country is to be supplied with cities that are markedly better than the horse and buggy models we still are using. The building of the Greenbelt Towns was a step in the direction of such full-scale experimentation. It was a very small step in relation to the magnitude and urgency of the problem and at best dealt with only one of the major factors in the decline of American cities. But the step was an important one and its value should not be underestimated.

In the boom days following World War I—and the situation is being repeated today—there was a tremendous outward expansion of the country's principal cities, but the network of suburban streets and lots and utilities was not laid out on lines essentially different from those which had existed previously in the intown areas. The structure of these areas had long since proved inadequate to meet the needs of the modern age in nearly every department of city life and as a result, vast sections were becoming blighted, with consequent loss in their use-fulness, in their real estate value, and in their ability to support essential municipal services.

Failure to achieve a type of city structure that meets the needs of contemporary living and contemporary business can prove disas-trous not only to the cities themselves, but to the nation whose economic life depends on their successful functioning. Bankrupt cities turn more and more to the Federal Government for financial help, but worse than that, they seriously obstruct the efficient con-duct of the nation's business.

It was for that reason that the Federal Government first undertook the Greenbelt Town experiments, hoping to develop a sound type of satellite community in place of the disorganized sprawl of suburban land subdivisions that had characterized past American practice. The Greenbelt Towns were started as adjuncts to another program de-signed to relieve unemployment and were not carried far enough to serve as complete demonstrations. Nevertheless, good beginnings were made and a sound foundation was laid for their completion through the purchase of adequate sites and the preparation of good basic town plans.

As programs are developed for their transfer from federal to private ownership, it is important that the essential features of the greenbelt experiments be preserved. They are, in brief:

> 1. The development of complete satellite communities capable of eco-nomic self-support and local self-government.
> 2. The preservation of greenbelts of open land around them to prevent their physical amalgamation with neighboring suburban territory and the consequent loss of the unity on which successful and economical govern-ment depends.

To insure that these purposes are served and that full opportunity is given for the ultimate completion of the communities as originally planned, it is recommended that the Greenbelt Towns be disposed of as complete units to a single development corporation and that sepa-rate tracts or parcels not be sold in a manner to destroy the essential unity of the development. To this end it is recommended that an effort be made to interest large investors, such as insurance companies, for carrying the projects through to completion and that the present valuations of the projects be written down to a point where such investment and continued development will be practicable.

BIBLIOGRAPHICAL ESSAY

This history of Forest Park draws upon a variety of sources. The most important deal with the locality of particular concern in this book, Forest Park and the Cincinnati metropolitan area. But I have also looked at materials produced elsewhere or about other places or related subjects, as part of the effort to verify and document the general prevalance of the "larger" modes of thought described in this work. Some of these sources were "primary"—artifacts or events, including books, articles, and essays—dating from one of the three chronological periods into which this study is divided. Others were "secondary," in that they described a chronological period of which they were not a part.

The Forest Park community generated rich resources for use by students of its history. Charles Dawson generously loaned to the Archival Collections of the University of Cincinnati not only the Forest Park Civic Association's "First Annual Report," but also copies of the *Forest Park Newsletter,* the organ of the Forest Park Civic Association; and *The Village Voice,* put out by the Forest Park Women's Club. Both the *Newsletter* and *The Village Voice* kept close track of social, community, and political affairs and reported on what the developer was and was not doing. The *Forest Park News,* which was started by Forest Park, Inc., a subsidiary of The Kanter Corporation, was filled with all kinds of civic information about Forest Park;

although suspected by some of pro-developer bias, *The News* struck this reader as reasonably balanced in its political coverage. The *Greenhills-Forest Park Journal,* housed in the Greenhills branch of the Public Library of Cincinnati and Hamilton County, was useful primarily as a source of supplemental information. The Forest Park city manager's office made available the records of the Forest Park municipal corporation; the most helpful of these were the minutes of the city council, the minutes and correspondence of the Planning and Zoning Commission, and the histories of the Women's Club and the Fire Department done by Forest Park residents Elizabeth White and Joe Valent. Forest Park, Inc., loaned a scrapbook of clippings, which simplified the task of tracing the Warner-Kanter Company's activities in beginning to develop Forest Park. The Hartzog Papers, at the Department of Manuscripts and Archives, Cornell University, proved enormously helpful, especially in connection with the period when Kanter took over the developer's role in Forest Park after the Warner-Kanter partnership broke up.

Students of the Cincinnati metropolitan area in the middle decades of the twentieth century are also fortunate to have readily accessible a broad range of sources. For this study, the Cincinnati Citizens Development Committee (CDC) papers at the Cincinnati Historical Society proved indispensable. The collection contains the records of both the CDC and the Cincinnati Community Development Company (CCDC), the organization which joined with Warner-Kanter to purchase North Greenhills and which oversaw the first five years of Forest Park's development (the papers contain nothing on that five-year period, however). The records of the Hamilton County Commissioners and the Hamilton County Regional Planning Commission, in the Hamilton County Courthouse, also yielded valuable information on Forest Park's early years. The minutes of the Cincinnati City Council meetings are under the care of the clerk of council, in Cincinnati City Hall, and the minutes of the Cincinnati City Planning Commission are housed in the planning commission's office in City Hall. These records, too, were particularly important for the early history of development in Forest Park.

Cincinnati's two metropolitan daily newspapers, the *Cincinnati Enquirer* and the *Cincinnati Post,* covered not only Forest Park but also other suburbs and the big city itself. Complete runs of both papers are housed in the downtown branch of the Public Library of Cincinnati and Hamilton County.

Among the best sources for changing views of the metropolis, its parts, and their relationships are the various studies prepared and published by the Cincinnati City Planning Commission. Of these, the most important for this book were the *Official Plan of the City of Cincinnati* (Cincinnati: City Planning Commission, 1925); the *Metropolitan Master Plan, 1948* (Cincinnati: City Planning Commission, 1948); and the ten volumes of supplemental studies prepared as part of the 1948 plan, all of which can be consulted at the Cincinnati Historical Society and in the Archival Collections of the University of Cincinnati. The 1948 plan, together with several revisions in the 1950s, 1960s, and 1970s of that plan for Cincinnati's downtown, have been analyzed in Geoffrey Giglierano and Zane L. Miller, "The Rediscovery of the City: Downtown Residential Housing in Cincinnati, 1948–1978," to be published in a forthcoming issue of the *Cincinnati Historical Society Bulletin*. I have also dealt with aspects of the history of the Cincinnati metropolitan area since the mid-nineteenth century in "Cincinnati: A Bicentennial Assessment," *Cincinnati Historical Society Bulletin*, Vol. 34, No. 4 (Winter 1976), 231–49; "Neighborhood, Community, and the Contemporary Metropolitan Crisis," in Ralph L. Pearson, ed., *Ohio in Century Three* (Columbus: Ohio Historical Society, 1977), 18–24; "Music Hall: Its Neighborhood, the City and the Metropolis," in Zane L. Miller and George Roth, *Cincinnati's Music Hall* (Virginia Beach, Va.: Jordan and Company, 1978), 15–64; and Henry D. Shapiro and Zane L. Miller, *Clifton: Neighborhood and Community in an Urban Setting* (Cincinnati: Laboratory in American Civilization, Dept. of History, Univ. of Cincinnati, 1976). All of these works contain additional documentation and explanation of some of the generalizations in this book.

Several other studies proved especially important in working out my approach to, and interpretation of, the history of community and neighborhood in urban and suburban settings. Alan I. Marcus, "In Sickness and In Health: The Marriage of the Municipal Corporation to the Public Interest and Problems of Public Health, 1820–1870. The Case of Cincinnati" (Ph.D. diss. Univ. of Cincinnati, 1979), explores the definition of the city in the early and mid-nineteenth century. Patricia Mooney Melvin, "Neighborhood in the 'Organic' City: The Social Unit Plan and the First Community Organization Movement" (Ph.D. diss. Univ. of Cincinnati, 1978), develops the thesis about the significance of neighborhood and city in the late nineteenth and early twentieth centuries which I have asserted in the introduction to this book. For a portion of the conclusion of this book, I drew on Martha Reynolds, "The Founding of the Clifton Town Meeting, 1961–1964" (typescript, June 1979, History Honors Seminar, McMicken College of Arts and Sciences Honors Program, Univ. of Cincinnati). William A. Baughin, "Murray Seasongood: Twentieth Century Urban Reformer" (Ph.D. diss. Univ. of Cincinnati, 1972), is the best account of Cincinnati metropolitan politics in the 1920s and 1930s. Kenneth A. Jackson, "The Crabgrass Frontier: 150 Years of Suburban Growth in America," in Raymond A. Mohl and James F. Richardson, *The Urban Experience: Themes in American History* (Belmont, Calif.: Wadsworth, 1973), 196–221; and especially Henry D. Shapiro, *Appalachia on Our Mind: The Southern Mountains and Mountaineers in the American Consciousness, 1870–1920* (Chapel Hill: Univ. of North Carolina Press, 1978), clarified my thinking about community and regionalism in America generally, and in the late nineteenth century and the first half of the twentieth, in particular.

Non-local primary sources for the period of the metropolitan mode of thought are abundant. While preparing this book I have consulted several which are recognized as significant works. Norman S.B. Gras, *An Introduction to Economic History* (New York: Harper, 1922), attempted a metropolitan interpretation of economic history which defined the metropolis as the basic unit of society, organizing the economy for a broad metropolitan area. Harlan Paul Douglass' *The Suburban Trend* (New York: Century, 1925), which appeared as a volume in the Century Country Life Books, treated suburbs as parts of evolving cities and concerned itself with urban-rural relations, rural centralization and urban decentralization, and the state and future prospects of the metropolis. Paul Studenski's *The Government of Metropolitan Areas in the United States* (New York: National Municipal League, 1930), which was funded by the Russell Sage Foundation, treated metropolitan areas as social and economic units and sought to devise a new form of government to integrate politically the localities which together formed the metropolitan community. R. D. McKenzie's *The Metropolitan Community* (New York: McGraw-Hill, 1933), a research monograph prepared under the auspices of President Hoover's Research Committee on Social Trends, addressed itself to the "era of city regionalism," which McKenzie said began about 1900, and called the metropolitan community a "supercommunity" which had become "the communal unit of local relations throughout the entire nation" (p. 7). Lewis Mumford began

The Culture of Cities (New York: Harcourt, Brace, 1938) with a close study of "New York and its immediate hinterland," and sought to establish "for the purpose of communal action, the basic principles upon which the human environment—buildings, neighborhoods, cities, region—may be renovated" (p. vi).

Works manifesting assumptions about the place of neighborhood in the metropolis during these years are James Dahir, *The Neighborhood Unit Plan: Its Spread and Acceptance* (New York: Russell Sage, 1947), and Saul D. Alinsky, *Reveille for Radicals* (New York: Random House, 1946). Writing this book prompted me to review the work of some of the Chicago school of sociologists on neighborhood, community, and the metropolis. Besides Wirth's essay on urbanism as a way of life and Harvey Warren Zorbaugh's *The Gold Coast and the Slum,* discussed in my text (Chapter I), I consulted Ernest W. Burgess, ed., *The Urban Community* (Chicago: Univ. of Chicago Press, 1926), and Leonard S. Cottrell, Jr., Albert Hunter, and James F. Short, Jr., *Ernest W. Burgess on Community, Family and Delinquency* (Chicago: Univ. of Chicago Press, 1973). Both works contain writings illustrating various aspects of the metropolitan mode of thought. Perhaps the most characteristic New Deal document on the metropolis is National Resources Committee, Research Committee on Urbanism, *Our Cities: Their Role in the National Economy* (Washington, D.C.: Government Printing Office, 1937), the preparation of which involved several Chicago scholars, including Wirth.

I found several secondary sources on greenbelt towns quite helpful. Paul K. Conkin, *Tomorrow A New World: The New Deal Community Program* (Ithaca, N.Y.: Cornell Univ. Press, 1959), places the greenbelt towns in the context of New Deal thinking about community generally. Joseph L. Arnold, *The New Deal in the Suburbs: A History of the Greenbelt Town Program, 1935–1954* (Columbus: Ohio State Univ. Press, 1971), traces the greenbelt towns from their conception through construction, settlement, organization, and sale after World War II. The fullest general study of Greenhills, Ohio, the Cincinnati area's greenbelt town, is Charles Bradley Leach, "Greenhills, Ohio: The Evolution of an American New Town" (Ph.D. diss. Case Western Reserve Univ., 1978).

Other aspects of urban and suburban community between 1920 and 1950 are treated in Barry D. Karl, *Charles Merriam and the Study of Politics* (Chicago: Univ. of Chicago Press, 1974), an extraordinarily good analysis of the relationships among different levels of government, foundations, academic disciplines, and urban professionals. Mark I. Gelfand, *A Nation of Cities: The Federal Government and Urban America, 1933–1965* (New York: Oxford Univ. Press, 1975), is a mine of useful information about the connections between Washington and the cities in this period. Roy Lubove, *Community Planning in the 1920s: The Contributions of the Regional Planning Association of America* (Pittsburgh: Univ. of Pittsburgh Press, 1964), is the standard work on the RPAA, while Mel Scott's *American City Planning Since 1890* (Berkeley: Univ. of California Press, 1969), the standard authority on the rise of the city planning profession, contains helpful information on a number of periods. Both can be usefully supplemented with Michael J. Austin and Neil Betten, "Intellectual Origins of Community Organizing, 1920–1939," *Social Service Review,* Vol. 51 (March 1977), 155–70, and with Carol Corden, *Planned Cities: New Towns in Britain and America* (Beverly Hills, Calif.: Sage, 1977). The Corden book concentrates on the post-World War II era but contains a helpful chapter on the United States government as community builder during the 1930s and 1940s.

Jon C. Teaford, *City and Suburb: The Political Fragmentation of Metropolitan America, 1850–1970* (Baltimore: Johns Hopkins Univ. Press, 1979), contains instructive chapters on annexation, consolidation, and metropolitan federation schemes during the era of the metropolitan mode of thought and into the 1970s. Kenneth Fox, *Better City Government: Innovations in American Urban Politics, 1850–1937* (Philadelphia: Temple Univ. Press, 1977), is illuminating on urban government. The best short survey of big city politics and the metropolis between 1920 and 1950 is Roger Lotchin, "Power and Policy: American City Politics Between the Two World Wars," in Roger Lotchin, Richard Meister, and Zane L. Miller, *Bossism and Bosses in American Urban Politics* [tentative title] (Boston: Schenkman Publishing Co., forthcoming). Lotchin also explores other important aspects of what he calls "metropolitanism" between the two world wars in "The City and the Sword: San Francisco and the Rise of the Metropolitan-Military Complex, 1919–1941," *Journal of American History,* Vol. LXV, No. 4 (March 1979), 996–1020, and in "The Metropolitan-Military Complex in Comparative Perspective: San Francisco, Los Angeles, and San Diego, 1919–1941," *Journal of the West,* Vol. XVIII, No. 3 (July 1979), 19–30.

Among the non-local primary sources for the community of limited liability, Morris Janowitz, *The Community Press in an Urban Setting:*

The Social Elements of Urbanism (Chicago: Univ. of Chicago Press, 1952; rev. ed. 1967), described in the text and from which I borrowed the phrase "community of limited liability," is the critical document. Although many regard Paul and Percival Goodman's *Communitas: Means of Livelihood and Ways of Life* (1947) as idiosyncratic, I find the revised second edition (New York: Vintage Books, 1960) an interpretation of planning in the 1920s and 1930s not uncharacteristic of the mode of social taxonomy prevailing in the mid-twentieth century and a book which in general is quite representative of what might be called community-of-limited-liability thinking.

The best single source for the new distinction between the city and suburbia is The Editors of *Fortune, The Exploding Metropolis: A Study of the Assault on Urbanism and How Our Cities Can Resist It* (Garden City, N. Y.: Doubleday, 1958). After an introduction by William H. Whyte, Jr., the book presents essays by Whyte, Francis Bello, Seymour Freedgood, Daniel Seligman, and Jane Jacobs which explore the automobile and the city, big city politics, slums, sprawl, downtown, and the issue of the Americanness of cities. For the urban politics produced by the distinction between the big city and suburbia, consult Robert C. Wood, *Suburbia: Its People and Their Politics* (Boston: Houghton Mifflin, 1958), and Edward C. Banfield and James Q. Wilson, *City Politics* (Boston: Joint Center for Urban Studies, Massachusetts Institute of Technology and Harvard Univ., 1963). Other examples which focus on the city and its diversity are Nathan Glazer and Daniel Patrick Moynihan, *Beyond the Melting Pot: The Negroes, Puerto Ricans, Jews, Italians, and Irish of New York City* (New York: Harper and Row, 1963), and Charles Abrams, *The City is the Frontier* (New York: Harper and Row, 1965). The latter is a general study of urban conditions which began in 1960 as an analysis of urban renewal supported by a grant from the Ford Foundation.

One of the first new suburban studies was David Riesman, Nathan Glazer, and Reuel Denney, *The Lonely Crowd: A Study of the Changing American Character* (New Haven: Yale Univ. Press, 1950), whose "hero," the "other-directed" personality type, is characteristically found in a suburban setting. Also see Will Herberg, *Protestant—Catholic—Jew: An Essay in American Religious Sociology* (New York: Doubleday, 1955); Gibson Winter, *The Suburban Captivity of the Churches: An Analysis of Protestant Responsibility in the Expanding Metropolis* (New York: Macmillan, 1962); and Betty Friedan, *The Feminine Mystique* (New York: Norton, 1963), all of which concentrated on phenomena associated with "suburbia." Other manifestations of the rediscovery of local community in the age of the autonomous individual include Roland L. Warren, *Studying Your Community* (New York: Russell Sage, 1955); A. C. Spectorsky, *The Exurbanites* (Philadelphia: Lippincott, 1955); Maurice R. Stein, *The Eclipse of Community: An Interpretation of American Studies* (Princeton: Princeton Univ. Press, 1960); Bennet M. Berger, *Working Class Suburb* (Berkeley: Univ. of California Press, 1960), especially pp. 12–13; Herbert J. Gans, "Urbanism and Suburbanism as Ways of Life: A Re-Evaluation of Some Definitions," in Arnold Rose, ed., *Human Behavior and Social Processes* (Boston: Houghton Mifflin, 1962), 625–48; Sam Bass Warner, Jr., *Streetcar Suburbs: The Process of Growth in Boston (1870–1920)* (Boston: Harvard Univ. Press, 1962); William M. Dobriner, *Class in Suburbia* (Englewood Cliffs, N.J.: Prentice-Hall, 1963); and Arthur J. Vidich, Joseph Bensman, Maurice R. Stein, *Reflections on Community Studies* (New York: John Wiley, 1964), especially Stein's essay, pp. 207–32.

There is a vast secondary literature bearing on community in an urban and suburban setting during the period of the community of limited liability. Gelfand, *A Nation of Cities,* cited above, deals with federal urban programs. Blake McKelvey, *The Emergence of Metropolitan America, 1915–1966* (New Brunswick, N.J.: Rutgers Univ. Press, 1968), contains useful information on both this and the previous period. Harvey S. Perloff, ed., *The Quality of the Urban Environment: Essays on "New Resources" in the Urban Age* (Baltimore: Johns Hopkins Univ. Press, 1969), analyzes the American economic and urban structure in the 1950s and early 1960s. Jean Lowe, *Cities in a Race with Time: Progress and Poverty in America's Renewing Cities* (New York: Random House, 1967), surveys the urban renaissance in the same period. Roy Lubove, *Twentieth Century Pittsburgh: Government, Business, and Environmental Change* (New York: John Wiley, 1969), covers the renaissance in Pittsburgh. For New York in the same years, see Robert A. Caro., *The Power Broker: Robert Moses and the Fall of New York* (New York: Knopf, 1974), a volume of controversial interpretations and useful information on the entire twentieth-century history of New York.

For discussions of the literature of suburban criticisim from the 1950s and early 1960s, see Scott Donaldson, *The Suburban Myth* (New York: Columbia Univ. Press, 1969), and Howard P. Chudacoff, *The Evolution of American Urban Society* (Englewood Cliffs, N.J.:

Prentice-Hall, 1975), 242–44. Raymond J. Burby, III, and Shirley F. Weiss, *New Communities U.S.A.* (Lexington, Mass.: D.C. Heath, 1976), analyze new communities, including Forest Park, created by private developers in the 1950s and 1960s. David R. Goldfield and Blaine A. Brownell, *Urban America: From Downtown to No Town* (Boston: Houghton Mifflin, 1979), is an American urban history text with several chapters on this period which, like the rest of the book, are noteworthy for their sensitivity to the spatial dimension and the role of suburbs in urban life. On "sunbelt" cities and suburbs after 1940, see Carl Abbott, "The American Sunbelt: Idea and Region," *Journal of the West*, Vol. XVIII, No. 3 (July 1979), 5–18; his *The New Urban America: Metropolitan Growth and Politics in the Sunbelt Since 1940* (Chapel Hill: Univ. of North Carolina Press, forthcoming); and Howard N. Rabinowitz, "Growth Trends in the Albuquerque SMSA, 1940–1978," *Journal of the West*, Vol. XVIII, No. 3 (July 1979), 62–74.

For this symptomatic history of community in urban and suburban America, the "secondary" sources on the community of limited liability serve double duty as primary sources for the community of advocacy, that recent past in which we still live. I have also benefitted from reading a variety of other non-local primary sources. Christopher Lasch, *The Culture of Narcissism: American Life in an Age of Diminishing Expectations* (New York: Norton, 1978), both analyzes the literature characteristic of the inward-turning tendency and stands as one of the most widely-read manifestations of that tendency. For other critiques of the social and policy implications of the tendency, see Warren G. Bennis, "Chairman Mac in Perspective," *Harvard Business Review*, Vol. 50, No. 5 (Sept.–Oct. 1972), 140–42; Warren G. Bennis, "A Future Beyond Push-Button Careers," *Technology Review* (March–April 1979), 12–13; Philip Roth, *My Life as a Man* (New York: Holt, Rinehart and Winston, 1974); Richard Sennet, *The Fall of Public Man* (New York: Knopf, 1977); Leon Botstein, "The Children of the Lonely Crowd," *Change* (May 1978), 16–20; and Fred Davis, *Yearning for Yesterday: A Sociology of Nostalgia* (New York: Free Press, 1979), which points out that contemporary nostalgia usually does not take civic objects, figures, or events as objects of yearning. Ellen Goodman, whose column is syndicated by the *Boston Globe* Newspaper Company—Washington Post Writers Group and appears in the *Cincinnati Post* and other metropolitan dailies, has been a persistent and rather sympathetic reporter of the inward-turning tendency. *Newsweek* columnist Meg Greenfield, especially in "Notes from the Swamp," *Newsweek,* August 13, 1979, p. 84, which expressed concern that the Carter White House took Lasch too seriously, has taken a more jaundiced view.

For views of urban and suburban life characteristic of the community of advocacy, see Milton Rakove, *The Changing Patterns of Suburban Politics in Cook County, Illinois* (Chicago: Center for Research in Urban Government, Loyola Univ., 1965); Herbert J. Gans, *The Levittowners: Ways of Life and Politics in a New Suburban Community* (New York: Pantheon, 1967); Stephan Thernstrom, *Poverty and Progress: Social Mobility in a Nineteenth Century City* (Cambridge, Mass.: Harvard Univ. Press, 1968); Milton Kotler, *Neighborhood Government: The Local Foundations of Political Life* (Indianapolis: Bobbs-Merrill, 1969); John B. Orr and F. Patrick Nichelson, *The Radical Suburb: Soundings in Changing American Character* (Philadelphia: Westminister Press, 1970); Daniel Patrick Moynihan, ed., *Toward a National Urban Policy* (New York: Basic Books, 1970), especially Moynihan's essay, "The City in Chassis," pp. 313–37; Louis H. Masotti and Jeffrey K. Hadden, eds., *Urbanization of the Suburbs* (Beverly Hills, Calif.: Sage, 1973); Daniel Bell, *The Coming of Post-Industrial Society: A Venture in Social Forecasting* (New York: Basic Books, 1973); Louis H. Masotti and Jeffrey K. Hadden, *Suburbia in Transition* (New York: New Viewpoints, div. of Franklin Watts, 1974); John D. Kassarda and George V. Redfearn, "Differential Patterns of Suburban Growth in the United States," *Journal of Urban History,* Vol. 2, No. 1 (November 1975), 43–66; George Sternlieb and James W. Hughes, eds., *Post-Industrial America: Metropolitan Decline and Inter-Regional Job Shifts* (New Brunswick, N. J.: The Center for Urban Policy Research, Rutgers Univ., 1975); Irving Lewis Allen, ed., *New Towns and the Suburban Dream: Ideology and Utopia in Planning and Development* (Port Washington, N.Y.: Kennikat Press, 1977); Peter O. Muller, "Suburbia, Geography and the Prospect of a Nation Without Important Cities," *Geographical Survey,* Vol. 7, No. 2 (April 1978), 3–8; William C. Baer, "On the Death of Cities," *Public Interest,* Vol. 45 (Fall 1976), 3–19.

I have also found useful the commentary on metropolitan affairs in the syndicated columns of Michael McManus and Neil Pierce, which appear in the *Cincinnati Post* and other metropolitan daily newspapers, and George Steinlieb's comments in *The New York Times,*

July 29, 1979, E5, about the evolution of a "new, swinging city around the core" surrounded by "the old industrial city that isn't making the transition." For an attempt to place neighborhood in historical perspective and connect "national" events after the mid-1960s to the neighborhood organization revolution, see Zane L. Miller, "The Role and Concept of Neighborhood in American Cities," in Robert Fisher and Peter Romanofsky, eds., *Community Organization for Social Change: A Historical Perspective* (Westport, Conn.: Greenwood Press, forthcoming).

Finally, my views on the community of advocacy have been informed by my participation in public life in the Cincinnati metropolitan area, as a member of: the steering committee of the Hamilton County Democratic party (1972–present); the Cincinnati Charter Review Commission (1975); the Cincinnati Architectural Board of Review 1976–1980); the Board of Trustees, Miami Purchase Association for Historic Preservation (1976–present); the Ohio Committee for Public Programs in the Humanities (1976–present); the Cincinnati Urban Conservation Task Force (1979–1980); the Cincinnati Historic Conservation Board (1980–present); and the Cincinnatus Association (1979–present). The last group is a "reform" organization, founded in the 1920s, which still acts as a watchdog in public affairs in Cincinnati and Hamilton County. All these types of participation have provided me with factual information unavailable elsewhere and exposed me to varied expressions of the mode of social taxonomy peculiar to the community of advocacy.

INDEX

Twentieth-Century America Series

DEWEY W. GRANTHAM, GENERAL EDITOR

Each volume in this series focuses on some aspects of the politics of social change in recent American history, utilizing new approaches to clarify the response of Americans to the dislocating forces of our own day—economic, technological, racial, demographic, and administrative.

VOLUMES PUBLISHED:

THE UNIVERSITY OF TENNESSEE PRESS: KNOXVILLE